SEARCHING

The One You've Always

FOR A GOD

Wanted Is Really There

TO LOVE

Chris Blake

WORD PUBLISHING

NASHVILLE

A Thomas Nelson Company

Published by Word Publishing
Nashville, TN

Scripture quotations used in this book are from The Revised Standard Version of
the Bible (RSV). Copyright © 1946, 1952, 1971, 1973 by the Division of Christian
Education.

Other Scripture references are from the Holy Bible, New International Version
(NIV). Copyright © 1973, 1978, 1984, International Bible Society. Used by permission of Zondervan Bible Publishers.

Cover Photography:
Man: Micheal Heissner, Stone
Sky: Yoshinori Watabe, Photonica

Cover Design:
Uttley/Douponce DesignWorks
www.uddesignworks.com

Library of Congress Cataloging-in-Publication Data

Blake, Chris, 1951–
    Searching for a God to love : the one you've always wanted is really there / Chris Blake.
      p. cm.
    Originally published: Nampa, Idaho : Pacific Press Pub. Association, ©1999.
    Includes bibliographical references.
    ISBN 0-8499-4226-8 (pbk.)
    1. Christian life. I. Title.
BV4501.2 .B5557 2000
231—dc21
                                              00-043334

Printed in the United States of America
00 01 02 03 04 PHX 9 8 7 6 5 4 3 2 1

CONTENTS

To my first family of life and laughter,
Marise, Bruce, Alison, and Janine,
and to their loved ones

To the memory of my father,
James Harlan Blake

~

ACKNOWLEDGMENTS

Any worthwhile work is the product of many minds. Because all truth is God's truth, I am first indebted to truth-tellers from diverse backgrounds, whether Hindu or atheist, ancient or contemporary. Whenever possible, to ensure accuracy I have checked the original source and context of anything quoted here.

Numerous people helped produce this book. For their generous comments on portions of the manuscript I am grateful to Bettina and Gary Krause, Gary Burns, Liz Rand, Maylan Schurch, Becky and Jeff Scoggins, Lynn Hawkins, Greg Nelson, Stuart Tyner, Richard Coffen, Andy Nash, Byard Parks, Jerry Thomas, and Marni Nelson. I especially appreciate my Union College colleague Mark Robison, who endured first drafts and consistently provided an astute sounding board.

To the many people who prayed for me and my writing (in particular Something Else and the four amigos), thank you. My students at Union College provided patience, feedback, and even a turn of phrase on occasion.

The people at Word Publishing have been excited and gracious in dealing with this manuscript. I appreciate Mark Sweeney, Ami McConnell, and my able editor, Janet Reed. In addition, my thanks extend to my agent, Greg Johnson, with Alive Communications.

Finally, I appreciate and love so much my wife, Yolanda, and our sons, Nathan and Geoffrey. They shouldered the brunt of months of living with a distracted husband and father. Each also gave valued feedback—including the classic advice, "Get some sleep, Dad." This book would not have happened without you. Thanks for believing in me and in the focus of this creation.

~

I don't know who God is. We're not up to that yet.

—ELEMENTARY SCHOOL STUDENT

There are many fine things which we cannot say if we have to shout.

—HENRY DAVID THOREAU

I am astonished at the boldness with which
people undertake to speak of God.

—BLAISE PASCAL

Whether we recognize it or not, we begin as agnostics. If we do not
acknowledge this, we will be too preoccupied with trivial gods to notice
the real God standing before us.

—LESLIE WEATHERHEAD

I cannot completely believe in a God that I can understand completely.

—LORALEE HAGEN

It's a great big universe and we're all really puny.
We're just tiny little specks about the size of Mickey Rooney.

—ANIMANIACS

Who alone stretched out the heavens,
    and trampled the waves of the sea;
who made the Bear and Orion,
    the Pleiades and the chambers of the south;
who does great things beyond understanding,
    and marvelous things without number.
Lo, he passes by me, and I see him not;
    he moves on, but I do not perceive him.

—JOB, CHAPTER 9

The people who sat in darkness have seen a great light.

—JESUS, QUOTING ISAIAH

~

I

EXCUSE ME,
YOU'RE STEPPING ON MY GOD

FOR SOME REASON, I felt like getting up. This isn't my typical early-Sunday feeling, but that morning instead of bringing in the plump newspaper for a browse, I entered our dark family room, located the remote, and turned on the television. During the first seven seconds, only sound emerged. A man was speaking—shouting, actually. His voice rose and fell as the screen's thousands of red, blue, and yellow pixels summoned the image of a televangelist.

Never before had I actually watched this show. The speaker paced the platform like a caged cat in a sleek blue suit, stalking and prancing, rumbling and wooing. With majestic emotion he told how "government and the media" collaborate in one evil conspiracy. He equated God's interests with America's interests, knew precisely God's plans and desires—the most intricate, God-smudged blueprints, the throbbing heart of life's great pulse—and claimed that everything happens "according to God's will." He carried God in his pocket.

At first I was merely amazed by the vastness of his narrowness. Slowly, though, my anger began to bubble. The sermon crawled with glittering generalities and yawning inaccuracies, quotations ripped from their context, opposing views clustered and characterized in the vilest light. Was his cause so good that he could behave so badly?

Following a crescendo summary, the preacher delivered an eyes-scrunched prayer that seemed directed toward the viewing audience. A moment after the "Amen," numbers galloped across the screen: "Call 1-800 . . ." Send money to receive a "free gift." Visa, Discover, and MasterCard logos appeared. An announcer with a voice like dark syrup supplied details. The speaker returned to personally urge viewers to "give abundantly and be blessed abundantly." In conclusion, he looked out and with polished sincerity appealed that "the Lord would come right now into your heart."

At this point a surprising conviction hit me. *Even if you're right about what you're saying, even if everything you say is true,* I thought, *I don't want it.*

I flicked off the set. The screen flashed and spit black.

. . .

Colors.

As I sit in the darkness in Griffith Park Planetarium in Los Angeles, that's what stuns me first. Kaleidoscopic magentas. Cool blues. Flaming oranges and stark whites. Jade and aqua, crimson and candlelight, dazzling colors wash in gauzy waves across the canvas of the universe.

Numbers.

More than 100 billion galaxies spiral in the void. The sky is thick with light, as if someone dipped a toothbrush in white paint and thumbed the bristles over black velvet. Hold a dime at arm's length: the coin covers 15 million stars in our Milky Way alone.

Some scientists estimate that a sun explodes with each tick of the clock. Infant stars, wrapped in linens of dust and gas, are born just as often. One tablespoonful of a neutron star would weigh about 5 trillion pounds on earth. "In the universe," writes Lao-tzu, "the difficult things are done as if they were easy."

Vastness.

Light travels 186,282 miles each second. At that speed a bullet rockets around Earth and grazes your ear seven times (ouch ouch ouch ouch ouch ouch ouch) in less than a second. The sun's light reaches us in 8.3 light-minutes. Neptune is about seven light-hours away. Andromeda, our closest spiral galaxy, is 2.2 million light-years away and stretches 100,000 light-years from edge to edge.

Gulp.

The lights come on, and I'm suddenly aware that my mouth hangs open. Leaving the planetarium, I pass the huge Foucault pendulum rocking from the lobby ceiling, monitoring our planet's predictable rotation. A car squeals out of the parking lot. Stepping outside, I stare straight up and drink in the whirling night. "The stars," observes Brennan Manning, "call us out of ourselves."

Then my thoughts turn to something truly wondrous. *Those intergalactic views are only half the picture.* Have you visited the Monsanto exhibit at Disneyland? There we're led to feel that we're shrinking to infinitesimal proportions—smaller, smaller, smaller. At one point an enormous human eye blinks at us through a microscope. Eventually we shrink into the center of an atom with its orbiting electrons and surging nucleus. In marvelous terror a voice cries out, "Dare I go on?" Some scientists claim we could go on, traveling deeper and deeper into the nucleus and its constituents. They also say that if you could harness and convert the energy, you could power your house for a day using the atoms in the period at the end of this sentence. The ink on an 8 by 11-inch sheet of paper would provide power for 150,000 days, more than 400 years.

Who are we to think we can comprehend a trillionth of this incredible power? How could anyone possibly know what animates galaxies and energizes each atom? In the polluted wake of some televangelists we may feel reticent to speak, worrying that the vastness of *our* narrowness will become apparent, but in every people group on earth the topic comes up. In French this power is called *Dieu*. In German it's *Gott*. In Spanish, *Dios*. In Hebrew it is *Elohim*. For Hindus it is *Brahman*. For Muslims, *Allah*. In another arena, the power is referred to as *Essence, Universal Mind, Life Force*.

In this book the power is called *God*. To millions of people "God" carries unpleasant associations. But a word is simply a symbol, not the object itself. By any other name a rose would smell as sweet, and by any other name God would still be, in Anselm's words, "That than which no greater can be conceived."

As a young child I attended Bethel Congregational Church, where every worship service Mr. Blakeslee, the organist, sat front and center behind a soft burgundy curtain. I could glimpse only the back of his pale, bald head. Somehow with my small eyes and ears watching and listening each week, I came to connect Mr. Blakeslee with God. God played unseen music with hidden hands and a mysterious face. Was He smiling or scowling? I had no clue. If I had chanced a guess based on the music, He would be minor-chord prone, majestic, gloomy, and loud.

For many of us who have carried similar images into adulthood, God remains inscrutable and distant. Is a grin playing on the lips, a tear moving, a glint of anger flashing? We try to discern the face of the player by the music, but all we know is the back of a bald head. We are also curious: What is this musician like away from the instrument and the score? Gentle? Petty? Vindictive? Fun-loving?

My friend Kim is thoughtful, fun, responsible, and skeptical. She's a believing unbeliever, one who believes in a God but who doesn't believe everything people say about God. At one time she "followed God," but too many things about that God didn't make sense; so she scrapped the whole idea. We talked last summer, sitting on the back of a houseboat one night when the Milky Way actually looked milky; Kim questioned why any God would allow little children to suffer and why God isn't more visible. After hearing about what she doesn't believe, I asked her what she does believe in, at the core of her being.

"I guess I believe in Christian values," she said sheepishly, and we both laughed.

"It seems a bit strange," I suggested, "to believe in those values but not in the Being who established them."

"I just don't see another way around it right now," she admitted.

This book is about falling in love with God, and it's written mostly for people like Kim. If you're an "unbeliever" who yearns for a God who is more than what televangelists and traditional religion are communicating—indeed, more than anyone could communicate—this book is for you. Frederick Buechner points out, "Many an atheist is a believer without knowing it, just as many a believer is an atheist without knowing it. You can sincerely believe there is no God and act as if there is. You can sincerely believe there is a God and live as though there isn't."

If you're a "believer" who feels squeezed and drained by a religious existence of deep weariness, unending frustration, and blasted hopes—to the point where even if your religion is "right" you don't know if you want it—this book is also for you.

STEP ONE

Let's admit something from the start: We cannot know God . . .

Agnostics contend we cannot know God. Often they say this because of God's transcendent nature, as caterpillars cannot know humans. Caterpillars can *experience* humans. They can crawl fuzzily up our fingers and forearms and swivel their heads quizzically, but they cannot *know* us because we transcend them.

But let's admit that we don't know even the people we live with. How deeply does a husband know his wife? How well do we know our parents, our children, our friends? The more we know, the more we suspect that we know very little. Like the six blind men of Indostan "reading" an elephant, we know in part at best.

The wonder is that even when we cannot know fully, we can love wholeheartedly. That which we do know—the kernel of a person that makes a person—we love. We believe Forrest Gump when he proclaims, "I might not be very smart, but I know what love is." We can and we do love the unfathomable.

Our search to understand God may produce only more confusion. *Life* magazine asked forty-nine people, both famous and obscure, the ultimate question, "Why are we here?" Garrison Keillor replied, "To know and to serve God, of course, is why we're here, a clear truth that, like the nose on your face, is near at hand and easily discernible but can make you dizzy if you try to focus on it hard." To their credit, many agnostics don't wish to strap God to any human framework. They maintain that any limitation we place on God is illusory; any claim to "know God" seems at once arrogant and naive. We are too feeble, too finite.

A short story describes beings in a distant galaxy whose home planet is warmed by multiple suns. Night never falls. While life in this sphere is fine enough, a terrible mystery consumes the thoughts of all inhabitants. Every 600 years the suns align in one monstrous eclipse, plunging the planet for a few hours into total darkness, and each time this happens, according to historical records, nearly all the inhabitants are wiped out. What is it in the darkness that proves fatal?

At last the moment of the eclipse arrives, and the inhabitants witness a startling sight. They see, for the first time, stars. Thousands upon thousands of shimmering stars. The vision sends them over the edge to insanity or to suicide. Why? Because suddenly they comprehend their true insignificance in the universe. They are a microscopic speck in a chartless ocean, a whimper in a hurricane, an M&M in the Milky Way.

The agnostic view takes into account our puny proportions and humble perspective when compared to God. However, agnosticism can actually end up limiting God. It is true: We cannot know God . . . unless God chooses to be known. In prematurely ending that sentence, the agnostic view steps on God by restricting this option. And while our knowledge of God can never be objectively measured, neither can we objectively measure truth, hope, or compassion. Would we give up on those?

Imagine a young man interviewing for a high-paying job with a major corporation. He glides through two interviews, shuffles past the formidable executive secretary, and finds himself face-to-face with the founder, owner, and CEO of the corporation. After the two exchange pleasantries, the young man speaks his mind.

"I know you're in control here," he offers generously, "so I want you to know something. You can do anything you like!"

"Oh . . . um . . . thanks," the owner manages to say.

"Unless," the young man continues, "you want to communicate personally with me or with any of your employees. That, of course, is impossible."

"Excuse me?"

"Well, you can't do that. You're too far above us. We can't appreciate you for all that you truly are."

At this point the owner assures the young man that he won't have to concern himself further with the prospect, and she escorts him to the door.

It's possible to hold mistaken assumptions about the "owner," isn't it? If God decides to communicate with us, who are we to deny that privilege? We can't enable caterpillars to know or love us, but (and this is an important point) we aren't God. We created neither the caterpillar nor the cosmos. Moreover, humans can comprehend infinitely more than caterpillars. As we'll explore later, God finds ingenious ways to interact with us.

Even if we act with the best intentions, if we deny God's ability or desire to communicate with us, we "step on" God.

STEP TWO

I enjoy running. That's when I do my best thinking, away from the madding crowd. At least I think I do. When my family lived one mile from Pismo Beach in California, I ran three mornings a week. Stepping out my front door, I'd pad down the hills of Brighton Avenue, circle a fence that confined a snarling dog, dodge through some firs, cut over the railroad tracks, zip across Highway 1, and be on the beach. Easy.

Once there, I felt as if I could run for hours. The wide white sand lay flat and firm, giving gently to my strides. The early morning fog would be lifting against the hills, the seagulls gliding and calling, the moist air suffused with salt and seaweed. Ahead of me sandpipers raced the spreading foam, their skinny legs a blur. Often I passed people on the beach—lovers walking hand in hand, another runner, a solitary soul thinking deeply, arms crossed, head down—and no matter who it was, I always called out, "Morning!" Nearly always I received a somewhat surprised smile and a greeting in return.

One morning a man didn't return my greeting. He stood alone, hidden in a heavy coat and gloves, but different from most beach walkers. He was inhaling a cigarette and listening intently to his headphones, swinging a metal detector across the sand much like the sightless wield a white cane. I called out "Morning!" and waved. He never noticed.

I understood his not wanting to hear or see the gasping, dripping man plodding by, but in hearing only the sound in his headphones he was missing the rhythmic roar of the surf and the squawking gulls. Looking only at his feet, he lost the splendor of the sandpipers and the lifting fog. With his coat and mind tightly buttoned, he could not appreciate the invigorating sensations all around him. He could never find with Shakespeare "tongues in trees, books in running brooks, sermons in stones and good in everything."

Too often we are like that man, swinging into God's revelations and not perceiving them. As Job confesses, "He passes by me, and I see him not." If we listen merely for life's metallic beeping, how can God get through? Our frantic society's beeps—the pressures of money's long, green madness and 1:15 appointments and advertising blitzes and bizarre relationship problems and every last honking hurry—can overwhelm us.[1] We lose the ability to sense and to make sense. We lose the ability to perceive.

We "step on" God when we become so busy and bothered that we do not discern that God is here.

STEP THREE

It's another misty morning, another run. Approaching me on the far side of the street walks a raven-haired wisp of a girl, about eleven years old, carrying a pink lunch bag and three books.

"Morning!" I call to her, and I smile.

Her response isn't one I'm used to seeing. Lowering her eyes, she quickens her pace, her body tense. She's clearly afraid.

Of course, she's right. Someone has taught her well: Don't talk to strangers. But I'm angry as I move beyond her. No, not at her. I'm angry at the people who took away an eleven-year-old girl's freedom to smile without fear and sing out, "Good morning!" I'm incensed at those who by their hideous actions spawned an epidemic of distrust.

Let's switch scenes. I'm talking with a friend. During the course of our easy conversation I mention the word *God*. Instantly his face stiffens, his eyes glaze over. It's obvious he wants no part of this discussion. His expression clearly tells me, *Let's forget about that, okay?*

And at once our freedom has been pinched. Our liberty to go beyond the banalities of bad weather, ball scores, and inevitable air disasters has been stepped on. We can't explore the meaning of life with candor and good humor in a safe atmosphere. We just can't. The possibility is gone. Vanished.

That scene is replayed on this planet a thousand times a day. I'm angry at those who bred this discomfort, this distrust, this reluctance bordering on abhorrence. Who causes these responses?

Mostly, religious people cause them.

Let me be clear in defining what I mean here by "religious people." I mean slippery, pushy evangelists attempting to cram others into their view of salvation. Deliver us from them.

I mean cautious churchgoers who care more about raising money than about raising literacy rates. Those who "disdain the world" but crave its publicity. Those wearing vanilla smiles who see no relevance in healing a poisoned environment

---

1. Poet e. e. cummings refers to "this busy monstermanunkind."

or in developing better housing for the poor or in upholding the rights and dignity of minorities.

I mean those who deny the true power of God and instead use church as a social coffee club, where the elite meet to greet. I mean those who distort and manhandle the Bible to the point where onlookers give up trying to make any sense of it.

I mean religious entertainers, including many neighborhood pulpit pounders, with their embarrassing, superficial antics. I mean those whose worship is all froth and those whose worship is as flat as road kill at rush hour. I mean pride- and hate-filled fanatics, from Belfast to Bosnia to the West Bank, who pulverize one another in the name of God.

I mean those who want to look good and who look the other way if someone else doesn't. I mean those who claim that the God of colors and numbers and vastness in the universe gets wrathful if a teenaged girl wears too much makeup. I could go on. You know what I mean.

Of course, religionists haven't cornered the market on bad behavior. (If you have trouble believing this, just pick up today's newspaper.) Unfortunately, however, religionists' actions are often connected to God. All of us at some time are embarrassed by our connections, whether by our workplace, our political party, our country, our race, our favorite athletes or musicians, our family. In our more lucid moments, we don't simply write these connections off. We understand that reality and the ideal don't often mesh.

How I wish I could adequately communicate this: *God's seekers are turned off to "religion" more than anybody.* "Religion" robs me of being able to talk with friends and relatives about my greatest love, my God. That's why, to a Christian God-seeker, it makes no sense to hear that someone isn't interested in God because she's "turned off by religion."

There exists a growing body of people who, according to a recent Gallup poll, are more interested in spiritual things. I found this to be true when walking through O'Hare Airport with the book *God: A Biography* tucked under my arm. Never have I seen so much interest in a book. While I stood in lines, travelers craned their necks to read the dust jacket, commenting on the fascinating nature of the concept. People today *are* interested in God. They are also wary and weary of religionists. We "step on" God when we reduce God to a packaged agenda, to a set of precepts easily held and manipulated.

It is possible to step on the limitless God of the universe to the point where not only can God not be found, but nobody's even looking.

~

I never knew how to worship until I knew how to love.

—Henry Ward Beecher

People despise religion; they hate it and fear it is true. To remedy this, we must begin by showing that religion is not contrary to reason.

—Blaise Pascal

We see things not as they are but as we are.

—Anaïs Nin

Surely we cannot take an open question like the supernatural and shut it with a bang, turning the key of the madhouse on all the mystics of history. You cannot take the region called the unknown and calmly say that though you know nothing about it, you know that all the gates are locked.

—G. K. Chesterton

We must respect the other fellow's religion, but only in the sense and to the extent that we respect his theory that his wife is beautiful and his children smart.

—H. L. Mencken

In thirty-five years of theological studies, I've come up with two incontrovertible facts: There is a God. And I'm not Him.

—A priest in *Rudy*

Religious certainty does not mean assurance without risk or doubt; it does not mean a fortress mentality and a strategy, but a life in ultimate relaxation, in confidence that the truth of God will establish itself even without massive human help. It follows from this that religious certainty without fanaticism is possible; doubt and adventure are also part of faith, as too is insight into the limits of and the need for tolerance.

—Hans Küng

A bruised ego leads to more doubt than a dearth of evidence.

—Ward Hill

In much of the Western world, the biggest problem is not skepticism but sentimentalism. Convictions have been transformed into clichés. Christian truths are unknown, because they are too well known.

—Becky Pippert

You will know the truth, and the truth will make you free.

—Jesus

~

2

STALKING THE WILD TRUTH

THE NEEDLES, THE tubes, the beeping chrome monitors, all filled her with horror. Sylvia harbored a paralyzing dread of life-support systems. While visiting a friend in the hospital, however, she determined to bravely steel herself. As she walked through the disinfected corridors, she tried not to peek at the machines in the rooms.

It was no use. She needed to get out. Trembling, she reached the nearest elevator and stabbed the down button. When the elevator door opened, a hospital attendant stood beside a gleaming chrome machine covered with tubes and dials. Sylvia hesitated, swallowed, and stepped inside. The door closed. She gazed straight ahead, her face a mask of apprehension. At last she blurted, "I sure would hate to be hooked up to one of those!"

The attendant looked down at the machine and up at Sylvia. "So would I," he said. "It's a rug cleaner."

Life is full of illusions. Even the language we use to clarify life can be tricky. Customers enter a hair salon to receive a "permanent," and six months later they return for another. Doctors attend medical school so they can finally practice, but I really don't want a doctor to *practice* on me. People declare, "It goes without saying that . . ." and then they say it. Or they write, "not to mention . . ." and then mention it. Moreover, speakers talk about what they'd like to do as if they're doing it. They announce, "We'd like to welcome you here tonight" or "I'd like to thank everyone who made this possible," and I think, *Well, then, go ahead and do it.* In the entire history of the Academy Awards, no one has ever actually thanked anyone for anything, though they'd like to.

Perhaps no word in the English language is freighted with more hidden meanings than the word *love*. So when we talk of loving God, do we mean love of "I love mashed potatoes," "love is a many-splendored thing," or your enemies"? Maybe this love is a quick infatuation, as heard in the song lyric, "Hello, I love you, won't you tell me your name?" Or co tugging curiosity, as with the hundreds who flocked to see the fac a burned tortilla, or the thousands who viewed the image of th on the concrete floor of a shower stall in a bathroom of Progreso Auto Supply in Progreso, Texas?[1]

Our ideas of love and God depend on our perceptions. Common wisdom holds that our minds are like parachutes, functioning only when open, but it's also possible to be so open-minded that our brains fall out. The story is told of Samuel Taylor Coleridge receiving a visitor who advised, "Don't teach your children what to believe. Let them grow up free to choose for themselves." Coleridge took him out to his "garden," a weedy, thistle-strewn patch of earth. The visitor was stunned. "You call this a garden?" he fumed. "There's nothing here but weeds!"

Coleridge replied, "That's true. I thought, however, that I would leave the flowers free to choose for themselves."

This garden we call modern society can appear overgrown. The wisdom of generations lies tangled and buried. The weeds inherit the earth. We grow up devotees of a vapid anythink. G. K. Chesterton concludes, "When a man ceases to believe in God, he does not believe in nothing, he believes in anything."

One night I was talking with a close friend and we got around to our beliefs on spiritual matters. He mentioned a belief he endorsed, and I wondered aloud how it measured up to reality, how it made sense.

"It doesn't have to make sense," he said.

My mind somersaulted. *If it doesn't have to make sense, then what ultimately matters?* Why not believe that flossing teeth brings salvation? Why not worship *TV Guide* or a jar of mayonnaise? We may as well follow Adolf Hitler or David Koresh, or be one of Marshall Applewhite's conscientious corpses wearing new Nikes. Certainly we don't comprehend all of our senses, and much of our "sensible" thinking is nonsense; yet on what basis do we make any decisions at all? Should we amputate our brains when we enter spiritual discussions?

Too often we inherit our thoughts from seeing only the obvious; our sponge souls soak in only what makes direct contact and little else. In seeing superficially we miss how life is not as much either/or as it is both/and—fair and unfair, complex and simple, parched and moist, bittersweet. At the start of College Writing each semester, my students encounter a twenty-five-second experiment in seeing, where they simply look at the following diagram and count the number of squares. Try it for yourself.

---

1. I've often wondered how people "recognize" these likenesses. Are original photographs somewhere in existence?

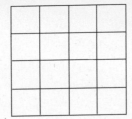

Some students count fast and shoot me a peek after three seconds that says, "Yeah, now what?" Then, glancing around, they notice others inspecting the figure, and look again. Many are still counting when the twenty-five seconds elapse. While the students call out how many squares they saw, I scribble the numbers on the board.

"Twenty-one!"

"Nineteen!"

"Twenty-five!"

"Thirty!"

"Thirty-two!"

By this time everyone is intently studying the square. What seemed so obvious at first is suddenly . . . different. I trace the thirty squares (yes, thirty). "Those of you who found more than thirty are into another dimension," I add, and we laugh. The point of the exercise will be brought to their attention many times during the course: *Be more than a sixteen-square person.* We discuss how those who found sixteen, twenty-one, and twenty-five squares were *right,* as far as they went, and how there's more to life than being *right.* As John Fischer told me, "An artist is one who stays a little longer." When we look at a tree, for instance, and see it merely as a tree, we miss a sanctuary; a living sculpture; a food source for woodpeckers, insects, and giraffes; a shade producer; a musical instrument in a breeze; a rooted tower; a means of transportation; a paper factory; a micro organic nursery of wriggling newborns; a source of poetry; a playmate; and dozens of other things. Looking beyond the obvious requires purposeful effort, particularly when the figure we're studying is "God."

Some people can look at the diagram for a month and see only sixteen squares. They stop looking, believing that once they are right they no longer need to seek, and thereafter muddle through life in the light of a 10-watt bulb.[2]

---

2. None is so blind as one who will not see.

In addition, those who located thirty are in greatest peril, because they may now believe that they are completely in the right in all areas. Religionists often see themselves as thirty-square people, along with stockbrokers and scientists, professors and postal workers, computer technicians and cabbies, and thus we shut ourselves off from seeing—in seeing, we become blinded.

In the midst of running from rug cleaners and chasing after charred tortillas, could we pause from our illusions to consider another view of reality?

REALITY IS NOT ALWAYS MULTIPLE CHOICE

I stared into the blue-white of Mendenhall Glacier outside Juneau, Alaska. My brother Bruce was describing how the seven-story ice calves into the bay, creating enormous ripples, exposing blue flesh like an open wound, though it doesn't happen often. In fact, he said, though he visits the glacier fairly frequently, he has never witnessed a calving. Then he related an unsettling tale.

A daring young man and woman a few years back decided to picnic near the edge of the glacier. They stumbled across the ice, threw down a blanket and a basket, and began enjoying their alfresco summer meal together, virtually dangling their feet over the cliff of ice. After a few delightful minutes, a terrific *crack* rent the air. While onlookers watched in horror, tons of ice under the couple collapsed into the frigid tidal lake. Their bodies were never recovered.

I stared once more at the massive glacier, then peered at Bruce. "Really?" I sputtered. "No way! That sounds like an urban legend."

"I understand that it happened," said Bruce somberly, "right there."

Of the many lessons that could be gleaned from this story, one appears preeminent. What the couple believed about the glacier didn't matter. In the end, all that mattered was the objective reality of the glacier. All the pair's beliefs merged with reality as the two dropped to the booming water.

This lesson runs counter to Gustave Flaubert's New Age creed, "The only reality is perception." Flaubert's statement acknowledges the complexity of life and our bewilderment with it, along with the power of perception. Whenever I teach, I make use of this power by asking students to examine and compare their perceptions; surely our perceptions create a vision of reality for us. The danger lies in extrapolating the vision until we believe that no objective reality therefore exists.[3] This illusion is particularly prevalent when people speak of

---

3. One of the problems the relativist faces is his belief that only his theory is absolute.

God as simply a subjective extension of our egos, projecting our own desires. "If that's God to you, fine," our society affirms. "Whatever works, honey."

What difference does it make what we think of God? Quite literally, all the difference in the world. Our view of reality is anchored in our view of God. For many the sour breath of life—the morning breath of God—permeates a lifetime. Whatever we worship does become God to us, but as with glaciers, an inexorable reality prevails.

Once a five-year-old girl brought a baby rabbit to her kindergarten class for show and tell. She had already dragged the box down two aisles when suddenly a fellow classmate wondered aloud, "What is this rabbit, a boy or a girl?"

The show-er couldn't tell. She looked to the teacher for help, but the teacher was at a loss for words. At last a small hand raised in the back. "I know, teacher!" offered the student. "Let's vote on it!"

Quiddity is a philosophical term meaning the essential nature of an object— what something actually *is*. Quiddity bangs against the slip-sliding worldview of let's-vote-on-it reality. Naturally, we don't whistle Flaubert's tune whenever we approach a traffic stoplight or ask for a bank withdrawal, because perception is not enough, then. "I thought it should have been green" or "Maybe I missed a few digits" doesn't cut it. In real life, a smorgasbord of choose-your-own realities is unacceptable whenever we deeply care about the results. We know better.

In Bangkok, Thailand, you can buy Peanuts apparel sporting a dog named "Snooby," polo shirts carrying the label "Ralph Laurence," and authentic Western wear from "Lavish Strauss." However, you would never know they aren't the genuine article if you didn't *know* the genuine article. A fake can be hard to detect. Police experts explain that the best way to recognize counterfeit money is to keep studying the original, to become so adept at recognizing the true currency that it becomes known by heart and by sight.

Studying the real God leads to authenticity. Any time we hear of those "called by God" to murder for peace, deceive for truth, or demean for love, we recognize a counterfeit. It's also good to remember that we would have no counterfeits without the genuine. The genuine God brings us a remarkably well-rounded life of physical, mental, and emotional balance. Keeping our balance, as G. K. Chesterton attests, is a challenging endeavor:

> It is always simple to fall; there are an infinity of angles at which one falls, only one at which one stands. To have fallen into any one of the [current] fads . . . would indeed have been obvious and tame. But to have avoided them all has been one whirling adventure; and in my vision the heavenly

chariot flies thundering through the ages, the dull heresies sprawling and prostrate, the wild truth reeling and erect.

STALKING THE WILD TRUTH

An obviously inebriated man was crawling under a street lamp at three A.M. Gliding by in his car, a police officer called out, "Hey, what are you doing there? Do you need some help?"

"I'm l-looking for my wallet," explained the man. "I l-lost it . . . on the corner of Third and Elm."

"Third and Elm?" exclaimed the officer. "This is Ninth and Spruce!"

"I know," the man replied. "But the l-light is better here."

We don't have to be drunk to pursue the truth about God where the "light is better." Human beings by nature gravitate toward an easy place, even if it's nowhere near the truth. In "The Wayfarer," Stephen Crane accurately describes our inclination:

> The wayfarer,
> Perceiving the pathway to truth,
> Was struck with astonishment.
> It was thickly grown with weeds.
> "Ha," he said,
> "I see that none has passed here
> In a long time."
> Later he saw that each weed
> Was a singular knife.
> "Well," he mumbled at last,
> "Doubtless there are other roads."

We must ask, Do we really want to get in touch with an objective reality? Do we aim toward the scintillating light of truth and freedom, or have we grown so dependent on our lies, our pains, and our prisons that any light in a blackened room sends us seeking after the comfort of familiar cold shadows?

I once had a student who was struggling with incredible pain; she had been sexually abused as a child, yet she still had to face the relative who had abused her. Though her life was unraveling and she recognized the need for help, she shunned counseling. Watching her slide lower and lower, I felt powerless because she would not honestly confront her problem and help herself.

One day as she was leaving class, I handed her a note with the simple message, "John 5:6." The scene portrayed in this verse involves Jesus and a man who had been ill for thirty-eight years. "When Jesus saw him and knew that he had been lying there a long time, he said to him, 'Do you want to be healed?'"

The next class, I sensed that she was different. After class she approached my desk and said with a glowing peace, "You'll never know how much that note meant to me."

The key for all of us is courageous honesty, an attribute easier eulogized than lived out. Are we brave enough to follow truth where it leads? *We must be committed to honesty before we can make any changes in our opinion of God.* When the groundbreaking book *The Day America Told the Truth* was written based on surveys taken across the United States, the published results stunned readers everywhere. Survey respondents had been advised, "We don't want surface answers to these questions. We don't want white lies. Please. No white lies. . . . We are looking for total honesty." This advice rose to sublime irony in the section on honesty, where the authors discovered that "Americans . . . lie more than we had ever thought possible before the study. . . . Lying has become an integral part of the American culture, a trait of the American character. We lie and don't even think about it. We lie for no reason. The writer Vance Bourjaily once said, 'Like most men, I tell a hundred lies a day.' That's about right. And the people we lie to most are those closest to us." We don't even need to open our mouths to lie; an arched eyebrow, a pause, a slight nod can communicate volumes of misleading information. "The cruelest lies," Robert Louis Stevenson reflects, "are often told in silence."

The truth is often painful to look in the face. I witnessed this in my father's U.S. history classroom when I visited one day and noticed a sophomore tapping her pencil on sheet after sheet of paper for the entire period. After class I asked Dad what she was doing. He told me that he had been attempting to impress upon students the immensity of the number 1,000,000,000 because people tend to talk about billions of dollars in a fairly offhanded way, so he promised that anyone who made a billion marks during the semester would receive an automatic A. He had the class make marks as fast as they could for one minute, then calculate how long it would take them, working at a comparable rate for twelve hours each day, seven days a week, to reach one billion. (A constant rate of 3 marks per second, or 129,600 marks per day, would require 7,716 days— about 21 years.)

"So why is she still doing it?" I asked.

Dad shook his head sadly. "Because, she told me, she wants an A in this class.

And she said she was willing to work more than twelve hours a day on it." He held up a fistful of papers covered with marks. "She's already done more than ten million. I've shown her the math and proved that she can never make it, but she keeps tapping her days away."

Confronted with the truth, many people react fearfully and illogically, perhaps buying into the relativistic language of the age. One definition of a fanatic is someone who, once the error of his or her ways has been clearly demonstrated, redoubles those efforts in the same direction. The bold success of Alcoholics Anonymous and spinoff Twelve-Step recovery groups is predicated on honesty—within the participants themselves, with other people, and with God. What changes the groups? Total honesty. The truth is elevating; the truth is humbling. The truth is stratospheric; the truth is earthbound. Anything less than truth results in wrecked lives.

How does being committed to truth lead to loving God? If our sincere quest is not toward total honesty and truth, we will wander in forests of deception, looking where the light is "better" and tapping on meaningless papers. What is acceptable we accept; we almost never do the unthinkable. If worshiping figments and loving fakes is just fine, if lying appears to be an acceptable way of life, our spiritual compass will be continually spinning. In the book of *Jeremiah* God laments, "They bend their tongue like a bow; falsehood and not truth has grown strong in the land; for they proceed from evil to evil, and they do not know me, . . . Heaping oppression upon oppression, and deceit upon deceit, they refuse to know me. . . . You will seek me and find me when you seek me with all your heart, I will be found by you."[4]

Among the disturbing findings in *The Day America Told the Truth* is that nearly half the people who responded honestly feel nobody knows them. Furthermore, one in four answered "nobody" to the question, "Who's for real?" God is for real. But if we aren't for real, if we aren't seeking the real, how can God be there for us? In addition to fracturing human trust, here is the most devastating aspect of posing and dissembling: God cannot *find* us to heal us, to save us.[5] When God appears, we aren't home. Some other person, some wavy, porous public image, inhabits our bony frame and brain.

Making contact can be unnerving, however. C. S. Lewis explains, "There comes a moment when the children who have been playing at burglars will

---

4. *Jeremiah*, chapters 9 and 29.
5. In the Garden of Eden, Adam and Eve "hid themselves from the presence of the Lord God," and an all-seeing God asked, "Where are you?" (*Genesis*, chapter 3).

hush suddenly: was that a real footstep in the hall? There comes a moment when people who have been dabbling in religion . . . suddenly draw back. Supposing we really found Him? We never meant it to come to *that!*"

A friend told me he once knelt and prayed for God's blessing and filling. Warm, dazzling light instantly enveloped him. Terrified, he opened his eyes and saw through the window before him that swift, dark clouds had parted to expose the naked sun. Reflecting on his fear when his request seemed actually granted, he confessed, "I'm not as cavalier about praying as I once was."

As is the case with real love, the wild truth leaves us confused, breathless with wide-eyed wonder, and liberated. The truth is as untamed as Einstein's hair, as prickly as a sea urchin with an attitude. The closer we get to truth, the closer we get to paradox. We learn that we must give to gain, serve to lead, be humble to be great. At the very least, truth startles us from our complacency. In his legendary commencement address to Duke University, Ted Koppel confirms that, "in its purest form, truth is not a polite tap on the shoulder. It is a howling reproach. What Moses brought down from Mount Sinai were not the Ten Suggestions."

KNOWING OUR NEED

How do we know God exists? Can we truly know that we're not alone here?

Human beings are remarkably open to different paths of knowing. We may use empirical methods, memory, and intuition, but nothing surpasses one avenue we use to know a bicycle or a box of chocolates. How do you know what you're sitting on right now will support you? How does a friend know that job will be good for her? *The best way to be certain is to test it.* When *New York* magazine sent John R. Coleman into the streets of the city for ten days to pose as a homeless man, he opened his report:

> Somehow, 12 degrees at 6 A.M. was colder than I had counted on. I think of myself as relatively immune to cold, but standing on a deserted sidewalk outside Penn Station with the thought of ten days ahead of me as a homeless man, the immunity vanished. When I pulled my collar closer and my watch cap lower, it wasn't to look the part of a street person; it was to keep the wind out.

We may resort to all types of theories about God, but the best way to be certain of God is to experience God, as billions claim to have done in the midst of splintering grief and soaring ecstasy. This experience comes even to people who don't believe in God. C. S. Lewis confessed that while he was an atheist he not only maintained that God did not exist, but he was also very angry with God for not existing and was equally angry with God for creating this world.

How important is *testing?* Parents and teachers think that if we can persuade others to *believe* the right things, they will act the right way. But studies don't support this. Bill McNabb writes in *Youthworker,* "In 1964 psychologist Leon Festinger concluded that research had in fact not supported the assumption that people's attitudes or beliefs will change their behavior. Festinger and others advanced the radical notion that the attitude-behavior relationship actually works the other way around—that is, people are more likely to behave their way into thinking than think their way into behaving." We believe *what we do* more than we do what we believe. Cognitive dissonance dictates that we cannot continue to do something and persist in believing it's wrong; rather, we rationalize whatever we're doing.

McNabb points out, "One week of building houses for poor families is worth five years of Bible studies on the importance of Christian service. We have taken with us scores of teenagers who did not believe in Jesus' admonition to serve, but came to believe it by doing it." Standing outside and looking hard will not convince us; we come to know the path by stepping into the jungle. To know is to risk. Action creates belief. Jesus insists, "Where your treasure is, there will your heart be also."

Knowing also goes beyond our senses. I once overheard a woman remark, "I've never seen God, and I can't believe in anything I can't see, hear, taste, smell, or touch." Sipping her Diet Pepsi, she concluded with a shrug, "So, I don't believe in God." At which point I wondered, *Have you ever seen a calorie? Or touched a calorie? How does a calorie taste?* As with all of us, she has yet to *experience* a calorie, yet calories fill conversations and dominate ad space, disappearing in an array of products from pudding to lite beer. Though we can't see, hear, smell, taste, or touch calories, we believe in them.

If calories function as a measurement of energy, what serves as a measurement for God? Typically we look toward tangible experiences as evidence of God's activity (which can be as easy as seeing grass grow), but a major obstacle to measuring God arises if we judge on the basis of "good" events only. An American football player kneels in the end zone after a touchdown to thank God, yet could God be just as much in his fumble or dropped pass? Imagine a player kneeling after being thrown for a five-yard loss to pray, "Thank you, God, for keeping me humble. With all the hype here, I need all the help I can get." We would know he was "shaken up."

James F. Sennett muses, "'If it works, that must be God blessing it.' So stated, no intelligent Christian would endorse this motto." The problem with if-it-works religion is that people hold such bizarre ideas of what and why something "works." We chalk up our good fortune to lucky clothes and numbers, planets aligning, and miracle food supplements, yet when we do acquire our desire and it turns out to be a terrible mistake, we distrust God all the more. When the economy crashes, the atmosphere buckles under stress, and violent gangs terrorize suburbia, blame God. Our reasoning is akin to my enduring a lengthy sneezing fit and then, instead of finding out what it is I'm allergic to, blaming the attack on my breathing. Obviously this breathing in—this inspiration— doesn't work for me.

The critical issue is need. Am I so self-absorbed that I stop at sixteen squares, believing that what I see is all that exists? Are my needs what the yelping advertisers insist? Here is a subtle foe. It's harder to feel our true need of God when a home entertainment center sits panting in the den. Cars, computers, and snacks cushion and divert us from recognizing real needs until a romantic breakup or traffic accident wreathes us in smoke, reminding us of life's fundamentals.

Modern Western society is afflicted by the curse of comfort, but our condition is nothing new. In the ancient book of *Deuteronomy,* Moses warns his people to beware, "lest, when you have eaten and are full, and have built goodly houses and live in them, and when your herds and flocks multiply, and your silver and gold is multiplied . . . then your heart be lifted up, and you forget the Lord your God . . ."[6] Fifteen hundred years later a being "like a son of man" says to the church of Laodicea, representing our age, "You say, I am rich, I have prospered, and I need nothing, not knowing that you are wretched, pitiable, poor, blind, and naked."[7]

We should make a distinction between the conceit of believing we don't need God and the conceit of believing God favors us. Christians can fit into the latter category, but going to church is not a surefire sign of this conceit. A lunch partner once said to me, "What bothers me is that Christians think they have an inside path to God. That's so arrogant!"

I asked, "What do you think about God?"

He pointed to his chest. "God is right here, inside me."

"H'mm," I said. "Christians are arrogant because they feel their need

---

6. *Deuteronomy,* chapter 8.
7. *Revelation,* chapter 3.

enough to look to an outside God to heal them, but you *are* God. And they're the arrogant ones." He kept stirring his coffee.

While God cannot be wholly contained in any theological system, going to church is no more spiritually arrogant than going for a walk is physically arrogant. The church is not a *Showtime!* for the saints but a hospital for the sick. It's a community designed to study and pursue deep quests: where we came from, who we are, where we're going. It's also a sanctuary for the bypassed, battered, baffled, and burned out. Our being wretched and pitiable doesn't mean we should stop visiting the hospital; in fact, in visiting the Doctor we more fully sense our needs. As He presses on our soul and inquires, "Does it hurt here?" we groan, and He says, "You must take this medicine. You need to apply this salve."

We're all hurting. Every being on earth is fighting some type of uphill battle. Mike Yaconelli, a popular Christian speaker, tells of agreeing to a friend's request that Yaconelli speak to the Northern California Toastmasters. Arriving at the event ten minutes before he was to speak, Yaconelli asked his friend to tell him a little more about the audience. His friend replied, "These people are the postmasters from every city in northern California."

> "Postmasters?" I said rather sheepishly. "I thought you said Toastmasters. TOASTmasters!"
>
> "No," he said, "why would I say that? I'm a postmaster."
>
> I had ten minutes to formulate the keynote address for the Northern California Postmasters. I wasn't allowed to talk about God or Jesus, of course, but I certainly didn't have much to say about the new bulk mail regulations. I did the only thing I could do, I decided to speak about issues we all struggle with—loneliness, insignificance, and meaninglessness. In other words, I decided to talk about our common longings.
>
> I was shocked.
>
> There were tears in many of their eyes during the talk, and I received a standing ovation when it was over . . . and I discovered something that day: People are longing for God. I had inadvertently touched base with their longings. They knew the loneliness I was talking about. They were experiencing the meaninglessness and insignificance of much of their lives, and they could not hold back the tears.

We are lonely for God. Our longing goes beyond knowing *about* God: We want to *know* God, to find a companionable friend beyond the noise.[8] Above

---

8. John Milton writes, "Loneliness is the first thing which God's eye nam'd not good."

all, our need for a God to love draws us. "When the conversation moves to the subject of knowing God," Tim Stafford observes, "listeners grow suddenly quiet and attentive. For a long time I thought this was a disapproving silence. I now know it is the silence that falls on a room of hungry people when someone talks of food."

THE TRUTH ABOUT DOUBT

Doubts have driven millions from God and steered millions toward God. Most of us hold healthy reservations on what we hear about God; doubtless we can become fanatical, self-serving, and woodenheaded.

Many commentators have expressed their views on doubt, particularly toward what appear to be God's startling concessions. Ellen White says, "God has never removed the possibility of doubt. Our faith must rest upon evidence, not demonstration. Those who wish to doubt will have opportunity, while those who really desire to know the truth will find plenty of evidence on which to rest their faith." Frederick Buechner points out the dilemma we pose for God in demanding both certainty and personal freedom: "Without somehow destroying me in the process, how could God reveal Himself in a way that would leave no room for doubt? If there were no room for doubt, there would be no room for me." God would rather deal with rebels than robots.

Of course, in the matter of faith there is no convincing some people. "Doubt becomes a way of life just as faith does," Calvin Miller writes. "Hard-core skeptics have often fallen in love with arguing as a lifestyle. They don't want to be convinced by the practical nature of the Christian faith. Argumentation is their greatest joy. Becoming a Christian would eliminate the argument and ruin their fun." And so the skeptic's challenge is set forth: "Explain God!" While to a large degree God is eminently logical and sensible, He cannot be reduced to a formula or encompassed by an explanation.[9] It is impossible for finite minds to fully comprehend infinity.

An anecdote about Albert Einstein demonstrates why complexity, including a complex God, cannot always be simplified.

---

9. God cannot even be accurately reduced to one gender, as God carries both male and female attributes. (For example, "So God created man in his own image, in the image of God he created him; male and female he created them," *Genesis,* chapter 1.) Unfortunately, the nongender alternative pronoun in English is *It,* an impersonal state that mucks up the picture even more than *He.* Where plausible, to avoid cumbersome phrasing, I'll use He. Substitute She if you prefer. In the interest of stability, I won't switch between genders.

One day a pesky reporter asked Einstein to describe his theory of relativity in a few simple words. He responded with the following story: A man was asked by a blind man to describe the color white. The man said, "White is the color of a swan." The blind man said, "What is a swan?" The man said, "A swan is a bird with a crooked neck."

The blind man asked, "What is crooked?" The man was becoming impatient. He grabbed the blind man's arm, straightened it and said, "This is straight." Then he bent it and said, "And this is crooked."

Whereupon the blind man quickly said, "Yes, yes, thank you. Now I know what white is."

Our doubtful questions about God and to God can take on a surreal quality. Are there any questions God cannot answer? All nonsense questions are unanswerable: Is it farther to New York or by bus? Is purple square or round? What's the difference between a toad? How can I live forever without plugging into the source of life? C. S. Lewis points out that most of our metaphysical questions are like these.

We spend too much effort braying our infallibility rather than bridling our strutting tongues. Two decades ago when I was starting to seriously seek God, my friend Larry undertook to "study with me." He and I met in his house to look into the Bible and talk about my doubts, and I asked Larry some hard questions: What happens to aborted babies? How does God "answer" our prayers for others and still honor their freedom of choice? Why does God allow so much suffering?

To each of these questions Larry provided a stunning answer. He said, "I don't know."

I couldn't believe it. I thought Christians presumed they knew everything. This was the one answer he could have given that appealed to me. Then he added, "I have some ideas, but whenever I don't reach satisfying conclusions, I pick that question up and hang it on a hook at the back of my mind. Later, I'll take it down and look at it again." He smiled his wry, tilted smile. "No matter how much I think I know," he concluded, "I want to keep growing."

God is a humbling mystery, but a mystery isn't something we know nothing about; it's something we don't know everything about.[10] We choose the smooth downhill path when we choose gods who will not trouble us with the fact of evil or the problem of suffering, when life's perplexing contradictions are evaded

---

10. We don't fully know *ourselves.* After Jesus disclosed that one of His closest friends would betray Him, the disciples asked, "Is it I?" They weren't certain of their own hidden motives.

and dismissed. Designer gods persuade us to pick daffodils, live and let live, and speak of love as though it were an easy thing, subject to no more disciplined effort than a languid stroll in a meadow.

Unfortunately, though, the world is a tough place. Marriages burst at the seams. People die from mistaken impressions. Dark flames of rage and despair lick about us. Living for God or the god-of-my-perceptions is the difference between fighting an insanely hot inferno with a fire hose or a can of diet cola.

As you read through this book, take what makes sense, cover it within your coat, and toss the rest away, or simply hang the remainder on a hook at the back of your mind to explore later. Too many people have surrendered their search for truth because they became riddled with tumors of doubt.

Our great need is to recognize our great need. And our deepest need burrows to the core of our lives.

Saying the "S" Word

Humankind's deepest need is one we fight against most feverishly. From birth till death, we dodge and disavow it. Though virtually everyone talks a good game of love and justice, we are essentially selfish creatures. We are born selfish, nurtured in selfishness, seduced by selfishness, rewarded for selfishness—and prone to deny it. The ancient Greeks called it *hubris,* a fatal flaw of pride. The Bible calls it sin.

We don't perceive our true condition because our self-centered atmosphere flows through our veins. Does a fish *feel* wet? We are immersed in self-absorption. Addicted to ourselves, we can't kick the habit. Our perceptions warp until goodness appears strange and evil tastes good. Jesus says, "The eye is the lamp of the body. So, if your eye is sound, your whole body will be full of light; but if your eye is not sound, your whole body will be full of darkness. If then the light in you is darkness, how great is the darkness!"

In *Hope Has Its Reasons,* Becky Pippert details her pilgrimage away from insisting on her own innocence:

> Slowly I started acknowledging my own faults. I began to deal with the root problems in my life and not merely the symptoms. I saw that my pride and self-centeredness lay deep within, far deeper than I had ever imagined. And I made an exciting discovery. The more I faced myself—my self-deceptions, pockets of unbelief, false confidences, controlling devices, and so on—the more I found freedom.

Once my wife, Yolanda, and I were planning to fly from Baltimore to Dallas. The flight was delayed after boarding, so we sat on the plane for an hour and a half. During the wait a man in front of us fell into a sound sleep. With the announcement that, owing to mechanical difficulties, the plane would not be departing, scores of disgruntled passengers grabbed their overhead bags and began to exit the aircraft. Startled, the man awoke with an expression so comical it activated Yolanda's shaking, silent laugh for about five minutes. The poor red-eyed fellow looked around, perplexed, and peered out the window, but because all terminals look the same he couldn't straightaway tell where he was. *Was he in Dallas, or was he still in Baltimore?*

Many of us look at "salvation" that way: Have we arrived, or are we still waiting for the trip? Is my life all right as it is? Can I tell by the people around me if I'm sitting on the right flight? One problem in our culture is we don't know we're lost. The other problem is we don't know we're found.

Our situation is something like walking out the back door of a house and plunging painfully into a deep pit someone dug during the night. We can't climb out; it's too slick and too steep. No one can hear our calls for help. There we sit, nursing our wounds and cursing our fortune. Suddenly a rope drops down from above. "Hold on!" a voice cries. "I'll pull you out."

Now, we can respond in many ways. We can say, "I didn't ask to be down here. It's not my fault I'm in this dank, smelly pit. So forget the rope. I'm not taking it."

We can say, "If you know where I am, you must have had something to do with digging this pit, so I'm not trusting you. No way."

We can say, "I'll accept the rope only if I can pull myself out. I don't want any help from you." But pulling ourselves up proves futile. It's much too far. After a few tries, we drop back to the bottom. "Thanks for nothing!" we wheeze.

Or we can hold on. It takes effort to keep our grip, yet we make slow and steady progress. When at last we reach the surface, eyes stinging from bright light, lungs filling with fresh air, we drop to our knees. "Thank you!" we gasp. "I was afraid no one would ever hear me or help me. I was afraid I'd be stuck there."

"You're welcome, my child," God says, wrapping us up in His arms.

Imagine what it would be like for a parent to ask a child in such a situation to hold on, and for the child to refuse, and eventually perish. What agony that parent must feel when no amount of begging or enticing can bring the child to a welcoming warm embrace! God endures this scene with His children every hour.

Some people believe that God is selective, choosing only those who cozy up to Him to curry His favor. In reality, salvation has nothing to do with favoritism and

everything to do with substance. In our pr[...]
presence just as we can't stare at the sun wi[...]
from God, rebellion against God. Preachin[...]
short of disclosing the true problem, not[...]
hurts living beings, including God. Sin ar[...]
separate ourselves from God we *inevitab*[...]
moon's phases. That's the sin problem—[...]
up to it. Who in their right minds wou[...]
are reluctant to address is the tendency [...]
looking others, picketing abortion clinics while keeping sile[...]
millions killed by promoting tobacco use overseas. Or claiming that matters or
taste are sinful. As horrible as sin is, it gets a bad rap whenever it becomes
twisted into something else.

We are especially uncomfortable with guilt. Listen to people discuss guilt in
general, and one message comes through with conviction: Guilt is bad. But it's
those who feel *no* guilt who are most dangerous—the psychopathic liars and
killers, Nuremberg war criminals, and hatemongers of the world who feel
totally justified in their ghastly acts. In August 1969, a small cult under the hyp-
notic direction of Charles Manson brutally slaughtered seven people in what
became known as the Tate-LaBianca murders. At his trial, after the court found
him guilty, Manson was asked if he had any comments before the judge handed
down his sentence. Wild-eyed and scraggly, Manson stood, pointed to the jury,
and seethed, "You have no right to try me! I did what I felt was right!"

Don't we all insist this for ourselves? No matter what heinous lie or hatred
we have perpetrated, we long to absolve ourselves of blame, twirling and ducking to avoid the penetrating missile of guilt. But guilt in itself is not bad. It's
faulty guilt that's tragic. It's unresolved guilt that's deadly. Without guilt—that
discomforting twinge of conscience—we would be a sorrier race than we are
now. As long as we're convinced we have never done anything wrong, we can
never do anything right. We complain to God that we're uncomfortable, and
God turns to us with a sad smile and says, "Good." How else would we change
our lack of compassion, our critical spirit, our greed, our lust for revenge?
Paradoxically, while each of us is—*just as we are*—a priceless gift of infinite
worth, none of us is "okay." We're all struggling children who need help.

What of the undeniable good that flares in us? Acts of unselfish sacrifice and
heroism can be witnessed every day, from exhausted mothers working overtime to
firefighters dying to save the life of a ninety-year-old. Insisting on our own innocence, though, is futile. As C. S. Lewis points out, "Everyone feels benevolent if

be annoying him at the moment." Joseph Cooke remarks, rd of any large group of people who, without external pressure illingly agreed together to suffer major inconvenience or loss for of other groups who were worse off. . . . When the chips are down cy always wins out over morality." Throughout history the "good" le, saints and prophets, reformers and martyrs, have found that the closer ey get to truth and to God, the clearer they see cruelty, selfishness, and deception crouching in us all. Literature mirrors this finding. The same conclusion is reached in *Hamlet, A Separate Peace, The Fall, Crime and Punishment,* and hundreds of other stories.

In William Golding's *Lord of the Flies,* an idyllic uninhabited island absorbs a crashed planeload of British schoolboys. With no adults on hand, Ralph and Piggy attempt to construct a "civilized" structure, but when Jack and his minions counter, the result is horrifying death. Their new society is peopled from eggs of the serpent's brood. Perhaps as much as any book, *Lord of the Flies* plays out how futile the quest for lasting peace and love is if it is based only upon human instincts. Rousseau's "noble savage" ideal is torched with the boys' island.

Our situation is like hearing from the doctor, "You must stop smoking. Plain and simple, it's killing you. You need to slow down—your blood pressure is too high. If you don't start eating less and exercising more, you're a prime candidate for a heart attack."

Some people respond, "I gotta find me another doctor."

What about you? Your conscience might be saying, "My life is out of control—it's running away from me. I feel empty and tired too often. My relationships are superficial, my promises are ropes of sand, my existence lacks purpose. The joy is seeping from my life."

It happens to all of us. The realization hits, *I need something more. Or maybe Someone more.*

What then?

Self-deception is at the base of sin's affliction. Our need is not first to avoid sin, but to recognize sin. Gary Krause comments, "The last thing we need is another New Age book, cassette, lecture, or video on discovering the god within and unleashing our innate goodness. The last thing we need is another slick millionaire self-help guru telling us how wonderful we are." Trying to fix the sin problem ourselves when we *are* the problem is like hearing from the bank that a checking account is overdrawn and responding, "That's all right. Here, I'll write a check to cover it."

A PRETTY GOOD PERSON?

Basically I think I'm a pretty good person. Unfortunately, I can also think that the glacier makes a peachy spot for a picnic. What matters is how God views me. The Bible asserts that God "sees not as man sees; man looks on the outward appearance, but the Lord looks on the heart."

In the film *Places in the Heart* a gang of hooded Klansmen pummel Moze, a black sharecropper, until his friend, blind Mr. Will, starts calling out their names. "That's Mr. Thompson, I've been selling him brooms for years. Sure as you're Mr. Shaw. And that's Mr. Simmons over there by the barn." The Klansmen know the game is up. Their hooded masks don't fool Mr. Will, because he knows them through another sense.

Our pretty good masks don't hoodwink God. "God is closer to us than we are to ourselves," says Augustine. God knows the germ within. He recognizes us not only by our actions but also by the DNA of our thoughts. God views us through His electron microscope and rubs His brow in sorrow. "This virus is a million times deadlier than AIDS," He sighs. "No living being can survive it. If it's unleashed in the universe, it will be hell."

G. K. Chesterton understood this. Many years ago the *Times* of London trumpeted the question, "What's Wrong with the World?" Chesterton responded in the letters section with characteristic directness: "I am. Yours truly, G. K. Chesterton."

How hard can it be to live and love perfectly? People who don't know music can't appreciate the subtleties or the difficulties inherent in a Mozart movement. The same is true with playing out godly purity, patience, faithfulness, self-control. I remember reading for the first time the following words from C. S. Lewis in *Mere Christianity* and being startled into a new comprehension of my condition:

> No man knows how bad he is till he has tried very hard to be good. A silly idea is current that good people do not know what temptation means. This is an obvious lie. Only those who try to resist temptation know how strong it is. After all, you find out the strength . . . of a wind by trying to walk against it, not by lying down. A man who gives in to temptation after five minutes simply does not know what it would have been like an hour later. That is why bad people, in one sense, know very little about badness. They have lived a sheltered life by always giving in. We never find out the strength of the evil impulse inside us until we try to fight it: and Christ,

because He was the only man who never yielded to temptation, is also the only man who knows to the full what temptation means—the only complete realist.

We are like skydivers plummeting from a great height with parachutes strapped to our backs. No matter how comfortable we become during the fall, shouting to each other over the turbulence, doing loop-de-loops, enjoying the wind in our hair, our end is certain death. The one way to survive is to admit we need a parachute. And when we pull the rip cord, we suddenly leave the crowd.

For those of us who are honestly searching and who earnestly desire what is right, who have sensed something we cannot shake from our minds, who have felt the breath of God on our skin—when we feel totally empty, a living being enters to fill what only He can fill. Dag Hammarskjöld concludes, "When you have nothing left but God you will become aware for the first time that God is enough."

· · ·

Jerry Levin served as a news correspondent in the Middle East boiling pot of Beirut when in an instant his life changed drastically. Walking to work one March morning in 1984, he felt a tap on his shoulder. Turning, he faced a young bearded man who pushed a handgun into Levin's stomach, propelling him toward a gray car with an open rear door. Levin didn't resist. He slid into the seat as the assailant jumped in beside him.

"Close eyes! Close eyes!" the man shouted. "You see, I kill." The car sped away. For the next eleven months, Levin, a fifty-one-year-old grandfather, was held hostage, blindfolded and chained to a wall in a tiny room. He was a Jewish agnostic, caught in the crossfire of fanatic religious terrorism. While in his prison, with no literature, no preachers, no tender counsel, no human interference of any kind, Levin became a believer in God. In fact, he became a Christian.

Outside, his wife had been praying fervently for him. Muslim, Jewish, and Christian friends joined in working for his release. One Muslim leader in Beirut commented that never in the past thousand years had so many people of differing faiths worked together on behalf of one man. On February 13, 1985, Levin wrestled out of his chains, lowered himself from his window, and escaped his captors.

"The irony," Levin said later, "is that all those people thought they were working for someone who was a godless man . . . I am convinced now that none of us is ever really godless. I know now that God is there for us whether or not we are there for God."

The wild truth is that God is there for us.

~

God, help us not to despise or oppose what we do not understand.

—WILLIAM PENN

To make an apple pie from scratch, you must first invent the universe.

—CARL SAGAN

The significance and joy in my science comes in those occasional moments of discovering something new and saying to myself, "So that's how God did it."

—HENRY F. SCHAEFER

What we suffer from today is humility in the wrong place. Modesty has moved from the organ of ambition. Modesty has settled upon the organ of conviction, where it was never meant to be. A man was meant to be doubtful about himself, but undoubting about the truth; this has been exactly reversed. We are on the road to producing a race of men too mentally modest to believe in the multiplication table.

—G. K. CHESTERTON

In the absence of any other proof, the thumb alone would convince me of God's existence.

—SIR ISAAC NEWTON

There is no book like the Bible.
There is none like it when your head is aching.
There is none like it when the day is without the sun,
     and the night without its stars.
There is nothing like it when your children are left motherless.
There is none like it when you bury your baby.
There is none like it when the springs of life are snapping.
There is none like when you reach the end of life's journey and pillow
     your head on its promises, and God stoops and kisses you to sleep.

—H. M. S. RICHARDS

~

3

BEYOND MOTHER NATURE

RECENTLY A CHURCH in Florida received a sweepstakes notice announcing that God, of Bushnell, Florida, was a finalist for the $11 million top prize. The letter said, "*God,* we've been searching for you." Centered between two official seals, the message requested God to "come forward." If God were to win, "what an incredible fortune there would be for *God!* Could you imagine the looks you'd get from your neighbors? But don't just sit there, *God.*"

The pastor of the church said his congregation was considering whether to mail in the entry, as the church could use the money. And if a different winner was chosen? "God would be disappointed," quipped the pastor.

In a sense, that sweepstakes notice echoed the thoughts and prayers of countless people. "God, we've been searching for You . . . come forward . . . don't just sit there, God."

In 1989, Voyager 2 had sailed more than 2.7 billion miles from Earth, discovered four new moons on Neptune, and sent us the news by radio signal transmissions *twenty billion times weaker than the battery power of a digital wristwatch.* With this sensitivity at our disposal, doesn't it seem we ought to be able to detect whether a creator God really exists?

I used to think of creationists as first cousins to the flat earthers, bumpkins who could not distinguish myth and symbolism from science. Creationists extended premises beyond their viable limits, left challenges to their beliefs unexamined, and no matter how much evidence piled up against them, continued to "believe." But the more one looks into it, the more it becomes apparent that intellectual blindness and complacent arrogance are found in the ranks of evolutionists as well.[1]

If you mark ten coins from one to ten and mix them in your pocket, what is the statistical likelihood that you could pull each coin out (and replace it) in exact numerical sequence? By mathematical law you have only one chance in

---

1. There are many varieties of evolutionists and creationists, and some overlap. For example, theistic evolutionists believe in a creator God, and nearly all creationists believe in microevolutionary adaptations.

10 billion. Now consider the chances of stomach, ears, kidneys, and capillaries developing at once. John T. Baldwin writes, "After subjecting Darwinian theory to the principles of probability theory, mathematicians Sir Fred Hoyle and Chandra Wickramasinghe expressed surprise at how so simple and so decisive a disproof of the Darwinian theory has escaped the attention of social scientists for so long. 'There can, we think, be no explanation other than intellectual perversity.'"[2]

Books such as Berkeley law professor Philip Johnson's *Darwin on Trial,* biochemist Michael Behe's *Darwin's Black Box,* and *Science* magazine editor M. Mitchell Waldrop's *Complexity* raise questions about macroevolution and the inherent problems of "irreducible complexity" and "self-organization."

"The most amazing thing to me is existence itself," says cosmologist Allan Sandage. "Why is there something instead of nothing? How is it that inanimate matter can organize itself? That's outside of any science I know."

Perhaps the larger question is not "creation or evolution?" but rather "purpose or accident?" Others illustrate it more simply by comparing the probability of life developing by accident to:

- a print shop explosion producing a dictionary
- a tornado passing through a salvage yard of scrap metal and creating a fully functioning car
- the disassembled parts of a watch shaken in a can for millions of years becoming a watch that keeps perfect time

Kip McGilliard, an associate professor of zoology with a Ph.D. in pharmacology, made his greatest spiritual discovery not in church but in a lab, peering through a microscope. "I was watching in amazement at the complex chemical reactions, and it just struck me," he recalls. "The complexity and order of these chemical reactions couldn't happen by accident. There must be an intelligent designer."

The probability of complex systems evolving naturally faces astronomical odds on every hand—and eye, cilium, and blood clot. How did the vital secretion of insulin into the bloodstream begin, and what prevented diabetic coma

---

2. Fred Hoyle and Chandra Wickramasinghe, *Why NeoDarwinism Does Not Work* (Cardiff, Wales: University College Cardiff Press, 1982). Quoted in *Ministry* magazine, September 1995. Donald Page of Princeton University's Institute for Advanced Study estimates the odds of human life existing to be one to 10,000,000,000[124].

before its appearance? *How* did a reptile become a bird?[3] Questions like these tend to punctuate my equilibrium. Kim Peckham estimates that reptile lungs developing into bird lungs would be as difficult as a piston engine changing to a rotary engine while it's running.

The last time I had the flu my body ached so much I couldn't stand up. An eyelash in my eye can incapacitate me. I know a man whose child was born without muscles in her eyelids, requiring several corrective surgeries. How often do you contemplate the muscles in your eyelids? But these are small matters. Think what a nuisance it would be to be without skin, what a *bother* to be missing a heart valve, what a *distraction* to be unable to assimilate food. Albert Einstein says, "There are only two ways to live your life. One is as though nothing is a miracle. The other is as though everything is a miracle."

Life is godly. Life glows. Life is vibrant, spicy, and liquid. We stand in awe as a human fetus floats and tumbles in the amniotic sac like a turtle in a tidal creek. When Stephen Jay Gould states his opinion that "a crab is not lower or less complex than a human being in any meaningful way," in one sense I understand his nuanced point. All of life amazes. On another level, though, I will admit some hierarchies. If faced with the choice of rescuing two crabs or one human being from death, I'll rescue the human every time; there is a distinction that is *meaningful*.

Science can be as baffling as religion. Each is a way of seeing, and each calls for an essential leap of faith. The "God of the gaps" scientific belief, that God occupies only those processes we don't understand, is a debilitating perspective—God

---

3. Much distance remains between the reptile and the bird. Some changes that must take place to move from reptile to bird:

- Arms greatly elongate to form wings
- Body streamlines so wings beating against it create air currents
- Wings change shape to provide lift
- Bones get lighter
- Skull gets thinner
- Body (including bones) becomes full of air sacs
- Air sacs and spaces in body connect with lungs for fast respiration
- Breathing in and out coordinates with wingbeat
- Heartbeat and metabolic rate speed up
- Outgrowths from skin elongate to form quills
- Quills develop thin, strong material with spongy interior
- Upper part of quill flattens out
- Side branches develop, forming barbs and barbules for the veins of feathers
- Softer, contour feathers and down feathers (for warmth) form
- Eyesight becomes sharper for long distance
- Eyes become able to adjust quickly for close observation
- Teeth and jawbones change to a thin, light beak
- The digestive process changes so that swallowed stones grind up food in the gizzard
- Brain becomes larger in proportion to the body
- A new nervous system develops as neurons in the brain are replaced
- Nearly all habits and instincts change, making way for nesting and migrating

shrinks as our discoveries increase until He is gradually edged out of His own universe. On the other hand, we're continually reminded of the limits of our understanding and application of science.[4] Computers that generate three million decisions a second can't handle the birth of twin zeroes, while a child spraying an aerosol can in a bathroom in Casper, Wyoming, widens a hole in the ozone layer over the South Pole. In 1994, astronomers discovered that a huge unidentified source of gravity is pulling the Milky Way at an average velocity of 1.5 million miles an hour in a separate drift from the general expansion of the universe.[5] "There are not supposed to be separate motions," said Marc Postman of the Space Telescope Science Institute in Baltimore. "We have yet to figure out exactly what is causing it."

Creationists, however, as is well-documented, have often been guilty of bad theology and worse science. Drawing sufficient conclusions from insufficient premises, they too create tomatoes out of tomato puree. "What religion worthy of its name," questions Harold Kushner, "would base itself on the hope that people would be too intimidated to find out how the world really works?" God is not against learning empirically.

In *The Battle of Beginnings: Why* Neither Side *Is Winning the Creation-Evolution Debate,* Del Ratzsch writes:

> Many creationists have failed to understand some of the basic distinctives of Darwinian evolutionary theory, much less the precise details that render many of the popular easy criticisms irrelevant. Many evolutionists have likewise simply failed to investigate the contents of the creationist case, are unfamiliar both with specific positions and with developments in recent decades, and confidently repeat criticisms that are simply irrelevant. It is difficult to fight an effective battle when one does not know what the opposition even looks like.

As Josh Billings says, "It's better not to know so much than to know so many things that ain't so."

Both sides have difficulties. Creationists have difficulty explaining the precise sorting in the fossil record; extinction patterns whereby the buried life in deep layers is extinct, while the stuff near the top is still living; and pseudogenes that

---

4. Sir Arthur Eddington remarks, "We often think that when we have completed our study on one, we know all about two, because 'two is one and one.' We forget that we have still to make a study of 'and.'"
5. It makes me wonder what else I haven't noticed.

imply common ancestors. Naturalistic evolutionists have difficulty explaining the notable lack of intermediate forms in the fossil record; the Cambrian explosion of fully developed complex forms; paraconformities that show little or no erosion over supposed millions of years; how significant mutations can be consistently beneficial as opposed to what we see today; and how to make DNA by natural processes.

Where did we come from? Stephen Jay Gould doesn't know what happened. The Leakeys don't know what happened. Stephen Hawking doesn't know what happened. Richard Dawkins doesn't know what happened. In spite of all the talk, they, along with creationists, have neither explained nor can they prove everything. Naturalistic evolutionists claim they don't have enough faith to believe in God. For me, I can't comprehend believing in evolutionary odds that are so improbable—I don't have enough of that type of faith. Annie Dillard observes in *Pilgrim at Tinker Creek*, "This view requires that a monstrous world running on chance and death, careening blindly from nowhere to nowhere, somehow produced wonderful us."

In 1993, Michael Ruse, a Darwinian philosopher of science, admitted that "evolution akin to religion involves making certain a priori or metaphysical assumptions which at some level cannot be proven empirically."

What's debilitating is any tendency to distrust anything that might lead away from what one already believes.

IT'S HARD TO BE FRIENDS WITH ENERGY

When I was in Alaska visiting my brother, we spent two days sea kayaking and camping on a deserted island. At twilight I set up my dome tent on the island about 80 yards from Bruce and 50 yards from the beach. In my short time around Haines I had witnessed a remarkable array of wildlife, including bald eagles by the dozens. Brown bear are also plentiful, and Bruce warned me, "They don't mess around." To prove his point, he recited a few intimidating tales, though I didn't require convincing.

I awoke in the hazy morning to the grunting and snuffling of a large animal outside my tent. By the full, deep resonance of the snorts I knew it was a bear, and while it's one thing to *talk* about being mauled and eaten, when you're lying in a zipped tent imagining the claw ripping through and the dripping maw plunging down, the prospect assumes fresh power. Somehow what came to mind was a Gary Larson cartoon of two polar bears looking at an igloo, and one bear saying, "Oh, hey! I just love these things! Crunchy on the outside and a chewy center!"

For the next few minutes as I listened to the sounds, I prayed for myself and Bruce and plotted what I could do. The bear seemed to be pacing past my tent. When the noises stopped, I cautiously unzipped the tent and stuck out my head. Then I stepped outside. Suddenly, I heard a snort behind me. I pivoted to face the animal. On the beach lounged a large harmless sea lion harrumphing and exhaling through its nostrils. The damp air had carried the sounds, and my imagination had done the rest. Bruce laughed his best seasoned-veteran "dumb rookie" laugh as I told him about it.

An hour later, we were finishing breakfast when we heard a huge *whoosh*. "Come on!" yelled Bruce. We rushed around and packed the kayak in seconds, then paddled furiously to keep up with the spouting humpback whale in front of us. As we chased it I thought, *This almost never happens in Nebraska.*

My reaction to the two sounds shows how we may view wildness as unbearably terrifying or a whale of a good time. The same reactions may occur when we encounter the wildness of God. What sort of power is this? Should I be cowering from it or chasing after it?

Often we hear of the "designs" or "creations" of Mother Nature as though this Mother carries a mind and a purpose of Her own. If so, then Mother Nature is merely another label for God. Or we may think of God as a Star Wars force—the energy in everything. It's hard to be friends with energy, though. In addition, the idea of a mindless energy source brings along its own baggage. In *Mere Christianity,* C. S. Lewis describes the Life-Force or Creative Evolution concept, where a Force without a mind or personality "strives" or has "purposes":

> One reason why many people find Creative Evolution so attractive is that it gives one much of the emotional comfort of believing in God and none of the less pleasant consequences. When you are feeling fit and the sun is shining and you do not want to believe that the whole universe is a mere mechanical dance of atoms, it is nice to be able to think of this great mechanical Force rolling on through the centuries and carrying you on its crest. If, on the other hand, you want to do something rather shabby, the Life-Force, being only a blind force, with no morals and no mind, will never interfere with you like that troublesome God we learned about when we were children. The Life-Force is a sort of tame God. You can switch it on when you want, but it will not bother you. All the thrills of religion and none of its cost. Is the Life-Force the greatest achievement of wishful thinking the world has yet seen?

Any Power that creates nature is by definition supernatural. By noting how nature is so precisely and intricately organized, we can discern that behind this Power is an intelligence. Philip Yancey writes, "'And God said, "Let the water teem with living creatures."' Behind that sentence lay a thousand decisions: fish with gills and not lungs, scales not fur, fins not feet, blood not sap. At every stage God the Creator made choices, eliminating alternatives."

Planning ahead requires not only intelligence but also passion and self-discipline. There is no great work begun without passion and no great work completed without restraint. The best creativity demands valuing, prioritizing, and reshaping.[6] Furthermore, each of these qualities originates from a free will, the ability to make up one's own mind to act. A computer may accomplish creative tasks, but somewhere in the background sat individual programmers with their own wills. When we consider that the Power has intelligence, passion, self-discipline, prioritization, and free will, it seems only reasonable to speak of this Power as a person. And if a person, then a personality follows.

. . .

If God has a personality and is at all accessible, who is this person? It's unlikely that God has ears, eyes, arms, hands, or sexual organs; yet we have few resources to think about God as a person outside of a three-dimensional reality. To many, God is *Aladdin's* Genie, as malleable as Robin Williams's character performing "You Ain't Never Had a Friend Like Me." Rub the magic prayer lamp and—poof!—he's Ed Sullivan, William Buckley, or Abu the elephant. God converts to whatever we wish for, with the applause sign always blinking. Some people view God as an old man, while others see Her differently. A Trinitarian God can be compared to three states of matter, as with water, or one light bending through a prism to create three primary colors and infinite expressions. All analogies fall short in the end, however.

The God of the Bible shows characteristics of a living paradox: male and female; friend and boss; lover and coach; child and warrior; large enough to run a universe, small enough for me. With respect to God's gender, we can readily see the Mother in Our Father; the absolute best maternal attributes—selflessness, tenacity, encouragement, humility, tenderness, immovable devotion—are traits of the biblical God. Almighty God is also a nimble nurturer.

---

6. One of my favorite *New Yorker* cartoons features a woman talking to a man at a restaurant table and proclaiming grandly, "I have such thoughts, I could write a book!" To which the man replies, "I have such ringing in my ears, I could write a symphony!"

What type of interaction may we experience with this God? Certainly it's not a mechanical interaction like we have with a car, which will run smoothly if we fix all its parts. Personal relationships don't work that way. It seems to me that we must move even beyond the clichéd "personal relationship" with God, for I can have a personal relationship with a gerbil. Beyond a personal relationship—this is my fondest hope with my mate and my children—is deep friendship.

The prospect of an individualized response brings fresh meaning to our connection. A folktale describes an African village that purchased a television set and a generator. For weeks all of the children and adults gathered around the set from morning to evening watching the programs. After a couple of months, though, the set was turned off and never watched again. A visitor noticed the dusty set and inquired of the chief, "Why do you no longer watch the television?"

"We have decided to listen to the storytellers," the chief explained.

"Doesn't the television know more stories?"

"Yes," the chief replied, "but the storyteller knows me."

The television isn't a person. Unlike God, the television's energy has no personality, no ability to care, no responsiveness, and no possibility of friendship.

WHY THE BIBLE?

When we're young, we hold weird ideas. Children can think that everyone with the same first name is a close relative, so Elizabeth Taylor and Elizabeth Barrett Browning are obviously sisters. And everybody with the same last name is related, including the Johnson brothers, Magic and Lyndon.

Some people never grow all the way out of that kind of thinking. They believe, for instance, that everything written about the Bible is coming from the same viewpoint. At one time, I felt intimidated by and strangely hostile toward the Bible. I saw that people could twist the Bible to mean anything they wanted it to, so why believe any of it? Someone would quote a Hezekiah 4:4 or Pheidippides 26:25, and I'd think, *You might as well quote Walt Disney, for all I care.* Because I didn't know much about the Bible and didn't care to know much, I lumped all the "Bible believers" together—Elizabeths and Johnsons.

But sometimes we grow up, and our ideas change. I eventually discovered that I needed to discriminate, that I couldn't lump "them" all together, because I met thoughtful, intelligent people who sincerely wanted to know the evidence for the existence of God, the historicity of Jesus, the reliability of the Bible.

We don't have to look far to develop questions about the Bible's reliability. Start reading in the book of *Genesis,* the first chapter. "In the beginning God . . ." Stop!

What does it mean, *beginning?* Who was there to report on this "beginning"? Moses? Hardly. How did he get his information? What type of "inspiration" was it? Did God whisper the words to him? And who is this God? A mountain of questions arises in the first four words.

Even beyond these questions rises the question of the Bible's whole purpose for existence. My friend Wayne told me about camping with his two sons. One warm, soggy night under a smudge of moon they traipsed along a path through a copse of pine. Wayne held the flashlight to illuminate the way, but within a minute his younger son asked if he could carry the flashlight. When he received it, the boy pointed the light into his own eyes—"so I could see better," as he later explained—and presently wandered off the path and conked his head on a tree.

Psalm 119 says, "Thy word is a lamp to my feet and a light to my path." The light is designed to illuminate life's path. Some aim the Bible into their own eyes, amassing knowledge and memorizing texts to no practical end. Like Wayne's young son, they crash into obstacles despite their "enlightenment." When we aim the Bible at how we should live, we can better see the broad picture and thereby miss the trees for the forest.

Ultimately, true enlightenment comes not in learning *about* God but in *encountering* God. God cannot be confined within the covers of a book. Occasionally Christians are guilty of entombing God in the pages of the Bible. Driving home one night, I heard a radio preacher announce, "When we open the Bible, God opens His mouth. When we close the Bible, God closes His mouth." God uses a million other means to communicate with us, including circumstances, friends, enemies, nature, literature, and our conscience. On the other hand, I think I know what the preacher was suggesting. There are many splendid reasons for listening to the Bible as God's Word.

But what about those other holy books? What makes one piece of writing holier than another? Can you tell just by looking? See how you fare in the following matching quiz:

1. ____ "For behold, ye do love money, and your substance, and your fine apparel, and the adorning of your churches, more than ye love the poor and the needy, the sick and the afflicted."

2. ____ "It is not righteousness that you turn your faces towards the East and the West, but righteousness is this that one should . . . give

A. The Bhavagad Gita
B. The Book of Mormon
C. The Qur'an
D. The Tipitaka
E. The Bible

away wealth out of love for Him to the near of kin and the orphans and the needy and the way-farer and the beggers and for [the emancipation of] the captives, and keep up prayer."

3. _____ "Religion that is pure and undefiled before God and the Father is this: to visit orphans and widows in their affliction, and to keep oneself unstained from the world."

4. _____ "Few are those people in the world who, when acquiring lavish wealth, don't become intoxicated and heedless, don't become greedy for sensual pleasures, and don't mistreat other beings."

5. _____ "To those who are constantly devoted and worship Me with love, I give the under-standing by which they can come to Me."[7]

Some passages from holy books appear to be almost interchangeable. What qualifies a text for inclusion in the Bible? Martin Luther King Jr.'s "Letter from a Birmingham Jail" is as insightful and eloquent in describing our high duty to enter the fray against evil as any letter Paul of Tarsus wrote from his prison. But King's letter is not in the Christian canon. Why not?

The Christian canon has aroused curiosity with the newfound interest in so-called lost biblical texts, often referred to as "the gnostic gospels." Christians have known about these texts for centuries, but the works were excluded from the canon on the basis of their lack of authenticity. A bit of background may be useful here.

The Old Testament was collected even at the time of Jesus as twenty-four books with three divisions: the Law (Torah), the Prophets, and the Writings.[8] Later, the books were arranged according to the type of literature they contain: historical, poetic, and prophetic. The twenty-seven books of the New Testament developed in a gradual process enacted by church councils. Early Christians accepted only books written by an apostle or a companion of an apostle. A work was judged on the basis of its harmony with the rest of Scripture, its inner consistency, and its adherence to general Christian experi-

---

7. Answers: 1. B; 2. C; 3. E; 4. D; 5. A
8. Some books were later divided up to create a total of thirty-nine books.

ence. When Diocletian (A.D. 303) decreed the burning of all Christian writings, persecuted believers were forced to decide which books they were willing to risk their lives for. Though wonderful, God-inspired writings have followed, the Christian canon of the Bible is set aside for a particular purpose, "for teaching, for reproof, for correction, and for training in righteousness."[9] God took extraordinary care to direct and preserve the Bible library—books such as *Isaiah, Luke, Ephesians, First Letter of John.*

While diversifying is generally a wise financial strategy, placing our trust in many stations instead of in one primary source isn't always a smart investment. "The kingdom of heaven," Jesus says, "is like a merchant in search of fine pearls, who, on finding one pearl of great value, went and sold all that he had and bought it." Mark Twain writes in *Pudd'nhead Wilson's Calendar,* "Keep all your eggs in one basket and—WATCH THAT BASKET." And in marriage, we experience greatest fulfillment when we wholeheartedly devote our deepest love to one only. The Bible remains a trustworthy guide.

THE SCARY OLD TESTAMENT GOD

For a long time I didn't like the God of the Old Testament. I didn't like the authorized massacres, the scare tactics, the inscrutable distancing. I still don't. A few considerations have tempered my thinking, though. First, when we look through a medical book, do we notice only the dreadful pictures—lip cancer, copperhead bite, birth deformities, smallpox? *What a revolting book,* we might think. *How could anyone benefit from this?* Outside their context, the pictures loom loathsome and offensive. We value them when we understand that those pictures identify ailments in order to point to a cure.

When Patty, a new Christian, read the Old Testament for the first time, she was aghast at the brutalities, ethnic cleansing, deception, rapes, and incest. "This reads like a cheap novel!" she exclaimed to a pastor. As I read the Old Testament book of *Judges* I felt the same revulsion (still do), and I recall pausing in the reading, placing the Bible facedown on my chest, to wonder what was going on. The Bible isn't a children's book. The sickening saga of the Levite and his concubine is a study in abnormal psychology. But disease pictures in a medical book do not reflect the ability of the physician; they illustrate the powerful need for healing.

Second, the Old Testament world was immeasurably different from ours.

---

9. *Second Letter to Timothy,* chapter 3.

The people of the time lived with a corporate personality in a rigid patriarchal culture based on oaths and covenants thousands of years old, and their writings reflect their culture. As I learn more about the customs and the rationales behind them, they become more fathomable, though not always so. They were probably as shocked by some of the actions recorded as we are stunned by aberrant behavior today.[10]

God reveals Himself to people in the Old Testament slowly, as if gradually opening a curtain in a dark room so they could grow accustomed to the light. Had God yanked the curtain cord and flashed His dazzling tenderness and terrible forgiveness, the ancients would have been blinded by the light, seeing nothing. Through the Old Testament we watch God struggle to reveal who He really is. G. K. Chesterton remarks, "The central idea of the great part of the Old Testament may be called the idea of the loneliness of God." God attempts the same revelation with us, of course, despite our 3-watt brilliance.

Third, an incident happened to me that helped me understand God's "strange acts," for as unpleasant as it is to admit, some Old Testament pictures do implicate the physician. When my sons Nathan and Geoffrey were five and two, we enjoyed visiting a nearby park where they could play and ride their Big Wheels—low-slung, plastic Harley-Davidsons with pedals. We'd pump on the swings, slide down the slides, crawl across the monkey bars. I'd spin them to Jupiter on the merry-go-round, then they'd hop on the Big Wheels to rumble on empty sidewalks. One day as they rode around me I noticed that someone had looped a swing around the top bar a few times, so I began unlooping. Straining on my toes, I had pushed the swing around once when I heard Nathan yell. I looked at Nathan, who was looking at Geoffrey, who was pedaling down the middle of the street.

"*Geoffreeee!*" The cry froze in my throat. I sprinted toward the normally busy street, looking both directions to wave off any approaching cars, but there were none. Geoffrey was oblivious. He seemed about to signal a left turn when I caught him, lifted the Big Wheel with his body in it off the pavement to the grass, jerked him up by a chubby arm and with one massive, back-bending spank on his bottom poured out my fear and rage at a world where two-year-olds can get squashed on their Big Wheels. I took little comfort in the sniffling hug and talk afterward. The image of Geoffrey bending toward the trees tormented me as I sat under an elm.

10. What would readers in three thousand years think of our culture, for example, if historians specifically highlighted the massacre at Columbine High School in Littleton, Colorado?

I didn't like what I'd done. I still don't. But he never rode his Big Wheel in the street again, a practice I'm not certain he would have relinquished if I hadn't administered pain, and that's a trade-off we can both live with. However, if someone had snapped a photograph of me yanking up and spanking my little boy, what sort of father would you see? In Old Testament language, here's how my behavior would be recorded: "And the father smote the son." You would miss our playground antics and quiet time with books and spontaneous hugs and my clothing and feeding him—without the context of the moment you could reach an unwarranted conclusion. Also, we tend to remember most vividly the unusual responses of our parents, children, teachers, presidents, and God—one more reason why the Bible is full of God's strange and remarkable acts. (Why does God allow Himself to be characterized like this?) The Bible depicts a mix of debauchery and magnificence, malady and remedy, and it's up to us to figure out which is which.

God raised His voice often in the Old Testament to get the attention of the children of Israel. They were mostly bottom dwellers in Kohlberg's stages of moral development, reacting solely to "punishment and reward," occasionally climbing up to "conformity" and "law and order," but we don't find evidence of spiritual growth beyond that. Nuances are completely lost on them—hence the two-by-four theology. Moreover, they forgot their lessons as quickly as an apple core turns brown.

Fourth, God doesn't agree with everything in the Bible. Much of the Bible is description, not prescription; reading a history book isn't necessarily a call to go and do likewise but to learn from the issues presented. The primary issue in the Old Testament is sovereignty: Who's in charge here? People worshiped every earthly thing, with the sun, moon, and stars kicked in as well, with the result that their lives were base and foul. A notable example appears when the Hebrews are enslaved in Egypt. Should they, along with the Egyptians, worship the sun god, Amon-Ra? Anubis, the jackal-headed god? Hathor, the cow goddess? Any local deities, such as the frog, cat, and crocodile? The Nile? Pharaoh? The ten plagues are directed at the worship of false gods. But once God is understood to be the all-powerful sovereignty, He then is deemed responsible for absolutely everything, the goodness and the gore. Thus, the Bible depicts God as causing events merely because they happen. Roger Rosenblatt writes in *Life* magazine:

> [God] will not tolerate the easy emotion or the shabby thought. He has no shabby thoughts Himself, though if one believes the Bible, He has behaved abominably from time to time. I will never understand, for instance, why

in the book of *Exodus* He kept hardening Pharaoh's heart after delivering the plagues, so that Pharaoh would continually renege on his promise to let Moses and His people go. It was God, not Pharaoh, who did the hardening. What was He out to prove? How tough He was?

Perhaps God hardens Pharaoh's heart as sunshine hardens clay, but the same sunshine melts a butter pat and warms a frigid nose. The receiving substance, not the sun, often determines the outcome.

The enigmatic book of *Job* is written to address human suffering and why a loving God allows it. From the beginning it is Satan who assaults Job and his family, yet a servant reports that "the fire of God fell from heaven." In another part of the Old Testament, in possibly the clearest demonstration of this discrepancy, we read, "Saul took his own sword, and fell upon it," and nine verses later, "Saul died for his unfaithfulness. . . . Therefore the Lord slew him."[11] Did God kill Saul? I looked in vain in the next chapter for: "CORRECTION: In the preceding chapter God was erroneously charged with killing Saul. We regret this error, and apologize for any misunderstanding this may have caused." Any newspaper today would print a comparable retraction.

When we consider that the issue of sovereignty is foremost in the minds of Bible writers, we can see possible discrepancies in God's motivation and His recorded acts. God may not even agree with what He is described as doing. (Why does God allow Himself to be characterized like this?) In *Who's Afraid of the Old Testament God?* Alden Thompson reflects, "It now seems strange to me that the Old Testament God has the reputation of having a short fuse. A God of incredible patience is a much more accurate description."

A telling example of God's patience and His desire to save and forgive is found in Jonah, the choicest Old Testament book on prejudice. After his cruise ship layover inside a fish, Jonah goes to Nineveh and says, "Yet forty days, and Nineveh will be overthrown." But when the city of Nineveh repents and is spared destruction, Jonah is sullen. He doesn't *like* Nineveh. He basically complains to God, "I knew this would happen! That's why I didn't want to come here. I knew you were a gracious God and merciful, slow to anger, and abounding in steadfast love. I knew you'd save them if you could." God then provides an object lesson to replant Jonah's perspective, pats him on the cheek, and patiently reasons with His petulant prophet. "Should I not pity Nineveh," He asks at the end, "that great city, in which there are more than 120,000 persons

---

11. *First Chronicles*, chapter 10.

who do not know their right hand from their left, and also much cattle?" His question hangs in the air like a lingering piano chord.

Could It Be Said Better?

A Jewish folktale finds the Lord God trying to determine who His chosen people will be. He first interviews the Greeks, asking them, "What could you do for me?" The Greeks promise God the finest art and the loftiest thinking. Then He interviews the Romans, who promise great buildings and wonderful road systems. After traveling around the world interviewing one nation after another, He interviews a small Middle Eastern group.

"Lord God," the Jewish people respond, "we aren't known for our art or power or roads. However, we are a nation of storytellers. If You were to be our God, and we were to be Your people, we could tell Your story throughout the world."

"It's a deal!" says God, and the rest is His story.

As seen in the evidence of the Bible, and especially in the life of Jesus, God loves stories. If you've ever played the game "telephone," however, you know that orally passing information along among even five people is fraught with peril. Whispering one sentence among twenty-five students in a classroom produces such garbling that the original is unrecognizable. "Give Jerry the blue hat before the amazing yellow ship comes to town" mutates to "Cherries on a blue hat bring the amazing yellow slip down." What happens, say, when the message is 30,000 sentences passed among 25,000,000 people over 150 generations? Jerry and the blue hat would be long gone. Binding agreements today are written down because they are more trustworthy that way. The same is true for the written Bible.

Why doesn't God dispense with the ancient words and just tell us in our heads how we should act? There comes a time when children must act freely to do what's right. It's part of growing into mature friendship. If God is always obviously directing, His children won't learn to make decisions on their own.[12] Why don't teachers just give their students the answers from the start? Because it's the process of learning that educates, so lessons can be applied to new, pressing, differing situations.

But couldn't God personalize all of His communication on an individual basis? On reflection, we can see the problems with such an approach. If Sharon

---

12. The pillars of fire and cloud during the exodus from Egypt, and the ensuing apostasies, demonstrated that God's perceptible presence doesn't ensure anything.

claims "God told me this," and Marcus declares "God told me that," how could you know which to believe? Better to have handy the original directions to discern the way, though we may still disagree in our analysis of them.

The Bible's unified storyline follows the fall and redemption of humanity, from Eden to Eden, yet the biblical books differ widely in style. When the distinctive personalities and writing styles of the authors come out, it's obvious that they were not God's stenographers. This inspiration process is one of balanced input—God's thoughts are written by human beings. Ellen White comments, "The Bible is written by inspired men, but it is not God's mode of thought and expression. It is that of humanity. God, as a writer, is not represented. [People] will often say such an expression is not like God. But God has not put Himself in words, in logic, in rhetoric, on trial in the Bible. The writers of the Bible were God's penmen, not His pen. Look at the different writers. . . . The divine mind and will are combined with the human mind and will; thus the utterances of man are the word of God."

REALITY CHECKS

Driving up from Los Angeles along the California coast on U.S. 101—El Camino Real, the king's highway—you catch sight of the Pacific Ocean at Ventura, at Goleta, and at Grover Beach. Each view is distinctive. Each watery horizon holds a minuscule fraction of the great Pacific. You can't see all of the Pacific from any point, and each site differs from all the other spots along the coast—widely differing from the sixty-four million square miles of open water with an average depth of fourteen thousand feet—but it is the Pacific, nonetheless.

So it is with seeing God. We touch a minuscule fraction of His face; we cannot fathom the fathomless. But it is His face, and the more we follow the contours of His coastline, the more we plumb His deeps, the more we shall know the shape of His cheek, the touch of His fingers, the sound of His voice.

• • •

Every semester an experiment takes place in one of my classes. The experiment is scripted and acted by a variety of characters. This semester the experiment involved our Humanities Division secretary, Janya Mekelburg, who is also a convincing actress. Twelve minutes into College Writing II, she threw open the classroom door as I was talking and dropped a stack of papers in front of me on my desk. She was barefoot, holding a light bulb, and along with her other bizarre attire sported a ruler sticking out of her blouse pocket.

"Here are the papers you wanted," she sneered.

"Just leave them there," I replied coldly.

"Excuse me," Janya said, "a *thank you* would be nice."

"Yeah, whatever." I placed my face in my hands, partly so I wouldn't smile as I saw the shocked, embarrassed expressions on students' faces.

"Hello?" she thundered. "*You* didn't have to stand in line behind five or six grumpy people waiting to make fifteen copies, stapled, on blue paper, and the stapler broke and the staple lady with the little green key chain around her wrist wasn't there so everything had to be stapled by hand!"

"Remember Philippians 4:11," I said with an air of superiority. "In whatever state I am, I am content."

Janya was livid. "Oh, save your scriptures for church!"

"You sniveling, ungrateful wretch!" I snapped.

"Hey, *peon* wasn't in the job description!" she roared. "Find someone else to do your last-minute copying. I quit!" She slammed the door behind her. I turned to the class and grinned.

"Okay, take out a piece of paper," I announced.

"Was that for real? Who was that?"

"Now," I continued, "I want you to write down *exactly* what happened, what was said, and what she was wearing, from head to toe. I'll give you five minutes. All twenty-one of you are eyewitnesses. Specifics are important. Go."

The students began writing. After five minutes they handed in their accounts. Some students were uncertain, some were as confident as though they were depositing hard cash. They had seen it with their own eyes, heard it with their own ears. When all the papers were in, I began writing discrepancies on the board. She was standing in line behind five, fifteen, and twenty people. She made six, fifteen, and five hundred copies. She was wearing shoes, boots, and was barefoot. I quoted Philippians 4:8, 11, 12, 13, 16, and 18. I called her a "filthy wrench," a "sniveling snit," and "a retch." Only one person mentioned the light bulb. Few noticed the ruler or the bare feet. Nobody saw the bandage on her hand.

Janya returned to the room, and we checked the perceptions against the reality. We laughed about it, talked about the experience, discussed the importance of the funnel we call *perspective,* and delved into other lessons. From twenty-one eyewitnesses we obtained twenty-one diverging eyewitness reports. No two reports were identical. That's the case every time.

I mention this experiment because I've heard people say they can't believe in the Bible because there are too many inconsistencies. I've also heard Christians vehemently defend the Bible as being totally logical and consistent. Let's admit it: The Bible is not totally logical and consistent. It's not a smoothly woven fabric. There are knots and tears and omissions. Why?

Only in fiction does the storyline run smoothly, swelling gradually to a climax. In true life we find "inconsistencies." A blonde, gum-popping waitress earns a Ph.D. in mathematics. A movie star becomes president. I can't find a sock. Those who invalidate the Bible because it doesn't fit "nicely" are missing one of the best reasons for believing. The difficulties, the absurdities, the discrepancies provide confirmation that the Bible is true. Some suggest that the New Testament was written merely to validate a young religious movement, but the Bible accounts are a far cry from lionizing propaganda. Examine these three scenarios:

1. You want to establish the reliability of the church's leaders as people to trust and follow. Would you show them as traitors (Peter), murderers (Paul), or skeptics (Thomas)? To convey respect, do you depict the pillars of the church abandoning their leader and quailing in a second-story hideout? That's not the style of Madison Avenue. That's no way to build a following.
2. If you're writing a script to establish a person's divinity, would you show Him exhausted, lonely, surprised, and killed? Would you have Him tell His disciples to buy swords and then rebuke them for using them? If you were making up some of it, you wouldn't include those, would you? Not unless you had to stick to what happened.
3. Suppose you wanted to prove the reality of the Resurrection. Would you have lowly women make the discovery? Moreover, if you're concocting a myth, you must synchronize the stories. Is one angel at the tomb (*Mark,* chapter 16), or are there two angels (*Luke,* chapter 24)? Perhaps the very fact of such a thing happening stuns you so that details are hazy. Indeed, when all the accounts mesh exactly, we may have some reason to doubt; perfect agreement betrays an attempt to "get our stories straight."

The differences in the four Gospel accounts are mind-boggling and faith-building. What we find in the Bible are accounts of real people who are stunned so often by a person (as my students were with Janya's behavior) that the details don't always fit. The differing accounts provide yet more evidence toward one awe-inspiring conclusion. It happened.

Other "contradictions" arise as Bible writers address different situations with varying advice. What else should we expect from a family letter that's written to so many people? A father writes to his impulsive child, "Be patient." To his child stuck in neutral, he says, "Get moving!" Is the father inconsistent?

Does consistency really matter? Lloyd Douglas describes a ritual he went through every morning as a university student living in a boardinghouse. Downstairs on the first floor lived an elderly, retired music teacher who was confined to a wheelchair. Douglas would bound down the steps, open the man's door, and ask, "Well, what's the good news?"

The old man would pick up his tuning fork, tap it on the side of his wheelchair, and say, "That's middle C! It was middle C yesterday; it will be middle C tomorrow; it will be middle C a thousand years from now. The tenor upstairs sings flat, the piano across the hall is out of tune, but, my friend, *that* is middle C!" This sure foundation resonated with the older and the younger man, just as the Bible's sure foundation resonates with many.

We long for middle C consistency and permanence in our lives primarily because Western society has adopted "the California syndrome." The Californian, writes journalist Neil Morgan, "has created a putty culture—yeasty, swollen, penetrable, unshaped, elastic, impermanent, but with a tendency to adhere at least for a time to anything solid." Thus we can sing the *Gilligan's Island* theme, but we can't recite the Ten Commandments. We know about O. J. Simpson, yet are ignorant of the Constitution that protects him. Mass media create a compatible, if flawed, corporate memory. In *Life after Television*, George Gilder observes, "TV news made the few hundred corpses in Tiananmen Square loom larger in our minds than the millions of deaths under Chairman Mao Tse-tung." Perhaps this explains why the April 1999 capture of three U.S. soldiers in Kosovo engenders more national outrage than the daily struggle of millions of U.S. children living in abject poverty.

One of the more challenging aspects of the Bible's reliability is found in its miracles; they also compose one of its strongest evidences. Miraculous prophecies of the Bible established the certainty for me that this volume had supernatural input. When I read the prophecies of *Daniel*, chapter 2, and compared them to history, and when I saw how Jesus fulfilled prophecy, it struck me with force that the odds of this happening were too outlandish—something more than human beings was at work here. To us, miracles are abnormalities that appear outside our understanding of the natural world. To God, miracles are "normals," the way things ought to be, and will be someday. I view prophecy and its ties to history and archaeology as the most compelling evidence of God's touch in the Bible, along with another type of miracle I've witnessed.

A new Christian convert was once challenged about whether the miracles of the Bible were true, beginning with Jesus' first recorded miracle. The skeptical questioner pressed his point home.

"How do you know the water was turned to wine?" the skeptic asked. "Were you there? Did you taste it?"

The other man paused to reflect. "No, I wasn't there for that miracle," he admitted. "But I was there when He turned my beer into furniture."

. . .

The Bible is actually a sixty-six-book library containing history, poetry, prayers, prophecies, letters, and memoirs. In it we discover at least thirty-eight widely varying writing styles in three languages, displaying the individuality of the authors. With the astounding diversity we find astounding continuity in its content and transmission.

All of the books in the New Testament were written between A.D. 50 and A.D. 100, and they comprise the best-attested collection of ancient manuscripts in the world, with more manuscript evidence than any ten pieces of classical literature combined. Next to the New Testament, the *Iliad* is the best preserved book, with 643 extant copies. The New Testament has 24,633 manuscripts in existence today, including more than 5,300 partial or complete Greek manuscripts.

The accuracy of the copyists of the Hebrew Bible is remarkable: scribes, lawyers, and massoretes preserved and transmitted the documents with practically perfect fidelity. They kept tabs on every letter, syllable, and word—no document has been as faithfully rendered over as wide a span of time. When the Dead Sea Scrolls were discovered in 1948, scholars were astounded at nearly identical biblical texts separated by more than one thousand years. William Shakespeare's texts are much less certain, containing at least ten times as many disputed readings as are in the New Testament.

Today we have literal translations, dynamic translations, and paraphrases. In 1990, Messianic Judaism opened up to me when I purchased a Jewish New Testament, translated by David H. Stern.[13] Look at a comparison of *John,* chapter 1, verses 19 and 20, in the Revised Standard Version and Stern's translation.

> And this is the testimony of John, when the Jews sent priests and Levites
> from Jerusalem to ask him, "Who are you?" He confessed, he did not deny,
> but confessed, "I am not the Christ." (RSV)

---

13. David H. Stern, trans., *Jewish New Testament* (Jerusalem, Israel, and Clarksville, Maryland: Jewish New Testament Publications, 1989). A helpful glossary of terms is provided on every spread.

> Here is Yochanan's testimony: when the Judeans sent cohanim and L'viim
> from Yerushalayim to ask him, "Who are you?" he was very straightforward
> and answered clearly, "I am not the Messiah." (JNT)

Could there have been such virulent anti-Semitism the past two millennia,
would there have been the pogroms, the unspeakable Holocaust, the countless
other atrocities, if the world had fairly understood it? Rabbi Yeshua bar-Yosef—
Jesus—was a Jew. All of the earliest leaders of Christianity were Jewish. The
writers of the New Testament—with the exception of Dr. Luke—were Jewish.
In reality, it *is* a Jewish New Testament.

The Old Testament, composed between about 1500 B.C. and 400 B.C., contains more than three hundred references to the coming of Messiah. All of the
references were made at least four centuries before He appeared. Jesus fulfilled
every prediction, from the place and time of His birth to the fine points of His
eloquent sacrifice. The odds of this happening are beyond calculation.

Though it's an ancient volume, the Bible transmits muscle and sinew to life
today. Harvard psychiatrist and author Robert Coles declares:

> Nothing I have discovered about the makeup of human beings contradicts
> in any way what I learn from the Hebrew prophets such as Isaiah, Jeremiah,
> and Amos and from the book of *Ecclesiastes,* and from Jesus and the lives of
> those He touched. Anything that I can say as a result of my research into
> human behavior is a mere footnote to those lives in the Old and New
> Testaments.

In *Mr. Holland's Opus,* Mr. Holland tries to convince a hesitant clarinetist
that she is missing the point of everything. Mr. Holland asserts, "There's a lot
more to music than notes on a page. It's about heart. It's about feelings, and
moving people, and something beautiful and being alive and having fun."

There's a lot more to the Bible than words on a page. It's about feelings and
moving people and something beautiful and being alive and having fun. It's about
living life to the fullest. As King David writes in Psalm 16 (NIV), "You have made
known to me the path of life; you will fill me with joy in your presence."

God is reliable.

~

Angels can fly because they can take themselves lightly.

—G. K. Chesterton

Joy is the most infallible sign of the presence of God.

—Leon Bly

The reason the mass of men fear God, and at bottom dislike Him, is because they rather distrust His heart, and fancy Him all brain like a watch.

—Herman Melville

Inventing a story with grass
I find a young horse deep inside it.

—James Dickey

It is not the business of the poet to save men's souls, but to make them worth saving.

—James Elroy Flecker

He prayeth well, who loveth well.

—Samuel Taylor Coleridge, *The Rime of the Ancient Mariner*

If we are unaccustomed to it, just slipping quietly into the presence of God can be so exotic and fresh that it delights us enormously.

—Richard J. Foster

Deep down in me I knowed it was a lie, and He knowed it. You can't pray a lie—I found that out.

—Huckleberry Finn

Prayer is most real when we refuse to say "Amen." We most love heaven when we will not end our conversations quickly.

—Calvin Miller

A wise lover regards not so much the gift of Him who loves, as the love of Him who gives.

—Thomas à Kempis

~

4

GOD IS RIGHT BRAINED

IN HIS PREFACE to *The Classics We've Read, the Difference They've Made,* Philip Yancey recounts a story that seems a slap in the face to purely naturalistic evolution:

> In 1962 Alexander Tvardovsky, editor-in-chief of the Russian literary maga-zine *Novy Mir,* took some manuscripts home to read in bed. He thumbed through them at a high rate of speed, making snap judgments and tossing most of them into a mounting pile of rejects. He came to a manuscript by an author unknown to him, with the simple title *One Day in the Life of Ivan Denisovich.* He read 10 lines. And then, as he later told a friend, "Suddenly I felt that I couldn't read it like this. I had to do something appropriate to the occasion. So I got up. I put on my best black suit, a white shirt with a starched collar, a tie and my good shoes. Then I sat at my desk and read a new classic."

Where does such a profound regard for beauty come from? Some may claim that our bodies were designed to respond best to tranquility and cheer, but the question is, Why are we built this way?

Of all the evidences of God's existence, none stands out as small and resonant and ubiquitous as a giggle. What kind of God creates us with the capacity for laughter? Does God ever laugh? Is God good-natured? We must face it: We are not likely to fall in love with a grouchy, overparticular, inflexible God.

If we see God's personality as humorless and robotic, we can come to believe that loving Him will make us strange. We fear, with some justification, that we will become judgmental and joyless in religion's thrall, that sooner or later we too may be raining spittle on homosexuals. We cannot trust a gloomy God. We espe-cially fear losing our identities, those core preferences that make us different, that make us who we are, which is why when Paul Simon sings, "Still crazy after all these years," we cheer. Acting religious would be caving in to the wrong crazi-ness—the craziness of conformity. We'd probably have to give up some bad habits; we might even have to give up slurping mint chocolate chip ice cream on

a sweltering day, roller coasters, Dave Barry and Jim Carrey, ska music, screaming stupid yells at a basketball game—we'd basically have to give up *fun*.

I suppose that's one reason why I was brought to God kicking and resisting.
What stood out for me in seeking God was a cramped, kill-joy mentality and
distasteful displays of obnoxiousness. God's disciples appeared to be glum company and poor tippers. Only when I sought God myself—by myself, for
myself—did my view change. I hadn't understood that God loves fun and that
God knows that life without fun is as barren as a bachelor's refrigerator. In *Who
Switched the Price Tags?* Tony Campolo writes:

> There isn't anything frivolous about having fun. Learning how to have fun
> is one of the most serious subjects in the world. Without fun, marriages
> don't work. When jobs aren't fun, they become intolerable and dehumaniz-
> ing. When children aren't fun, they are heartbreaking. When church is not
> fun, religion becomes a drag. When life is not fun, it is hard to be spiritual.

George MacDonald concludes, "It is the heart that is not yet sure of its God
that is afraid to laugh in His presence." (I think of this sometimes in church
sanctuaries.) Humor is a fundamental part of God's personality and one proof
for God's existence. Let's look closely at our seventh sense—the sense of
humor—and how it matters infinitely.

HUMOR ME, GOD

Five-year-old Josh was being unruly during church. After several parental
warnings, he continued to snicker and kick the pew in front of him. Finally his
exasperated mother picked him up and headed for the back door. On the way
down the aisle, Josh popped his head over Mom's shoulder and yelled out, "Pray
for me!"

. . .

When the young man and woman walked in midway through the morning
church service, every eye followed them. Wrapped in white with sashes around
their waists, barefoot, and carrying blankets, they moved to the front row.
After the service they sat cross-legged on the grass outside our church building. A vapor of stale perspiration enveloped them as I crouched to visit. The
man had very short hair. He said his name was David, and he wasted no time
with small talk.

"Brother," he said in a flat voice, "there are three keys to heaven. No killing. No sex. No materialism. The Spirit gives life; all life is from the Spirit."

"Do you believe in Jesus?" I asked.

"Yes, He was the prophet of God."

I tried to be gentle when I suggested, "Jesus ate fish, didn't He?"

David stiffened. "That was a parable. The fish represented people."

"I see," I said, not seeing. "How do you know it's a parable?"

"By the Spirit. No one can know except by the Spirit. The Spirit gives life; all life is from the Spirit."

"Why don't you carry a Bible?" I inquired. "The Bible helps me to be sure I'm not just following my own way. How about you?"

"The Bible says not to take scrip for your journey, neither two coats, neither shoes."

"And you think that means take no Bible with you? I've never heard that one. Where's it found?"

"It's in Matthew."[1]

I changed the subject. "What about when God told Adam and Eve to be fruitful and multiply?" I wondered if "be fruitful and multiply" might be a parable for using bananas on flash cards.

"That was the result of sin," David explained grimly.

"But God told them that before sin came into the world."

"In heaven we shall be as the angels. The Spirit gives life; all life is from the Spirit."

"Well, all right," I said, extending my hand. "It's good to meet you."

David placed his hand on his chest. "Handshake from the heart, brother."

I stood to leave.

"Do you have a dollar for some holy spaghetti?" David was looking toward me.

"For some what?" I said.

"For some holy spaghetti," he repeated. "At the store down the street. For some holy nourishment."

I looked at him and his silent partner and considered this for a moment. "Okay," I said finally. Reaching in my wallet, I produced a dollar bill, for which David extended his hand. I was sorely tempted to retract the bill and sing, "Money from the heart, brother!" I resisted temptation.

The couple rose together and walked through the gate toward the holy store. Neither had smiled once in the time they had "attended church."

---

1. *Matthew,* chapter 10. A "scrip" (King James Version) is a bag.

• • •

Why do I relate more to Josh than to David? Why does Josh's "irreverence" delight and David's "reverence" repel? Josh affects no artificial holiness. He's enjoying himself and God's creation, and he hasn't reduced God to a formula. Josh is real.

David, on the other hand (although an extreme example), represents the religion believing unbelievers want no part of—withdrawing from meaningful involvement in life or "finding the Lord" and becoming baptized in pickle brine. While some religionists imply that belief should be incomprehensible, laughter frowned upon, and creativity feared, the God of the Bible appears to prefer an approach of defiant optimism. From blooming violets to blasting quasars, our universe thrives on positive energy. In David's quest to follow God, he had missed that God is, most important, a God of yes: yes to interacting with society, yes to zestful curiosity, yes to wellsprings of gratefulness in the midst of the garbage heaps of life.[2]

Humorless people are unattractive. They walk through life as serious as a heart attack, and they often end life the same way. What a tragedy it is when we are so earnest that we cannot embrace ecstasy. When an infinite God is seriously packaged and reduced to something more practically manageable, the molten zeal flows, the righteous bearing is hoisted, the simplistic solutions are trumpeted.[3] Small, impudent people may claim to represent the living God as they close Him up in a box kept on the pew for occasional viewing, but the lion of Judah they uncover is small and mild, defanged and declawed. "If you would defend a lion," Duncan Eva says, "let him out of the cage."

Humor is, like food and music, a matter of taste. In my mind the funniest things come not from the movies or stand-up comics but from real life. At a local talent show a few years ago, one of the entries was "The Singing Dog." When a woman and her mutt walked onstage, the woman proceeded to howl a mournful tune, expecting her dog to join her. The dog, however, sat impassively. Again and again the woman began her baying, but the dog did nothing. Keenly feeling the woman's embarrassment, we in the audience wondered how long the agony would last. Then Tony, our quick-thinking master of ceremonies, rescued the situation by calling out, "Isn't that amazing, ladies and gentlemen? It's a ventriloquist dog!"

---

2. "The Son of God, Jesus . . . was not Yes and No; but in him it is always Yes. For all the promises of God find their Yes in him" (*Second Corinthians,* chapter 1).

3. Benjamin Disraeli described a zealot as "one of those men who think the world can be saved by writing a pamphlet."

As with most parents, Yolanda and I have enjoyed gales of laughter thanks to the antics of our children. Fortunately, children haven't built up layers of sophistication—they're transparent (literally, "beyond parents"). Without hauling out the family videos, I'll share one sample. When Geoffrey was young, he and I dined in a Chinese restaurant he enjoyed. We had been greeted and seated when he suddenly leaned across the table and whispered, "Dad, do Chinese people know how to count?"

Startled, I lowered my voice. "Yes, son, they do. Why do you ask?"

"Well," he replied, "every time we walk into this restaurant somebody walks up to us and asks, 'How many?'"

Finally, Mary Louise Gilman, editor of the *National Shorthand Reporter*, collected thousands of courtroom bloopers, actual questions asked by lawyers in courtrooms. Here are a few choice ones:

Q: The truth of the matter is that you were not an unbiased, objective witness, isn't it? You too were shot in the fracas?
A: No, sir. I was shot midway between the fracas and the navel.

Q: She has three children, right?
A: Yes.
Q: How many of them were boys?
A: None.
Q: Were there any girls?

Q: What happened then?
A: He told me, he says, "I have to kill you because you can identify me."
Q: Did he kill you?
A: No.

Q: When he went, had you gone and had she, if she wanted to and were able, for the time being excluding all the restraints on her not to go, gone also, would he have brought you, meaning you and she, with him to the station?
Mr. Brooks: Objection. That question should be taken out and shot.

Q: And lastly, Gary, all your responses must be oral. Okay? What school did you go to?
A: Oral.

Q: How old are you?
A: Oral.

Q: Doctor, before you performed the autopsy, did you check for a pulse?
A: No.
Q: Did you check for blood pressure?
A: No.
Q: Did you check for breathing?
A: No.
Q: So, then it is possible that the patient was alive when you began the autopsy?
A: No.
Q: How can you be so sure, Doctor?
A: Because his brain was sitting on my desk in a jar.
Q: But could the patient have still been alive nevertheless?
A: It is possible that he could have been alive and practicing law somewhere.

God's sense of humor is shown most clearly in His crowning act of creation—us. However, God also sees His children tormented, abused, killed—when I consider all that, I would be disappointed if God were too mirthful. Yet sometimes behind His eyes of pain I catch a smile like a spreading sunrise and laughter like a supernova.

God Is Right Brained

There is a winsomeness in God, a rollicking, frolicking goodness that tickles and refreshes. We can see it in a vein of a leaf, in skipping rocks on a smooth lake, in the infinite variety of human voices. But undoubtedly the most glorious creation of God is the human brain. About the size of a grapefruit, it's the one organ we cannot transplant and be ourselves. In the human brain there are perhaps one trillion neurons, or nerve cells, and the number of possible interconnections between these cells is greater than the number of atoms in the known universe.

Nobel laureate Roger Sperry observes that in the brain "there are forces within forces within forces, as in no other cubic half foot in the universe that we know." Dr. Paul Brand adds:

I have been inside a human brain on maybe a half-dozen occasions. Each time I have felt humble and inadequate, a trespasser entering where no man was meant to. Who am I to invade the holy place where a person resides? Perhaps if I worked on brains daily, I would grow more callous and unimpressed. But I think not—the brain surgeons I know still talk of their subject in hushed, almost worshipful tones.

The human brain can be divided into many groupings, including left brain and right brain. Simply put, the left hemisphere of the brain is analytical, the right hemisphere is creative; the left is serial, the right is holistic. We know and don't know much about the human brain, but the bigger question is, What is *God's* brain like? Some view God as a great unblinking cosmic stare—uninvolved, unmoved. Does God really care about you, your dog, bending birches, starlings, leaping dolphins? Albert Einstein confides, "I want to know God's thoughts . . . the rest is details."

God has to be the epitome of balance to fashion the endlessly intricate mechanism of life and our capacity to enjoy it, a divine blend of logic and laughter. Using His left brain, God eliminated flutter problems in butterfly wings long before scientists eliminated flutter on bridges.[4] God knitted amino acids, formed retinas, and shaped palates into complexities beyond comprehension. But it becomes increasingly clear that once the Judeo-Christian God analyzed and set up life so that "it was good," God chose to interact with us as a right-brained being, using metaphor, music, and movement to reach us.

Though He numbers the hairs on our heads, God is not a statistician. Life is less like counting the seeds in an apple and more like counting the apples in a seed. Go figure the calculus of a soul, but first factor in the joy of stretching in the morning. Add to that the roaring of the wind, the rising of the sap, the aroma of baking bread. God definitely has diversity on the brain. Not content with a firefly and a potato bug, He conjured up three hundred thousand species of beetles and weevils.

God is more a poet than a police officer. He's more an acrobat than an accountant, more a midwife than an anesthetist. He values relationships more than rules. He's more interested in our nearness than our neatness. He desires more to be loved than to be understood.

One of the most revealing creations of God is the miracle of human sexuality. Of all the myriad options possible, God chose a delirious fitting together that has also frankly led to unbelievable pain. A purely analytical God would have had us reproduce asexually by mitosis—it's much less messy, and the risky potential for

---

4. According to poet Wallace Stevens, "All of our ideas come from the natural world: trees equal umbrellas."

hurtful wickedness would be eliminated. Instead, a right-brained God designed sex to engage our deepest emotions, knowing the powerful bond it produces between a loving husband and wife to be worth the inherent dangers. It's an astounding decision, one that shouts volumes about the sacredness of committed love.

Given the choice of flawless perfection or life, God makes the same choice earthly parents make when they choose to have children: fussing, burping, messy, disobedient, imperfect . . . life. It's the choice Jesus from the town of Nazareth made. Instead of becoming a monkish Essene, hidden and shielded from the world's evils and ills, He came in contact with despair and decay, and hope and healing sprang from His fingertips wherever He touched. Confronting the frothing demoniacs, rebuking the mourners of a dead boy, and wading out of the terrified crowd to touch a festering leper, Jesus said yes to life.

We must not restrict God's creative, holistic activity to religion. God is at work in the world in sweet corn, a soccer kick, and an escalator. God speaks through astronomers, artists, psychologists, and historians.

Some people say, "Better to leave theology to the theologians." To the theologians? If what they mean by *theology* is inconsequential, arcane nitpicking that judges the menu as more important than the meal, I will gladly leave it to the professionals. But if theology means the discussion, study, or experience of God, then I will bring it to breakfast. I will carry it in my car. I will open it in my classes. I will sing it in the shower. The prophet Jeremiah declares, "If I say 'I will not mention Him, or speak anymore in His name,' there is in my heart as it were a burning fire shut up in my bones, and I am weary with holding it in, and I cannot."

When snorkeling at Hawaii's Hanauma Bay I saw a sea turtle flipping slow motion out to a sea canyon. I was so awestruck by the sight that I momentarily forgot where I was and involuntarily said out loud, underwater, "Thank you, God." I sounded like Darth Vader, but it occurs to me that I could say it more often. God is our passion and our prize—our banana split, our walking stick, our eyes.

PRAYER—COMMUNICATION WITH A FRIEND

Unusual maps fascinate me, whether of ocean floors or the surface of the moon. The first time I saw a world map created in the former Soviet Union, I was intrigued to find the U.S.S.R. stretching across three-fourths of the world; the United States was split in half on either side. Hanging on my office walls are maps of "Native American Tribes" in North America (I live in "Dakota"), a "Down-Under Map of the World" with Australia dominating top center, and a photo of the Milky Way galaxy. Each map gives a different perspective on reality. If for some reason I'm feeling stressed, I'm calmed when I look at the Milky Way's innumerable stars and think, *How does this matter in all of that?* I think about how God views the universe, the earth, me. I'd love to see God's map of the cosmos, and in a way I can—through prayer.

I don't know how prayer works. I don't understand exactly how God "speaks" to us, how He honors our personal freedom yet accomplishes His designs, or why some *obviously* good answers don't occur, and some obviously bad requests seem to gain positive responses. I can't comprehend why God seems to intervene in seemingly small matters when children are dying. So when I share what appeals to me about prayer, it's not with the idea that I have God all figured out. I do know this: Somehow prayer enables God and ennobles me.

Often we labor under the illusion that prayer must be something formal, something desperate, something absolutely magical. Sir Eric Roll tells the story of a little boy who was overheard praying fervently, "Tokyo, Tokyo, Tokyo." Later, when he was asked why, the boy replied, "Well, you see, I've just taken my geography examination in school, and I have been praying to the Lord to make Tokyo the capital of France."

Prayer isn't about miraculously changing the world atlas. Prayer is primarily communicating with God—as vital to spiritual health as breathing is to physical health. And if you were not interested in your spiritual health, you would not be reading these words right now.

A common problem with prayer comes in not hearing an answer. In praying we can feel like Ernestine, Lily Tomlin's nasal telephone operator character, asking: "Have I reached the person to whom I am speaking?" A man once confessed to C. S. Lewis, "I can believe in God all right, but what I cannot swallow is the idea of Him attending to several hundred million human beings who are all addressing Him at the same moment." In his answer, recorded in *Mere Christianity*, Lewis presents the possibility that God's time is different from our time:

> Suppose I am writing a novel. I write "Mary laid down her work; next moment came a knock at the door!" For Mary who has to live in the imaginary time of my story there is no interval between putting down the work and hearing the knock. But I, who am Mary's maker, do not live in that imaginary time at all. Between writing the first half of that sentence and the second, I might sit down for three hours and think steadily about Mary. I could think about Mary as if she were the only character in the book and for as long as I pleased, and the hours I spent in doing so would not appear in Mary's time (the time inside the story) at all.

God is not hurried along in the Time-stream of this universe any more than an author is hurried along in the imaginary time of his own novel. He has infinite attention to spare for each one of us. He doesn't have to deal with us in the mass. You are as much alone with Him as if you were the only being He had ever created.

God is not too busy for us, nor is He unwilling to respond. Bill Hybels writes in *Too Busy Not to Pray,* "I get tired of hearing about 'secrets to prayer' to get past God's reluctance, to reveal the little-known way to pester our way into His presence." We don't need to beg God. God is better than that. The Bible does say we need to persist in prayer. Why?

When he was thirteen, Nathan said to me, "I want a Mercedes." Through deft questioning, I came to realize that he meant his mother and I should go out *now* and buy a Mercedes for him, though he would allow us to drive it until he received his driving permit. He seemed sincere enough, though obviously addled.

Understand, I love to give things to Nathan; I gain great pleasure in giving, and I especially enjoy surprising him with gifts. He doesn't have to beg me to do it—I'm looking for opportunities to give. But I didn't buy him the Mercedes he asked for. Three considerations came to mind: (1) Did he truly mean it? (He quit asking shortly afterward.) (2) Did he really need it? (3) Would I be doing him more harm to grant his request than to deny it? In the case of the missing Mercedes, my finite wisdom seemed to register *no, no,* and *yes.*

Persisting in prayer may indicate the depth of our desire, and as countless cautionary tales point out, we should be careful what we ask for. Furthermore, our motivation can be a problem. A critical distinction looms between a child-like dependence on God and a childish demanding of God. Part of prayer maturity is learning not to get what we want but to want what we get. It may be appropriate for a one-year-old to view Daddy primarily as a giver of horsy rides and ice cream, but one would hope a thirty-one-year-old would hold a more complete view of him. We truly love God when we love Him more than the gifts He offers.

When God refuses to perform just because we say so, He frees us from our false, idolatrous notions. Richard J. Foster reflects, "For me, the greatest value in my lack of control was the intimate and ultimate awareness that I could not manage God. God refused to jump when I said, 'Jump!'" For this reason, I'm somewhat uncomfortable with aspects of the "claiming promises" approach to prayer, as though we can hold a grudging God's feet to the fire with

"Remember? You *promised.*" Most of life is conditional to some degree—my promise to take the children to the park Sunday may be contingent on a thunderstorm rolling in or the car expiring.[5] On the other hand, promises are designed to be kept. Asking, believing, and claiming God's promises have resulted in astounding answers to prayer.

Jesus' prayer, "Thy kingdom come, Thy will be done" allows the wiggle room God deserves, especially with absurd or selfish requests. Often God takes an indirect route to answer our prayers. The mother of Augustine prayed all night that God would stop her son from going to Italy because she wanted him to become a Christian. While she was praying he sailed away to Italy, where he converted to Christianity. Naturally, his mother believed for a time that her prayers had gone unheard. As with any healthy relationship on earth, a friendship with God is characterized by mutual freedom.

The book of *Psalms* merits a subtitle: *Raw Prayers from Passionate Believers.* I used to wonder why some psalms are in the Bible, for they are riddled with doubt and violence. (What prayers would you publish if you were God?) Psalmists fume, harangue, question, and scold. They also laud, celebrate, confess, and exalt. Alden Thompson writes about his growing experience with the psalms:

> I developed the habit of being quite careful of what I did and said in God's presence. My prayers were polite. Any agony of soul was kept well under cover. . . . Now bring the two problems together: the violent and passionate words of the psalms and my polite little prayers to the great God of the universe. . . . I finally awoke to the fact that God's people had been quite frank with Him all along. I had simply robbed myself of a great privilege. . . . If David and the psalmists could be open with God, why couldn't I? And that was the beginning of a real friendship with my God.

Huckleberry Finn discovered that he couldn't pray a lie. Richard J. Foster admits, "Who we are—not who we want to be—is the only offering we have to give." God is interested in honest communication, but with God we go to another level.

God knows we cannot live in peace with unresolved guilt, so Jesus says for us to first clear up any tension or misunderstanding with another person, then

---

5. The farmer may be praying for that thunderstorm. People pray for contradictory answers, and God cannot always honor both requests.

confess our specific sins to God to receive the healing of memory.[6] It's as hard to absolve yourself of your own guilt as it is to kiss the top of your own head. God cleanses our wounds and sets us free.

King Frederick II, an eighteenth-century king of Prussia, was visiting a prison in Berlin when a story of confession developed. The inmates tried to convince him that they had been framed, duped, and unjustly imprisoned. Amid their protests of innocence, the king spotted one man sitting alone in a corner, oblivious to the commotion. When the king asked the man what he was there for, the prisoner replied, "Armed robbery, Your Honor."

The king asked, "Were you guilty?"

"Yes, sir," he answered. "I entirely deserve my punishment."

The king then issued an order: "Release this guilty man. I don't want him corrupting all these innocent people."

When we pray, we should ask for mercy, not justice.

BREATHING STYLES

Prayer is spiritual breathing; but unlike the involuntary act of breathing, prayer involves conscious effort. How does one find time to fit prayer into a busy schedule? My friend Rose prays whenever she's alone driving a car. Martin Cossins uses the times he awakens in the middle of the night as cues that something needs to be prayed about. I enjoy praying when I'm moving by myself—while walking, taking a shower, or mowing the lawn.

Dave Zehring, a pastor in Arizona, prays when he's stopped at red lights. He used to be frustrated by them; now they're positive motivation. Vic Pentz, a pastor in Washington, prays while watching the news on television. He says, "The human needs depicted on the screen cause me to pray silently for them." Richard Foster prays for people who are distressed in classes or in meetings. He comments, "It's exciting for me to see some of their heaviness lift as the meetings progress." My brother enjoys fasting and praying for a week in the desert.

Frank Laubach developed the idea of "flash prayers," so that "to *see* anybody will be to pray! To *hear* anybody, as these children talking, that boy crying, may be to pray!" Thomas à Kempis practiced the presence of God. An anonymous seventeenth-century nun said, "Prayer is living life with an Audience."

In his superb book *Prayer*, Richard J. Foster writes, "There is a principle of

---

6. Terry Muck asked hundreds of spiritual leaders, "How do you know when you need to pray?" Their most common response was, "I get irritable with people."

progression in the spiritual life. We do not take occasional joggers and put them in a marathon race, and we must not do that with prayer, either. . . . We will discover that by praying we learn to pray."

Finding your style of prayer is as individual a matter as finding a style of breathing. We cannot exist for long by having others breathe for us; we must breathe on our own. Yet despite our individual styles, everyone engages in the same two steps of breathing—inhaling and exhaling. In the case of prayer, most people are expert exhalers, letting God know precisely how things are "down here" and what we expect Him to do about it.

Inhaling is listening to God. We are often impatient in this, as restless as a ten-year-old in a tie; *yet who of us would dare to inhale only 5 percent of our time?* Listening requires taking the time to wait on God, to clear away distractions. This process calls for focus and patience. We can live by breathing the constant question, "What would you have me do?"

Dr. Wilbur Chapman writes about his encounter with an American missionary known as Praying Hyde. "Mr. Hyde, I want you to pray for me," Chapman said, and describes what happened next:

> He came to my room, turned the key in the door, dropped on his knees, and waited five minutes without a single syllable coming from his lips. I could hear my own heart thumping. . . . I felt hot tears running down my face. I knew I was with God. Then, with upturned face, down while the tears were streaming, he said, "O God." Then for five minutes at least he was still again; and then, when he knew that he was talking with God there came from the depths of his heart such petitions for me as I had never heard before. I rose from my knees to know what real prayer was.

Listening is the communication skill learned first, used most, and taught least. Few high school graduates have a clue what the seven types of listening are.[7] Paul Tournier notes, "It is impossible to overemphasize the immense need humans have to be really listened to. Listen to all the conversations of our world, between nations as well as those between couples. They are, for the most part, dialogues of the deaf." In our God conversations we may move to three deepening levels: talking *about* God, talking *to* God, and talking *with* God. Even reading the Bible, as we listen to God's counsel, can be a form of listening prayer.

---

7. Supporting, analyzing, paraphrasing, judging, prompting, questioning, and advising.

Following God is a fascinating, challenging endeavor, one not always viewed aright. The quickest way for a sailboat to travel across a lake is not usually found in aiming straight across. By tacking the boat back and forth, a sailor maintains a full sail and optimum speed, although an uninformed observer sees many apparently inefficient, needless side trips. These side trips may take the form of helping an autistic girl, volunteering with a community service organization, or simply smiling at a stranger; yet in undertaking them, we arrive quicker at our true destination. The key to an effective life is not in setting our own course and sticking to it but in responding to the powerful wind of God's Spirit. This makes the difference between living on nervous energy or on deep energy. C. S. Lewis writes:

> The real problem of the Christian life comes where people do not usually look for it. It comes the very moment you wake up each morning. All your wishes and hopes for the day rush at you like wild animals. And the first job each morning consists simply in shoving them all back; in listening to that other voice, taking that other point of view, letting that other larger, stronger, quieter life come flowing in. And so on, all day.

Prayer helps free us from worry, our "natural fussings and frettings." The English word *worry* comes from the German *würgen,* which means "to strangle, to choke." The opposite of faith is not doubt but worry, for doubt can eventually strengthen faith, but worry always drains us. Jesus preaches this in His Sermon on the Mount. He cautions:

> I tell you, do not be anxious about your life, what you shall eat or what you shall drink, nor about your body, what you shall put on. Is not life more than food, and the body more than clothing? . . . But seek first [God's] kingdom and His righteousness, and all these things shall be yours as well. Therefore do not be anxious about tomorrow, for tomorrow will be anxious for itself.

Once for a teaching lesson I filled a large vat with five gallons of water while energetic seventh and eighth graders clustered around me. "This water," I announced, "is our trust in God. Five gallons of faith." I held up a bottle of cooking oil. "This oil represents our worry."

I poured in one cup of oil. "Now, Eric"—I chose smiling Eric, always ready for anything—"I want you to mix this little worry into our large faith so that the worry disappears." Happy to oblige, Eric churned the water to a froth. We waited a half minute for the water to stop spinning.

At first the oil couldn't be seen in the movement, but as the water stilled, six oil globules congealed on top. Then, amazingly, the globules flattened, moved toward each other, connected, and formed an oily film.[8] In the end, the one cup of worry covered five gallons of faith. Worry and faith cannot coexist, just as oil and water don't mix.

As we're stilled in bed after a spinning day, worries congeal, expand, and cover our peace of mind. We must trust God purely, entirely, giving our worries to Him. It's said that if a problem is not large enough to be handled with prayer, it's not big enough to worry about. Particularly, we pray, *God, take these worries of mine and bury them under your love. I do not fear tomorrow, for I know you are already there.*

The world brings pressure to our door; Jay Kesler points out that there are two ways of handling pressure. One is to become like the bathysphere, the miniature submarine used to explore ocean depths where water pressure can crush a conventional submarine as easily as we can flatten an aluminum can. Bathyspheres are protected with plate steel several inches thick. This also makes them rigid, slow, and cramped.

At the same depths we find another way to handle pressure. Swimming about the bathysphere are the denizens of the deep—supple, quick, and free. Rather than sporting thick skins, these fish compensate for the enormous external pressure through equal internal pressure. Like the fish, we don't have to be hard and inflexible in facing stress. We can appropriate God's peaceful breathings within to offset the pressure without.

"The most important thing that ever happens in prayer," says Brennan Manning, "is letting ourselves be loved by God. 'Be still and know that I am God' (Psalm 46). It's like slipping into a tub of hot water and letting God's love wash over us, enfold us. . . . The awareness of being loved brings a touch of lightness and a tint of brightness and sometimes, for no apparent reason, a smile plays at the corner of your mouth." Prayer is breathing for eternity. Prayer is propping open our heart to a friend.

God is personal.

. . .

God of creation, sovereign of light and sound, wetness and wonder, darting tad-

---

8. This surprised me as well as the students. The best way to learn anything is to teach it.

poles and pelicans on the wing, conductor of symphonies of creeks and seashores, I pray, and at times I know not why. Can you hear me?

I pray in the midst of a sick, sad, toxic environment, and I long for relief. I admit that I have played too many roles in the sadness. Please forgive me for those. I pray also that I may listen to You more, so that I may hurt others less.

I pray, thanking You for breath and brains and ladybugs, for dewy roses and lamps and off-key singing, for parks and libraries and redwoods, for curling waves and running laughter.

I pray on the edge of infinity always, believing that You are with me and also waiting, whispering peace, on the other side of whatever I'm facing. Deliver me from worry. Grant me Your inner hush.

I pray, God.

~

The birds sing with beauty.
Blood stains the turning earth.
What does it all mean?

—INNER-CITY HIGH SCHOOL STUDENT

I do not believe that sheer suffering teaches. If suffering alone taught, all the world would be wise, since everyone suffers. To suffering must be added mourning, understanding, patience, love, openness, and the willingness to remain vulnerable.

—ANNE MORROW LINDBERGH

Why must some of us deliberate between brands of toothpaste, while others deliberate between damp dirt and bone dust to quiet the fire of an empty stomach lining?

—ADAH PRICE, *THE POISONWOOD BIBLE*

Tyger! Tyger! burning bright
In the forests of the night,
What immortal hand or eye
Could frame thy fearful symmetry?

—WILLIAM BLAKE

God is light, and in him is no darkness at all.

—*FIRST LETTER OF JOHN*, CHAPTER I

It's the cracked ones that let the light through.

—PAUL MOORE

Any god who promises to fulfill all of our desires is the devil in disguise.

—DONALD W. MCCULLOUGH

When Mother Teresa was passing through a crowd in Detroit, a woman remarked, "Her secret is that she is free to be nothing. Therefore God can use her for anything."

—EDWARD FARRELL

Jesus wept.

—*JOHN*, CHAPTER 11

~

5

FREEDOM'S MORTGAGE PAYMENTS

ALL IS NOT right with the world. Something has gone wrong. It's spattered across the morning papers pitched on our porches. We see it shuffling on street corners in the afternoon heat. We hear it in a siren's whoop at three A.M. We feel it slap us in a name: Hiroshima. Oklahoma City. Pompeii. Chernobyl. Jonestown. MyLai. Rwanda. Auschwitz. It claws at our minds from the inside, a monstrous dread standing between us and falling in love with God. It leads to a question each of us grapples with—or should.

WHY SO MUCH SUFFERING?

If we're human, we're touched by suffering. Seared. Hounded. Crippled. Suffocated. Devastated. Headlines shout about murder and fiery deaths. Behind every running sore of war on the planet lurk untold tortures and mind-numbing rapes. I cannot get my mind around the fact that every sixty seconds, thirty-three children die from starvation.

Beyond the news reports lie quiet tragedies. A child cringes at a classmate's taunts; a parent cringes also. The Beatles sing of Eleanor Rigby and all the lonely people, and we all relate. Rumors stalk and stab us. Nobody escapes. You have lost a loved one. I watched my father, wracked by cancer, slowly die.

In the summer of 1969 humans first walked on the moon, a crowning achievement for our species. But thirty years later we cannot stop poverty or sexual abuse here at home. Nothing has quelled bigotry. All the accurate-to-a-picosecond, CD-ROM-genius of humankind is weaker than the instinct of human selfishness. What other excuse can we offer? Mark Twain growls, "Man is the only animal that blushes. Or needs to."

"The chief and only thing wrong with the world is man," writes Carl Jung. And yet we know that the claw-hand of suffering moves past humanity's reach. Floods, hurricanes, blizzards, earthquakes, tornadoes, and volcanoes all wreak havoc, battering the belief—or at least the love—out of many. Nature is a tough book to read. We might wish to stop reading when we add to the tiger's fearful symmetry scorpions, mosquitoes, and the praying mantis who chews off her mate's head while copulating. Finding God in all of nature is a frightening assignment.

I arrived in Guatemala in 1976, two months after the earthquake that killed twenty-three thousand people. Entire villages were pushed under bulldozers, and many people slept outside, afraid of collapsing walls. One night I was awakened by a strong aftershock. I turned on the light and rode the rolling floor like a surfer on a wave. The animist nationals held an interpretation for the earthquake and aftershocks. "The great serpent is moving," they explained. That phrase has stuck with me over the years.

In my country, the "great serpent" is a joke, a punchline for comedians, a red-tailed grinner on fireworks boxes. Often in cultures where people actively worship "spirits," the warring between good and evil seems more pronounced, more raw. Dabbling in the occult opens demonic doors. Even those in modern society who have firsthand experience with the battle will state uncategorically that evil is real and that an intelligent force, more haunting than any Alfred Hitchcock horror, colder than any Stephen King story, is behind it. Dr. M. Scott Peck in *People of the Lie* reveals this intelligence as he describes two dramatic, tortuous exorcisms in his detached, clinical style:

> In common with 99 percent of psychiatrists and the majority of clergy, I did not think the devil existed. . . .
>
> When the demonic finally revealed itself in the exorcism of this other patient, it was with a still more ghastly expression. The patient suddenly resembled a writhing snake of great strength, viciously attempting to bite the team members. More frightening than the writhing body, however, was the face. The eyes were hooded with lazy reptilian torpor—except when the reptile darted out in attack, at which moment the eyes would open wide with blazing hatred. Despite these frequent darting moments, what upset me most was the extraordinary sense of a fifty-million-year-old heaviness I received from this serpentine being. It caused me to despair of the success of the exorcism. Almost all the team members at both exorcisms were convinced that they were at these times in the presence of something absolutely alien and inhuman.

He reaches other conclusions about an actual devil: (1) It is not a snake; it is a spirit that takes control of a body, and this is a rare occurrence. (2) The best definition for Satan is "a real spirit of unreality." It lied continually. (3) Satan's threats are empty. "The only power that Satan has is through belief in these lies." (4) Owing to its extraordinary pride and narcissism, notions of love and sacrifice are totally foreign to it.[1]

Peck contends that "the central defect of evil is not the sin but the refusal to acknowledge it." Consistent, destructive lying, or "hiddenness," characterizes evil. Evil people are masters of pretense and disguise, of "scapegoating," and are intolerant to criticism. They are also the world's bullies, and worse. Jacobo Timerman met the evil in an Argentine prison:

> A man's hands are shackled behind him, his eyes blindfolded. No one says a word. Blows are showered upon him. He's placed on the ground and someone counts to ten, but he's not killed. He is then led to what may be a canvas bed or a table, stripped, doused with water, and tied to the ends of the bed or table with his hands and legs outstretched. And the application of electric shocks begins. The amount of electricity transmitted by the electrodes—or whatever they're called—is regulated, so that it merely hurts, or burns, or destroys.
>
> It's impossible to shout—you howl. At the onset of that long human howl, someone with soft hands checks the state of your heart, someone sticks his hand into your mouth and pulls out your tongue to prevent you from choking. Someone places a piece of rubber in your mouth to prevent you from biting your tongue or destroying your lips. A brief pause. And then it starts all over again. With insults this time. A brief pause. And then questions. A brief pause. And then words of hope. A brief pause. And then insults.
>
> What does a man feel? The only thing that comes to mind: They're ripping apart my flesh. They didn't rip apart my flesh. They didn't even leave marks.

For countless inhabitants of earth, Timerman's ordeal approximates what they also endure from birth, with brief pauses, but they use another name for "that long human howl": Life. Most believing unbelievers cite "the world's suffering" as their number-one obstacle to believing in a loving, compassionate God. It's the reason why millions of sensitive people give up altogether on God.

---

1. Establishing unquestionably the existence of Satan is beyond the scope of this book, though we'll be looking at some Bible references. Anecdotal evidence such as Dr. Peck's may or may not be persuasive. It was noteworthy to me personally when a friend, a former devil worshiper, informed me that he came to believe in God because he was so certain of the existence of the devil.

"Why doesn't God stop the suffering?" they ask. "End the endless hurting." To do so makes such glorious good sense. Why doesn't He?

Epicurus (341–270 B.C.) posed an ancient dilemma: "Either God can stop suffering and will not, in which case He is evil, or God wants to but cannot prevent suffering, and thus is impotent. Would He in either case deserve our worship?" In *J.B.,* Archibald MacLeish's play on the sufferings of Job, the conundrum appears in clever wordplay: "If God is God He is not good; if God is good He is not God." William Blake inquires of the snarling tiger, "Did He who made the lamb make thee?"

If we are ever to fully love God, we cannot look away from suffering, excusing conditions as being "not that bad." We know differently. Instead, we must look suffering in the eyes, unblinking, to find what is behind it and why it doesn't end. For answers, we need to go back to before the beginning.

THE COSMIC CONFLICT

Before the beginning of Earth dawned the genesis of suffering. In the concluding book of the Bible, *Revelation,* the story unfolds in chapter 12:

> Now war arose in heaven, Michael and his angels fighting against the dragon; and the dragon and his angels fought, but they were defeated and there was no longer any place for them in heaven. And the great dragon was thrown down, that ancient serpent, who is called the Devil and Satan, the deceiver of the whole world—he was thrown down to the earth, and his angels were thrown down with him.

Phoenician and Egyptian literature, Greek and Roman mythology, the Gilgamesh epic, and the Rig Veda all contain creation accounts, but no account portrays the inception of evil as definitively as does the Bible. Before the beginning of life on this planet, in the beginning of sin and suffering, was a war. It wasn't a war of laser swords à la Luke Skywalker and Darth Vader, but a war of concepts, a battle for minds and affections. The battle was for the trusting love of all inhabitants of the universe, and Lucifer was "thrown down."[2] At issue with the first traitor—the great dragon Lucifer, who is later called Satan—are the same issues we face today. Who deserves to be God? What is God like? According to the Bible, Lucifer was once a different being altogether:

---

2. Later, Jesus tells His disciples, "I saw Satan fall like lightning from heaven."

You were on the holy mountain of God;
in the midst of the stones of fire you walked.
You were blameless in your ways
from the day you were created,
till iniquity was found in you. . . .
Your heart was proud because of your beauty;
you corrupted your wisdom for the sake of your splendor.[3]

While Lucifer wants to be God, God labors with Lucifer because he is not the source of life, and to say otherwise is to deceive. Deception, however, is the devil's method, as Jesus details, "He was a murderer from the beginning, and has nothing to do with the truth, because there is no truth in him. When he lies, he speaks according to his own nature, for he is a liar and the father of lies." God is at a disadvantage, for God will not stoop to manipulating half-truths (nor will His followers).

As Dick Winn says, this conflict involves not an offended deity defending his dignity, but a loving God defending reality. "The central core of the great controversy," he contends, "is Satan's deceptive accusations about the character of God, because those who accept Satan's portrayal of God will turn from God. They will break faith with the Lifegiver, and thus they will die. Our Father, therefore, has one overriding goal: to reveal Himself as He really is." The charges the dragon levels at God are the complaints that remain today.

God is against freedom.

God is against personal expression.

God is anti-fun.

God is power hungry.

God's subjects serve Him out of greed or fear.

God is unforgiving.

God is arbitrary.

God will torture you if you don't agree with Him.

God cannot be trusted.

When Lucifer arrived on earth, he became Satan, in charge of an "unseen world." *Revelation* reports, "His tail swept down a third of the stars [angels] of heaven, and cast them to earth."[4] The Bible depicts these fallen beings as our

---

3. *Ezekiel,* chapter 28.

4. Thus God, the perfect parent, lost a third of His children. This should put to rest the notion that parents are always somehow to blame when a child "turns out bad."

most formidable enemies: "We are not contending against flesh and blood, but against the principalities, against the powers, against the world rulers of this present darkness. . ."[5] A hidden war for human loyalties is apparently being waged in this unseen realm, even as I write and you read these words.

We might ask, "Why didn't God squash Lucifer like a fly? Wouldn't that have saved untold agony?" The downside to this approach is that, certainly at the beginning, "rubbing out" the lone dissenter would not have endeared God to a watching universe. All would have served God thereafter out of fear, not love. The ultimate effects of evil would not have been evident.

When our sons were very young, Yolanda got them a ball of white fluff, which the boys named Buffy. We watched with delight as the kitten hunted pieces of string and attacked menacing curtains. She nibbled and purred and pawed the litter box. After a few months we decided it was time to let her run free on our country property. Our cul-de-sac contained only six other homes, so traffic was light.

The first day we let her out, she romped about with giddy glee. I left for work. When I returned home that evening, I noticed a spot of white on the pavement in front of our house, and my heart lurched. *Oh, no. Oh, no.* I drove closer until I could see her. Squashed on the street.

I still remember the look, the revolting death mask, on that kitten as I tried to scrape a shovel under it. If you've ever scraped up a pet, you'll relate. Grieving, disheartened, my spirit as flat as the crushed body, I remember thinking, *This is the work of the enemy. This is what it would have for each of us. For my wife and children. For every being on earth.* And I stopped scraping. I leaned on my shovel and prayed, "God, help me never to aid this enemy of yours, this agent of death. Alert me whenever I'm helping the wrong side. Enable me to always be angry about evil, and to use only good means to fight it."

Evil is a mystery. Sometimes I ask people, "What if Satan and his legions died *today?* Do you think all suffering would stop tomorrow?" They sadly shake their heads no. Human evil would still exist. We would still be free to cause distrust and pain. To stop the hurt we must be radically changed from the inside.

Look again at the list of charges the dragon fires at God, beginning with "He is against freedom." *Each one can be applied truthfully to the dragon.* The legendary mark of the beast mentioned in the Bible (see *Revelation,* chapters 13 and 17) is characterized by lies and force. Ellen White observes, "The kingdom of Satan is a kingdom of force; every individual regards every other as an obsta-

5. *Ephesians,* chapter 6.

cle in the way of his own advancement, or a steppingstone on which he himself may climb to a higher place. . . . There can be no more conclusive evidence that we possess the Spirit of Satan than the disposition to hurt and destroy those who do not appreciate our work or who act contrary to our ideas." No matter how noble our aims, we are on the side of the beast when we use coercion and deception.

The Face in the Mirror

When I wake up in the morning, it's easy to view everything as relative, for life is complex. Labels of "good" and "evil" lose their distinction when we uncover personal motives, cultural colorings, and misperceptions. Customs such as enthusiastic belching or exposing the sole of your foot prove that actions may be right in one setting and wrong in another. Yet even the dogmatic will admit that some actions transcend this theory of relativity. Rape is never right. Child abuse is unacceptable.

Beyond "wrong" lies evil, just as beyond our atmosphere lies deep space. Without delving into definition (evil darkens, spreads, and stains past definition), evil is antilove, antilife—live spelled backward. To catch a fresh glimpse of evil's reality, we need only look at the face in the mirror, as Isabel Allende writes in *Paula:*

> Sometimes, when I was alone in some secret place on the hill with some time to think, I again saw the black waters of the mirrors of my childhood where Satan peered out at night, and as I leaned toward the glass, I realized, with horror, that the Evil One had my face. I was not unsullied, no one was: a monster crouched in each of us, every one of us had a dark and fiendish side. Given the conditions, could I torture and kill? Let us say, for example, that someone harmed my children. . . . What cruelty would I be capable of in that situation? The demons had escaped from the mirrors and were running loose through the world.

Adolf Eichmann organized anti-Jewish persecutions during World War II, in particular the loathsome concentration camps. Captured by U.S. forces in 1945, he escaped until 1960 when Israeli agents found him living in Argentina and smuggled him into Israel for trial. During the trial one of the witnesses entered the courtroom and looked for the man who had put him through so much misery. When his eyes landed on Adolf Eichmann, the witness fell to his knees, broke down, and wept. When at last he stood, he told the hushed room why he had cried. He wept, he confessed, because at that moment he knew that within himself was the same tendency to evil that was in Adolf Eichmann.

Freedom's Mortgage Payments

A Danish atheist with the unlikely name of Christian Fog befriended me and accepted a supper invitation to our house. After the meal we talked about God. "Why is it," he asked as we sat on the sofa, "that your God won't stop the suffering? Even an earthly father keeps his children from hurting each other."

"What do you think causes the most suffering in the world?" I responded. "Is it our fists or our words?"

He reflected a moment. "Our words," he said finally. "The spoken and the unspoken."

"So for God to keep us from hurting each other," I said, "He would have to control our words, and to do that He must control what creates our words. He must control our thoughts. "We fight world wars to prevent such oppression. You were alive when a man named Hitler wanted to control people's thoughts. How would you like a God like that?"

Christian stared at me. "I see what you mean," he said. "Yes, I would rather be free."

Years ago, I attended the funeral of the much-loved two-year-old child of a close friend. My friend had found his son floating facedown in a pond. The funeral service seemed especially tragic, and I remember thinking, *The coffin is too small.* One other thought loomed during the service. A person leaned on the pulpit, looked out over a sea of tears, and uttered, "We must recognize that whatever happens is God's will."

When I heard those words, I wanted to stand up and shout, "No! This is *not* God's will! Not my God!" Decorum pinned me in my seat that dreary day. We need to distinguish between what God allows and what God desires. Many think of God's will as equivalent to God's desire, His want. From the Bible's *Second Letter of Peter,* though, we learn that God is "not willing that any should perish." Yet it happens.

One sunny morning when my son Geoffrey was five, he and I were eating our bowls of Cheerios and discussing why he couldn't go over to his friend Cleidson's house to play "right now." Suddenly Geoff grew pensive.

"Dad," he said, looking at me intently, "God doesn't always get His way either, does He?"

I sat momentarily stunned. My eyes misted over when I replied, "No, son. He doesn't."

Not everything that happens is as our God would have it. The all-powerful, all-knowing master of the universe doesn't always get His way because His way is also the way of freedom. *Freedom is sacred to God.* God would rather have us free than have us safe. God would rather have us free than have us forever saved. Otherwise, He would force us to be saved, to be gentle, to be unselfish and kind. God understands that sullen submission breeds resentment and rebellion. God knows love cannot be forced.

We can compare God's situation to my family's purchase of our present house. When Yolanda and I bought the house, we did so with the idea that it would be a center of love for our family, a place of warmth and light, a sanctuary for companionship, security, and honor. But with the house we also purchased something else: a mortgage. The bank actually owns "our" house, and we must make payments to the bank. Please understand this: *It is not our desire to make those payments.* We make them because they come with the territory, the house.

The "house" God has bought is freedom, human free will. The mortgage payments on the house are the sufferings that result from our free choices. For now, Satan, the prince of darkness, is the bank. Jesus calls him "the ruler of this world," yet adds, "don't be afraid, for I have overcome the world."

UNNATURAL DISASTERS

One night Yolanda and I stood in our kitchen mesmerized by a spectacular lightning storm. Earlier that day the Weather Channel's forecaster had pointed at our town on a map and announced cheerily, "Look at this, folks. Look at Hagerstown, Maryland. They're about to be crushed."

While our children slept, we watched arm in arm in the darkness, marveling at the show, the power of hundreds of thunderous strikes. All at once a deafening clap sounded and sizzling raced through the house. Instinctively, with a "*Yeeow!*" we yanked each other from the window. Upon inspection we found that one light bulb, the television, and the VCR were "gone." We had been hit by a bolt.

The next day I called the store where we had purchased the television. Our service contract was still in effect, but the representative coolly informed me that lightning strikes are not covered by the contract because they are "an act of God." I paused on the line, hovering like a hummingbird, considering.

"He gets blamed for a lot of things, doesn't He?" I said finally.

She said, "Yes, sir, He does."

Understandably, we become confused. When Christians pray, "Thank you, God, for this nice day," or for "the sunshine," or "the needed rain," we're saying that God controls the weather. He's also, then, apparently in charge of flooding in the Midwestern states, Bay of Bengal typhoons that maroon hundreds of thousands, droughts in eastern Africa that starve millions, and killer quakes in China. "Weather" we like it or not, we have to accept both sides.

It's hard to love a God who controls all that. Is it merely a matter of our unfortunate positioning, as a grain of sand is beautiful until it gets in your eye? The lightning bolt is lovely until it nukes our brains. Maybe we should just stay out of God's way?

When I read newspaper accounts of tragedies where some are killed and some are spared, and a tearful survivor says, "God saved my family," I think about the people who had lost loved ones. What do the grieving think of God when they read those words? The message appears obvious and terrible: *If God saved theirs, then He killed mine. God didn't want my loved ones saved.* Even when God is "praised" He often indirectly takes the blame. I wonder how much of a favor we're doing Him when we make such pronouncements.

Paul of Tarsus observes to his Roman audience that the Earth itself longs to be "set free from its bondage to decay and obtain the glorious liberty of the children of God. We know that the whole creation has been groaning in agony until now; and not only the creation, but we ourselves." This decay colors the white mold on my peach this morning, the cancerous black lesions on a rainbow trout, the rusty blight on a billion grain heads. Who is responsible? As Jesus teaches in His parable, "An enemy has done this." As the Guatemalans say, "The great serpent is moving."

Some would say that the state of the world is neither good nor bad—it simply is. Here we have to pause; if we consider fly-specked, blank-eyed starving children with stick arms and legs, and toxic deformities, and swerving drunk drivers, and any thing gloved with promise and gutted by disease as "all right" or "good enough," we don't need to read on. Something has gone wrong.

PAIN—GOD'S GREAT GOOF?

Upon accepting an award, comedian Jack Benny quipped, "I really don't deserve this. But I have arthritis, and I don't deserve that either."

Life is not fair. The wicked triumph. Evil prospers. Virtue is mowed down like cut grass, swallowed like spring water, chomped and spit out like bubble gum. How should we respond to injustice? Which view of evil and suffering reflects reality? Is pain an illusion? Could there be a God of evil as well as a God of good? Various commentators have made worthwhile observations on these questions. C. S. Lewis asserts that Christians believe "a great many things have gone wrong with the world that God made and that God insists, and insists very loudly, on our putting them right again." Columnist Ann Landers writes a provocative dialogue:

> "Sometimes I would like to ask God why He allows poverty, famine, and injustice when He could do something about it."
> "Well, why don't you ask Him?"
> "Because I'm afraid God might ask me the same question."

It is fitting that the civil rights movement in the United States was launched in Christian churches and that the movement's leader, Dr. Martin Luther King Jr., was above all a minister of the good news about Jesus, humanity's freedom fighter. God's followers ought to be light bearers wherever soul darkness threatens. In King's words, "Injustice anywhere is a threat to justice everywhere."

Suffering itself is a complex thing. In *The Road Less Traveled*, M. Scott Peck maintains that "the attempt to avoid legitimate suffering lies at the root of all emotional illness." Those who delay gratification and choose to face up to unpleasant realities and difficult decisions are healthier and happier. But does life have to be so hard, so filled with rocks? Couldn't God have fashioned an undulating pathway of ease to enlighten us? As Ward Hill explains:

> Why couldn't God make things more *obvious*? Why not give us a book so clear that honest men and women wouldn't disagree over it? Why couldn't every time someone tells the truth, a halo gleams overhead, and the opposite invokes the Pinocchio principle? Because there is something valuable, something *holy* in the struggle. We are given sufficient evidence, not coercive evidence.

Any musician who has strained to master a piece, any athlete who has sweated and grunted to achieve victory, any woman who has carried a child nine months in her belly *knows* something holy breathes in the struggle. Our joy rises from overcoming. As we explore in the concluding chapter, heaven will also bear its struggles, though of a different nature.

One summer while vacationing with family and friends in Colorado, a group of us climbed Mt. Princeton to 14,197 feet (at that altitude, every foot counts). The last half mile or so was all rocks—sharp, tipsy, sliding, aggravating, dangerous. We scrambled, gasping, to the summit.

"Hey, welcome to the top!" a woman called out. Another smiling person offered to snap our photos with the magnificent panorama in the background, after my pulse rate had lowered to 180. A couple handed around clusters of purple grapes. We discovered that the dozen or so people sitting on Princeton's head had arrived from France, Nebraska, Colorado, and Washington. We talked about the ascent and similar climbs, about food and rest, and we warmly welcomed all who joined us. We instantly formed a community in a gathering of total strangers.

That day another company of our friends, spouses, and children visited St. Elmo, a nearby ghost town. They told us afterward of sluggish crowds of hot, spoiled tourists elbowing into the chipmunk-feeding area, of whining kids, and of how people appeared bored, distant, and snappish.

What made the difference? The climbers had endured and striven for a challenging, worthwhile goal, and through our suffering a community was born. The St. Elmo tourists had endured driving slowly and shuffling along jammed sidewalks, and some had striven to be first in line. For them, any irritation in a day of expected comfort produced a huffy complaint. For us, any relief in a day of expected suffering produced grateful camaraderie.

Look at most disaster-relief situations, and you'll find strangers banding together to heft sandbags by a rising river or neighbors picking up fences after a windstorm. "Ten thousand difficulties," declares John Henry Newman, "do not make one doubt."

What of the very existence of pain in our bodies? How can we love a God who *created* pain? In their classic book *Where Is God When It Hurts?* Philip Yancey and Dr. Paul Brand collaborate to show how pain is in one sense a gift. Dr. Brand, a hand surgeon, specializes in treating victims of Hansen's disease (leprosy), a malady that acts as an anesthetic, numbing the pain cells of feet, hands, ears, nose, and eyes. For thousands of years people considered leprosy to be highly contagious. Largely through Dr. Brand's research, we now know that of all infectious diseases, Hansen's is probably the least contagious and that "in ninety-nine percent of the cases, HD only numbs the extremities. The destruction follows solely because the warning system of pain is gone."

How does this absence of pain lead to destruction? Persons with HD have been known to reach directly into a fire to retrieve dropped food, walk barefoot over shards of glass, wash with scalding water, and work all day gripping a handle with a protruding nail. If they tear ligaments in an ankle, they simply adjust by walking crooked. Dr. Brand tries to sleuth out the cause of the injury and infection. *Are your shoes too tight? How do you open jars? Show me precisely what you do when you work.* His patients destroy themselves piece by numbed piece.

At one point Dr. Brand and his associates attempted to devise an artificial nerve cell and warning system to activate if, for instance, a patient turned a key too hard. At first the warnings employed buzzers and blinking lights, but the experiment failed because the patients ignored them. Just as pain is unpleasant, so also the stimulus had to be sufficiently undesirable, so the doctors "upgraded" to electric shocks. But despite placing themselves in grave peril, "even intelligent people" switched off the signal to do what they wanted.[6] They preferred to go their own way. After investing five years of work and more than a million dollars, the team abandoned the project.

Although it can rage out of control, specific pain alerts us to the fact that *something is not right.* Without pain in this life, we would exterminate ourselves as a race. No film or book creates empathy like the experience of a heartbreaking trauma. After separating my shoulder, I wince with those who separate theirs. Having felt the arrows of insult and rejection myself, I know more of how others must feel.

Pain also makes us mindful of transcendent values, as Yancey shows:

> We could (some people do) believe that the purpose of life here is to be comfortable. Enjoy yourself, build a nice home, engorge good food, have sex, live the good life. That's all there is.
>
> But the presence of suffering complicates that philosophy. It's much harder to believe that the world is here just so I can party when a third of its people go to bed starving each night. It's much harder to believe the purpose of life is to feel good when I see teenagers smashed on the freeway. If I try to escape the idea and merely enjoy life, suffering is there, haunting me, reminding me of how hollow life would be if this world were all I'll ever know.

Alexander Solzhenitsyn writes of his imprisonment in the gulag, "It was only when I lay there on rotting prison straw that I sensed within myself the first stirrings of good. . . . So, bless you, prison, for having been in my life." Even of Jesus it is written, "He learned obedience from what he suffered."[7] We need not

---

6. Dr. Brand notes how wise God is in placing pain out of reach.

7. *Hebrews,* chapter 5.

look for suffering. It will find us. Longing for suffering is a sign of sickness, not holiness. One measure of maturity is the ability to reconcile two apparently contradicting ideas. Though suffering can lead to character growth, we should not thank the terrorist for enhanced airline security. Though death can be a welcome relief, it is of Satan's realm.

It is not God's desire that people suffer and die. We clearly see this in the Garden of Gethsemane, when Jesus asks His Father three times that the cup of suffering be taken away. If you've ever asked for something three times, you know that Jesus seriously wanted out. The pain that stretched ahead, particularly the agony of separation from His Father, seemed unbearable. But what enemies devise for our harm, God turns to our good—as we allow Him. God in reality is a God of *recovery*. Jesus embodies the recovery model as evil sniffs and savages Him on the cross. The universe's most monstrous event, the murder of God's Son, becomes the universe's most glorious event.

What of the Bible's injunction: "Rejoice always, pray constantly, give thanks in all circumstances; for this is the will of God in Christ Jesus for you"?[8] We should make a distinction between *in* and *for*. As James Hilt brings out, "Thanking God for evil as well as good presumes evil also finds its source in Him. This is a terrible distortion. God should not be thanked for anything of a fallen nature—anything that finds its source in this planet's rebellion against God. This includes accidents, health problems, natural disasters." God can be thanked *in* all things, but not *for* all things. In all circumstances we can know that nothing, neither disease nor discouragement, devil nor death, will be able to separate us from the love of God.

We tend to think that life should be fair because God is fair. But God is not life. God is behind life, the author of life, the energy of life, the hope of life, the end of life; He is not life. A painter, while "seen" in her painting, is not the painting, and will not be seen truly, especially if the painter's enemies and "friends" have access to mar the product. Life is like the back side of a tapestry, its tied threads all jumbled with indistinct, muted colors and clashing patterns. We can *sort of* make out the picture. But it's not until we get to the front of the tapestry, the other side of this life, that we experience the full design, the whole image, the reason for every knotted red and gray and black and white, and gasp, "Oh, *that's* how it looks!"

What more could God do? How does one keep freedom sacred and not allow people to make hurtful choices?[9] Would we rather have a planet populated with

---

8. *First Letter to the Thessalonians*, chapter 5.
9. In Feodor Dostoevsky's *The Brothers Karamazov*, the Grand Inquisitor is furious with Jesus for allowing people the freedom to choose, because obviously they cannot handle their freedom.

unthinking automatons? Would I have God reverse natural laws at my whim, abolishing the law of gravity if I fall, dismissing E=MC², and reconfiguring molecules if I mash into a maple? What on earth could we count on? Like a parent giving too much license to a child, continuing to shield and "bail out" bolsters irresponsibility and becomes the ultimate act of sabotage.

God maintains that the real universe is composed of laws that will not be changed; it is up to us to abide by them.[10] The law of gravity will not change simply because we feel like diving off a bridge. Similarly, the laws for peace and joy—as found, for example, in prayer and the Beatitudes—will not change. They are the physics of love. Admittedly, people get hurt as a result of gravity, but to argue against gravity misses the grave point that without the law we wouldn't be here to argue at all, and without the pull of love, we wouldn't care if we weren't here anyway.

It is also the unhappy case that, should I decide to dive off a bridge, I may land on an "innocent" person. Sin is in part a random destroyer. Jesus speaks to this when He says that no one who was killed under a collapsing tower deserved accidental death.[11] The effects of sin, those mortgage payments of freedom, collide with the constant of universal laws. Fortunately, the ethos of God's justice and mercy will make it right . . . someday.

"Humankind cannot bear very much reality," observes T. S. Eliot. Consider the problems we humans pose for God. *We want to live.* But we don't want to be connected to the Source of life. *We want freedom.* But we don't want to be free to hurt ourselves or to have others free to hurt us. *We want to love.* But we don't want to give up our natural selfishness to follow the Selfless One.

A brilliant pre-law student named Kevin once complained to me about the pathetic state of this planet. He was familiar with the biblical paradigm of evil and with God's response.

"If you were God," I said, "how would you do it better?"

An incredulous look swept over him. "I've never been asked that before," he replied.

Go ahead, concoct a better approach to our imperfect world. Design a realistic way, based on the laws of the universe, to have people keep their individuality and continually create love unselfishly—*without* freely plugging

---

10. The bigger problem for me is not why God doesn't "intervene" more but why God "intervenes" at all. What an incredible risk God takes in doing so. Like any parent, only God knows why He enters into such actions.

11. *Luke,* chapter 10.

into the Creator of love. Then stand back as the critics shoot your theory full of holes.

WHAT GOD WANTS

God does have another solution. He promises, "If you follow the Son, you will be free indeed." God promises freedom—His actual will—in four forms.

Freedom from the guilt of evil. Little is more freeing than a clear conscience. Unresolved guilt creates emotional cripples. God promises, "If we confess our sins, he is faithful and just, and will forgive our sins and cleanse us from all unrighteousness."[12] Of course, God also commands us to ask for forgiveness directly from anyone we have hurt and to forgive others that we may be forgiven. Through His sacrifice, Jesus provides freedom from guilt. This is called justification.

Freedom from the power of evil. A life that does not cause others to suffer is a holy life. A life that truly liberates is a godly life. Ultimate freedom is wanting to do only what we should do—what God desires for us. This is sanctification.

Freedom from the presence of evil. For now we're bound to this planet, though we may *sometimes* think, *Stop this spinning ball, I want to get off.* We can take comfort that in *Revelation,* God promises there will come a time for His children when "he will wipe away every tear from their eyes, and death shall be no more, neither shall there be mourning nor crying nor pain any more." This is glorification.

Freedom from the misconceptions of evil. Evil will be completely unmasked. Because God's character is the epicenter of the cosmic conflict, our clear-eyed view of God, especially His connection with our pain, is imperative. Falling in love with God is impossible unless we understand His part in the world's suffering. God is a God of recovery. This is realization.

The great unseen war can become clear if we think of God as a physician. Evil misrepresents suffering, just as telling a four-year-old, "Your father drugs people to unconsciousness. Then, when they are helpless, he has them stretched on a table, cuts their bodies with knives, and sends them the bill!" misrepresents the actions of a surgeon.[13] Another misrepresentation comes through God's "friends" who state, "The Doctor says that if His patients don't take their medicine, He will kill them." This doesn't lead to love, of course. (Can we possibly love some-

---

12. *First Letter of John,* chapter 1.
13. Leslie Weatherhead proposed this analogy.

one, knowing he will kill us if we don't?) Those who say, "The Doctor told us that if His patients don't take their medicine, they will die," present a truer picture. This compassionate doctor reasons and pleads, but the decision is finally ours.

We need to know at a fundamental level whether we can trust God. Is God at all responsible for the blunt pain and treachery of life? Are the infinitely lined hands cupped and caked with blood? Can the charlatans we see and hear actually be God's representatives? Would eternity be pleasurable? Fortunately, God answers these questions in the person of Jesus, the rabbi from Nazareth.

Possibly the most moving modern portrait of suffering is in Elie Wiesel's *Night*, written from his perspective as a youth in German death camps. In one scene the young Wiesel and the other camp inhabitants move forward in a single file, compelled to look at the hanging of another child, with "the face of a sad angel," who, being so light, was not yet dead.

> For more than half an hour he stayed there, struggling between life and death, dying in slow agony under our eyes. And we had to look him full in the face. He was still alive when I passed in front of him. His tongue was still red, his eyes not yet glazed.
>
> Behind me, I heard the same man asking:
>
> "Where is God now?"
>
> And I heard a voice within me answer him:
>
> "Where is He? Here He is—He is hanging here on this gallows."

Though Wiesel is not suggesting such, and though we must never answer the question glibly, that is where God was, a sad-faced Jewish Child hanging on a gallows in the shape of a cross. Whenever I am tempted to complain of injustice, I look to the ultimate injustice of God's Son, my Messiah and a true innocent, hanging on a cross.

Jesus came to do His Father's will. "I have come down from heaven, not to do my own will, but the will of him who sent me." He said to Philip, "He who has seen me has seen the Father." A little later He assures the disciples, "I do not say to you that I shall pray the Father for you; for the Father himself loves you."[14] Richard Coffen states, "While on this earth Jesus actually did what God wanted, and He has been the only person ever to fully do what God wants." Looking at Jesus, we gain the truest picture of God's approach to evil and suffering. What did Jesus do when He lived on this earth? Coffen continues:

---

14. These three quotes are in the book of *John*, chapters 6, 14, and 16.

Did He kill people? No, He raised the dead to life. Did He inflict disease on others? No, He healed the sick wherever He went. Did He molest little children? No, he told His disciples, who wanted to keep children from disturbing Him, "Let the children come to Me." Did He strike people with blindness? No, He opened the eyes of the blind. Did He make people go deaf? No, He healed people of their deafness. Did He make people lose their power of speech? No, He freed the tongues of those who couldn't talk.

At the foot of the cross is where virtually every question of mine about God gets answered. How does God view us? What is He willing to give up for me? Watch Jesus groaning and twitching, and you know that God cares. God understands. *We are not abandoned.*

God paid on the cross the mortgage payments of suffering, yet He and His children—every sentient being on earth—suffer every second. Make no mistake, just as Jesus was lashed with a soldier's whip, so also our heavenly Parent is lashed with our tears. Isaiah contends, "In all their affliction he was afflicted."

Do we love God only when life is dripping smooth and sweet? The inescapable question is, Do we love freedom or not? Are we willing, as countless soldiers have been and *as God is,* to give up everything for freedom's sake? The rap against religion is that it's too cramping, too restrictive. We have no idea of the immensity of freedom.

Terrors and tortures are never God's desire. Our long human howl will end with singing the song of the Lamb of God, and His paramount plan will put an end to evil without taking away the freedom to choose. Someday, God will buy back the bank. For the sake of my freedom, God invests so much and is Himself so touched by the mortgage payments. When I look at the world's suffering (the minuscule portion that I can fathom) and why God endures it, I love Him all the more.

God is liberating.

. . .

God, I turn away from the cancer of violence and emptiness that surrounds me. I will not be consumed. Thank you for freedom. Enable me to hold and defend it for others as sacredly and tenaciously as You do. Remind me of the evil force behind lies and of the true power of love and truth. Keep my eyes open to the pain sin causes. Help me to see all of life's suffering from the perspective of the foot of the cross. I give myself to You, trusting in Your peace. Amen.

~

I love humanity! It's people I can't stand!

—Lucy in "Peanuts"

You can pick out the actors by the glazed look that comes into their eyes when the conversation wanders away from themselves.

—Michael Wilding

If you have love in your life, it can make up for a great many things you lack. If you don't have it, no matter what else there is, it's not enough.

—Ann Landers

A body tends by its weight toward the place proper to it—weight does not necessarily tend toward the lowest place but toward its proper place. Fire tends upwards, stone downwards. By their weight they are moved and seek their proper place. Oil poured over water is borne on the surface of the water, water poured over oil sinks below the oil: it is by their weight that they are moved and seek their proper place. . . . My love is my weight: wherever I go my love is what brings me there.

—Augustine

There is no surprise more magical than the surprise of being loved. It is the finger of God on our shoulder.

—Charles Morgan

I am a kind of paranoiac in reverse. I suspect people of plotting to make me happy.

—J. D. Salinger

If you're coming to help me, you are wasting your time. But if you have come because your liberation is bound up with mine, then let's work together.

—Aboriginal woman from Australia

Nothing could more surely convince me of God's unending mercy than the continued existence on earth of the church.

—Annie Dillard

Now the tax collectors and sinners were all drawing near to hear Him.
And the Pharisees and the scribes murmured, saying,
"This man receives sinners and eats with them."

—Luke, chapter 15

~

6

THE WORLD'S GREATEST LOVER

AMONG MY FAVORITE movies is the romantic comedy *Groundhog Day*, which I consider one of the most spiritual films ever made, and I'm picky about entertainment. In commending a film to students I'm especially picky, but when I ask a class what they think of *Groundhog* and hear, "Oh, that was so boring. It was the same thing over and over," I sense an opening for true education.

Phil Connors (Bill Murray) is an egocentric, disdainful, wisecracking TV weatherman who detests covering the annual Groundhog Day in Punxsutawney, Pennsylvania. To Phil, the event is a hick festival, filled with bad theater and lowlife amusements in a town that's simply unworthy of his time. He's teamed this year with Rita (Andie MacDowell), the new director and endlessly optimistic foil to Phil's sardonic attitude. After filming the groundhog's "appearance," they get caught in a giant blizzard (which he failed to accurately predict) and are forced to stay in town. When Phil wakes up the next morning, however, it's February 2, again. And it's February 2 the next morning, and the next morning, and the next morning . . .

Eventually he gets over his time-lag disorientation and resolves to make the most of a day that will be without lasting consequences. Recklessly he indulges his every fantasy—crime, wealth, gluttony, sex—but each leaves him unfulfilled. Then he falls for Rita and, using his godlike knowledge, works to gain her affection. She sees through his orchestrations, though; no matter how he tries, he can't manipulate love. In a masterful spiritual gem, a hopeless Phil admits to Rita, "I've come to the end of me. There's no way out now." After abducting the groundhog, Phil commits suicide. When he wakes up the next morning, February 2, he says, "Aw, nuts!"

What's left? He's tried it all. What would you do? At one point after Phil confides to Rita what's happening, she watches him toss cards into a hat and comments, "So *this* is what you do with eternity."

Almost by accident, Phil takes another tack. He aspires to artistic pursuits—reading poetry, playing keyboard, carving ice sculptures—and pours himself into selfless service for every person in Punxsutawney. With religious fervor he gets to know the local residents and invests himself in them with genuine caring. Wherever he can help, he's there. Phil becomes a different person. He's fulfilled at last. Each new-old day is a freshly anticipated adventure. He is reborn.

What does this have to do with a God to love? And how might the message affect our lives?

THE "SO THAT" PRINCIPLE

Visualize a perfectly healthy person. Let's be more precise. Picture a twenty-seven-year-old male. You can see that he's in fabulous shape. He works out with weights and stretches for strength and flexibility. For daily aerobic exercise he runs eight to ten miles or bicycles thirty miles. His hobby is rock climbing.

Moreover, he eats only what's healthful for him: Piles of fruits and vegetables. Mounds of alfalfa sprouts. Barrels of oat bran. He drinks quarts of water between meals, sleeps eight hours a night, and approaches sweets as though they were radioactive.

His physician says she's never seen a healthier human being. His triglyceride and cholesterol counts are marvelous, as is his blood pressure. The guy never touches tobacco, alcohol, or other addictive drugs. He doesn't even take aspirin. Since the day he was born, he's never been in a hospital. Once, he had a cold—it lasted half a day. Two days later, he finished first in an Ironman triathlon.

Is this person healthy? Is he fit? Before you answer, let me tell you a little more about him.

Yesterday, on the way out the door to his daily workout, he kicked his dog, screamed obscenities at his wife, and brushed past his children without saying a word to them. At work, he lied to his boss, angrily blaming a coworker for a mistake he made. Later, he bragged about "getting out of that one." All in all, it was a typical day for him.

This man is impatient, unkind, and conceited. His physical training schedule and dietary needs come first—always. Family and acquaintances know that he's disloyal; integrity is a foreign concept to him. He feels no desire to stretch his mind. He sees no need to change anything about himself. He finds no ultimate purpose. He is morally and spiritually bankrupt.

Now, is he healthy?

Being healthy involves more than just our physical selves. Think of a light bulb, for instance. If the outer glass is sound but the filament is broken, is it a "healthy" bulb? The health of a light bulb is determined by only one aspect: *whether it produces light*. That's the sole reason for its existence. Whatever prevents it from producing light makes the bulb unhealthy. As with human beings, the true condition of the bulb is exposed when it gets shaken up.

Once while my family and I were visiting Sea World in San Diego, California, our camcorder malfunctioned. Since we rarely get the chance to visit Sea World, I decided to buy a new-on-the-market disposable paper camera to record a few fun moments. As I was at the counter unwrapping the camera, the salesman caught my eye and said, "You realize you have to turn the camera in to a film store after you finish the roll."

I chuckled. "Right," I said. "How else could you get to see what you've taken?"

The salesman shrugged with a half-smile. "I don't know," he replied. "But last week a woman threw her disposable camera in the trash and then wanted to know when she was going to get her pictures."

That woman isn't alone. Humans are masters at confusing means and ends. We work long hours just to get ahead, and when we've gotten there we work longer hours. We spend a fortune on facial cosmetics then choose to not wear a seat belt. We buy a comfortable sofa and cover it with plastic. We throw our lives away in trivialities and expect to see profound results. What we often miss is an understanding of the "so that" principle. The light bulb exists *so that* we can have light. A camera exists *so that* we can see the pictures. Light bulbs and cameras aren't ends in themselves; they're only means to an end.

So why should people be healthy? Answers to that question include, "So I'll look better," or "So I'll have more energy." Those are pretty good reasons, but they don't go far enough. Some abysmally shallow, selfish people are gorgeous. Maximum security prisons are jammed with people with boundless energy. Beyond gorgeousness and energy lies another, higher goal.

Love is the highest reason for our existence. Love is to people as light is to light bulbs. Whatever prevents us from loving makes us unhealthy. Loving involves our minds, our bodies, our souls. Everything we do should be done *so that* we can love better—studying algebra, eating organically, praying, running errands, listening to music. Love is the goal of human life. As Phil discovered, nothing else matters. Nothing else lasts.

John Richard Green muses, "What seems to grow fairer as life goes by is the love and grace and tenderness of it; not its wit and cleverness and grandeur of knowledge, grand as knowledge is, but just the laughter of children and the friendship of friends and the cozy talk by the fireside and the sight of flowers and the sound of music."

The highest love is loving God. Unless we are in love with God, we are not fully alive or awake. We are sleepwalking, settling for mundane, pallid days.

Jesus says, "I have come *so that* you may have life, and have it to the full." He arrived to present the fundamental importance of love and to expose God as the greatest lover of all.

Making Love

Perhaps this is the place to clear up a skewed, steamy picture. What do you think of when you hear the word *lover* or the words *making love?* When those last two words bump together, they attract attention like the beach attracts waves. We've been brainwashed. "Making love" implies the sexual act of copulating, and in analyzing the phrase we find we're not really talking about creating or building or shaping love; we're talking about making sex. "They were making sex" doesn't sound as romantic, of course. And when two people have made sex outside of marriage, to be truly accurate we sadly need to describe what else they were probably making. They were making tears. They were making lies. They were making regrets. Because these are what accompany the mere making of sex without the responsibility and depth and nourishment of committed love. Sex can be a part of love, but it is not love.

Somehow we get tricked into thinking that God is keeping the *good stuff* from us, and if we just break free from God, we'll enjoy life more. Don't we know that God desperately wants the absolute best for us? What arrogance to pretend otherwise. C. S. Lewis observes, "We are half-hearted creatures, fooling about with drink and sex and ambition when infinite joy is offered us, like an ignorant child who wants to go on making mud pies in a slum because he cannot imagine what is meant by the offer of a holiday at the sea."

How do we make love? In the case of couples, watch him washing dishes for them. He's making love. See how she runs errands for him. She's making love. Look at how the two keep confidences, support, and smile through the troubles they go through. They're making love. Witness his opening up his insecurities to her. He's making love. Hear her confront and encourage him. She's making love. Listen to them discuss the meaning of life. They're making love. The sexual act is designed to be bonding and sweet and luminous, but anyone knows the act is wasted unless the right stage is set and the actors know their parts.[1]

---

1. Harold Kushner writes in *Who Needs God,* "Why do we keep certain parts of our bodies covered out of a sense of shame? The answer, I suspect, is not that sex is dirty, but rather that sex is holy. Without realizing how we feel, we have inherited that outlook from ancestors who saw the presence of God in the ability of a man and a woman to create life out of their love for each other. The parts of the body which we cover are the ones that contain the secret of generating and sustaining life, and because the creation of life is holy, we cover them out of an instinctive memory of reverence."

The role of a lover was poetically spelled out by Paul of Tarsus in his most famous passage:

> If I speak in the tongues of men and of angels, but have not love, I am a noisy gong or a clanging cymbal. And if I have prophetic powers, and understand all mysteries and all knowledge, and if I have all faith, so as to remove mountains, but have not love, I am nothing. If I give away all I have, and if I deliver my body to be burned, but have not love, I gain nothing.
>
> Love is patient and kind; love is not jealous or boastful; it is not arrogant or rude. Love does not insist on its own way; it is not irritable or resentful; it does not rejoice at wrong, but rejoices in the right. Love bears all things, believes all things, hopes all things, endures all things.
>
> Love never ends.[2]

Marriage furnishes a vibrant metaphor for God the lover. The Bible specifically presents Jesus as bridegroom to His people, the bride. As with all earthly marriages, trust and communication are imperatives with God, and our life together is not all fun and games. Moreover, when we seek spiritual highs and intimacy without commitment, we set ourselves up for counterfeit oneness. Allison Lamon remarks in *View,* "If we seek emotional gratification from God without committing 'for better or for worse,' then we are trying to have the spiritual equivalent of premarital sex with God. A fling. Marriage vows do not read 'as long as our excitement shall last' because that can and will change."

Promiscuous people become consumers in marriage, testing and rejecting while carelessly ripping themselves and others apart. The same is true with promiscuous worship. Note the first of the Ten Commandments: "You shall have no other gods before me." Whether we worship food, exercise, sex, entertainment, job, art, or money instead of God, according them ultimate honor and loyalty, we are unfaithful. We will inevitably make tears and lies rather than love.

A LOVER WHO LOVES IMPARTIALLY

Another distorted picture of God the lover frames Him as caring only for His distinctive people. Is it true? Does God love the whole world, or does He attend to a mere fragment?

---

2. *First Letter to the Corinthians,* chapter 13. Along with Paul and Jesus, I believe in righteousness by love more than righteousness by faith.

God showers His care on everyone; He doesn't "take sides." Jesus affirms this when He tells us that to be followers of God we also must love our enemies, for the Father "makes His sun rise on the evil and on the good, and sends rain on the just and the unjust." God makes His sun shine on the bottle-sucking infant who sleeps in a crib and on the bottle-sucking infant who abuses his wife. He sends blood coursing through the arteries of those who love Him and those who despise Him.

The belief that God looks after His favorites only, the freshly scrubbed and honey scented, His chosen few, is as wrong as the belief that the sun orbits the earth. God *can* look after us better when we allow Him to do so—by following His directions, for instance—but that is not God's choice; it's ours. C. S. Lewis says, "He shows much more of Himself to some people than to others—not because He has favourites, but because it is impossible for Him to show Himself to a man whose whole mind and character are in the wrong condition. Just as sunlight, though it has no favourites, cannot be reflected in a dusty mirror as clearly as a clean one."

I like the dialogue that takes place in chapter five of the Bible's book of *Joshua*. Joshua, planning to conquer the walled city of Jericho, looks up to discover someone holding a sword.

Joshua asks: "Are you with us or against us?"

The angel responds: "No, I am of the host of heaven."

To the angel, the question is irrelevant. It's the same for us today.

The question for us is not, "Is God on our side?" but rather, "Are we on God's side?"

The world of sports provides a stunning laboratory for the "God is on our side" phenomenon. Years ago I watched a championship college basketball game in which one coach sat with patience and dignity on the bench. I knew that upon accepting the head coaching position, his first move had been to add an educational counselor to his staff. His reputation was that he cared more about the character of his players than about their performance. The opposing coach spent the entire game ranting along the sidelines. He screamed. He swore. He gave every indication of incurring a grand-mal seizure.

Who won the game? The ranting coach's team won, one of the biggest upsets in college basketball history. Afterward this coach shared what he considered to be the main reason for the victory. He looked out at twenty-three thousand people in the arena and millions more watching television and announced, "God was with me." It made me wonder. Maybe his was merely an affected expression of humility, but to many of us watching the sideline antics, the screaming, the shoving, the cursing, God made a weird choice.

If God was on *his* side, then—Mark Twain's classic "War Prayer" calls this "the unspoken part"—God *wasn't* on the other team's side. What a devastating implication, and a surefire way to build resentment against such a God. In every contest, He would be against half the participants. But could God have been just as much on the losing team's side? Might He be "with me" just as much when I lose, when I don't find my car keys, when I don't make the team, when my dad doesn't recover from cancer? God becoming Immanuel, "God with us," is a fact not borne out by victories or defeats. "Us" isn't the Seahawks or the Spartans or the Screaming Eels, nor is "us" our country or our religion. "Us" is the human race, all of God's children.

I remember watching the end of an NFL Super Bowl as the Buffalo Bills' kicker was lining up for a game-winning field goal. The TV camera caught New York Giants players kneeling and holding hands, praying on the sidelines. If they were praying for the Bills kicker to miss (he did), that sickens me, and I believe it sickens God. Prayers like that are pure voodoo, using verbal pins. The story is told of Yogi Berra, the all-star catcher for the New York Yankees, watching an opposing batter step up and draw the sign of the cross with his bat in the home plate dust. Berra, a Catholic himself, reached out and swept the plate clean, saying, "Why don't we let God just watch this one?"[3]

We also need to realize that God so loved the world that Jesus died for people we don't even like. Jesus died for Goliath, too. There's more to the David-and-Goliath story than a rugged country boy clobbering a nasty old giant. Some children (and adults) may infer from the story that there are good people and there are bad people, that God doesn't love these bad people as much, that they deserve the bad things that happen to them, and that maybe it doesn't even matter if we add to their pains. Retired U.S. Army Colonel Harry Summers observes, "It always makes it easier to fight a war if you demonize people so that you're not killing human beings, you're killing the devil."

The gospel is better than that. God's love for all of us is like a mother's crazy, tenacious love for her child. The best modern illustration I've found of the love of God is curled up in the children's book *Love You Forever*, by Robert Munsch. I can't get through the book without crying. A mother holds her baby and rocks him back and forth, back and forth. While she rocks him she sings, "I'll love you

---

3. Joseph C. Hough, dean of Vanderbilt Divinity School, contends that God does not intervene in sports: "From my perspective, the Christian message is that God will help you bear up under anything. You will not escape tribulation or suffering or defeat, but God will give you the grace to bear it with dignity and courage."

forever, I'll like you for always, as long as I'm living my baby you'll be." She continues to pick him up, rock him, and sing to him from infancy through adolescence to adulthood. Eventually she drives across town at night to prop a ladder against his open window. Her love is relentless.

God is that crazy-loving mother.

A Lover Who Takes Risks

Love is risky. God's greatest risk is us; His greatest disappointment is us; His greatest triumph is us. Like a wise teacher who gives her students the reins and walks beside them, He involves us for our benefit so that we will develop.

One of the most popular exotic fish is the shark, which can grow to eighteen feet in the boundless sea. But if you catch a small shark and confine it in a small aquarium, it will stay small. Sharks can be fully mature yet only six inches long. Similarly, human beings can be fifty years old yet small-minded, their love stunted and gnarled. This condition comes into focus most clearly with Jesus' claim that the church is His body, and we find His body disoriented, crippled, anemic. Annie Dillard reflects, "What a pity that so hard on the heels of Christ come the Christians."

I'm holding in my hand a 1976 press kit containing newspaper clippings, photos, and testimonials from a remarkable church, one of the largest Protestant churches in the United States. This interracial urban church carried on an extensive ministry of impressive humanitarian aid. It rehabilitated more than two hundred people from drug habits and financed the education of more than one hundred students in medicine, law, teaching, and other human service fields; many students lived in dormitories provided by the church. Moreover, the church provided care in its own facilities for senior citizens, medical convalescents, orphans, and disabled children. Clippings included testimonials from a variety of sources, including the *Congressional Record,* the *San Francisco Chronicle,* and the *Washington Post.* Also quoted was a former CBS-TV affiliate News Bureau Chief who, after working on a documentary on the church, had been so touched by the "magnificent example" of the pastor in working to "stand courageously against all forms of injustice, to relieve human suffering of every kind, and to establish brotherhood among peoples of wide-ranging backgrounds" that he quit his job at CBS to work full-time for the church. I've never seen a more impressive church press kit.[4]

---

4. To be fair, not many churches *have* press kits.

The pastor was a member of a 1.4 million-member Christian denomination, and by 1976 he had been pastoring for twenty-five years. He had also served as a public school teacher and, for two years, as a foreign missionary, establishing programs for orphans. More recently, he had begun a foreign agricultural mission on thousands of acres to produce food for distribution to critical hunger regions. He had received numerous awards, including one from the *Los Angeles Herald* for "Humanitarian of the Year." In 1976 he was appointed chair of the San Francisco Housing Authority. With his wife he had adopted at least nine impoverished children of different racial backgrounds. They lived next to one of the church's large animal refuge shelters, which took in and cared for sick and abandoned animals.

You've probably heard of People's Temple Christian Church, Rev. Jim Jones, pastor.

Two years later, 909 church members lay dead in a distant South American country, victims of mass suicide and murder. After a visiting U.S. congressman was killed, Jones told his followers, "Everyone has to die. If you love me as I love you, we must all die." On November 17, 1978, a vat of purple Kool-Aid laced with cyanide provided what had been billed as "white night," a mass suicide ritual members had practiced for months to test their loyalty to Jones.[5] Though some defected and attempted to escape, friends and families died with their arms around each other. News of the tragedy in Jonestown, Guyana, shocked the world. How could this happen?

We now know that the Temple's ties to Christianity were exceedingly slim. Jones, known to his followers as "Father" or "Dad," demanded total allegiance, scorned the Bible, and meted out public beatings and threats to any who challenged his authority or considered leaving. He chose mistresses from the Temple's members, developed a drug addiction (he nearly always wore sunglasses), and expected all followers to turn their life savings over to him. Jones himself was the object of cult worship. When his corruption, sadism, and paranoia came to light, he demanded darkness—for all.

Here in grim detail we see the immense risk God takes in allowing human beings to represent Him. Even people who do wonderful things can be (or turn) rotten on the inside. Phil in *Groundhog Day* at one point makes all the right gestures to attract Rita, but his motives are dishonorable. Moreover, we can do

---

5. After loudspeakers would awaken members from their sleep, they would line up to be given a "poison" drink. Minutes later, Jones would inform them that the drink wasn't poisonous and they had "passed the test."

horrible things with good intentions. Our bizarre inclinations caused Blaise Pascal to declare, "What a chimera, then, is [humanity]! What a novelty! What a monster, what a chaos, what a contradiction, what a prodigy! Judge of all things, feeble worm of the earth, depository of truth, a sink of uncertainty and error, the glory and shame of the universe."

In *Revelation,* God says, "I know you—you are neither hot nor cold. I wish you were one or the other. But because you are merely lukewarm, I will spit you out of my mouth." If you've ever sipped a soft drink that's been sitting out for hours, you know the feeling. Life is a stage on which we play our parts. Lukewarm players acknowledge the other actors but not the author. If luke-warm players act their parts woodenly, if their words hang heavy with chill, they blame the author—or claim the theater is too stark or too lively, the tickets too expensive or too cheap, the distractions unwarranted, the floor gummy, the seats unyielding. While the hot players deliver despite all obstacles and the cold players don't participate, the lukewarm carry their bitter, stale flavor into every tainted production.

What hot lifestyle is God looking for from His followers? At the conclusion of the film *Schindler's List,* Oskar Schindler breaks down and cries. Surrounded by 1,100 people he has rescued, he laments, "I could have got more . . . I didn't do enough." His car was worth ten people, his gold pen—another person. Heartbroken with the crushing impact of his massive waste, he sobs, "I spent so much money." Sometimes I wonder, will I arrive at the same end, weeping for all the wasted money and years? I believe that in God's eyes Schindler moved from cold to lukewarm to hot; yet we shouldn't be motivated solely by pity or desperation. Schindler became obsessively driven as circumstances dictated that he had to be. But his compulsion isn't necessarily what God is looking for in us. When we're consumed by fretting and remorse, feeling guilty when we relax, we lose the pleasure of living. How, then, can we stay balanced?

We retain our balance and our joy by remaining amateurs. The Latin root of *amateur* is *amator,* "lover," from *amare,* "to love." God's greatest desire for us, for the world, is that we love with abandon, with recklessness, as people who play their parts, not for silvered rewards or from shadowed guilt, but for the pure exhilaration of loving. "Above all," says Peter, "hold unfailing your love for one another, since love covers a multitude of sins." What a difference would exist if this world were filled with hot amateurs instead of lukewarm profes-

---

6. Amateurs also strive for excellence, but they do it for love, and it lifts their performances above those of the mere professionals.

sionals.[6] Responding to our amateurish love, God is like a father who shows off the garish tie his five-year-old has given him. Though our offerings are pitifully rendered, God's eyes sparkle with gladness.

As Eric Liddell, Christian missionary and amateur runner in the 1924 Olympics, enthuses in *Chariots of Fire*, "When I run, I feel His pleasure." This is our hot lifestyle, our fiery delight.

Judging by the Bible, God is not after risk-free people who manage to arrive at death safely. God revels in "thirty-square" people, tough and creative, thick-skinned and broad-minded, with oceans flowing through our veins. Unfortunately, as Peter Marshall observed, we're usually like deep-sea divers in full diving suits, marching forward to bravely pull out the bathtub plug. Madeleine L'Engle says, "We are not all called to go to El Salvador, or Moscow, or Calcutta, or even the slums of New York. But none of us will escape the moment when we have to decide whether to withdraw, to play it safe, or to act on what we prayerfully believe to be right."

A LOVER WHO CHANGES US

God asks us to be His lovers—to love Him, His children, and His creation. We are called to see beneath the facades that front us every moment. In *The Weight of Glory*, C. S. Lewis writes, "There are no ordinary people. You have never talked to an ordinary mortal. . . . It is immortals whom we joke with, work with, marry, snub, and exploit—immortal horrors or everlasting splendours. . . . Your neighbour is the holiest object presented to your senses." We can change the world only as our view of the world is changed.

Along with Sydney Opera House, my favorite building (apart from cathedrals) is the Library of Congress in Washington, D.C., a relatively obscure wonder with the richest interior of any structure in the country. On my first visit, I entered the library's Great Hall and stood transfixed, my chin rattling my knees, at the splendor of bas-reliefs, arches, paintings, domes, arabesques, mosaics, statues, friezes, columns, and festoons. More than forty painters and sculptors with the aid of a small army of architectural craftspeople fashioned the building into a remarkable work of art. Statues depict Shakespeare, Newton, Herodotus, Bacon, Plato, Moses, and dozens more. Memorable thoughts on philosophy, art, science, history, poetry, commerce, and religion are carved into marble walls. I stayed for two hours. Toward the end of my visit, I chanced upon a thought with no attribution carved high on a wall. Of all the words I saw, these jarred me most: "The true Shekinah is man." The Shekinah, the visible, holy presence of God on earth, is within *us*.

We catch a glimpse of the Shekinah when we watch great lovers. Jesus says, "If a man loves me, he will keep my word, and my Father will love him, and we will come to him and make our home with him." We are God's dwelling place—God's home. Paul of Tarsus says, "We are the temple of the living God; as God said, 'I will live in them and move among them, and I will be their God, and they shall be my people.'"[7] As we invite God in, we become walking, sitting, talking, running holy temples. What an incredible concept! Do we plead for God's Holy Spirit to inhabit us, to captivate us? Do I provide a welcome within? Dwight Moody tells of continually begging God to fill him with His Spirit, until

> one day, in the city of New York—oh, what a day!—I cannot describe it; I seldom refer to it; it is almost too sacred an experience to name. Paul had an experience of which he never spoke for fourteen years. I can only say that God revealed Himself to me, and I had such an experience of His love that I had to ask Him to stay His hand.

Imagine: "Stop, God! Please, I can't take any more love. Stop pouring your love on me."

God not only lives in us, but He also lives in those around us. "I tell you the truth," says Jesus, "as you have done to one of the least of these brothers and sisters of mine, you have done it to me." God is present in disguise on our planet. The "least" are emaciated AIDS victims and street people, hardened prostitutes and prison inmates, helpless nursing home residents and welfare babies.

But surprises abound in God's kingdom. The "least" are also the new pariahs of society: pushy telemarketers and preowned-car salesmen, manipulative faith healers and cult members, furious gang bangers and skinheads, well-oiled politicians and attorneys. While not all merit our trust, all deserve to be treated with dignity and respect. And according to Jesus, though they may not earn our like, each one deserves our genuine love. This outrageous love calls for the risky direction of the divine lover, with a humbling recognition that at times I am the least of these.

. . .

To "believe in God" is not nearly enough. The critical issue is what difference God makes in our lives. We can believe that Saturn has rings and not ears, as

---

7. See *John*, chapter 14, and *Second Letter to the Corinthians*, chapter 6.

Galileo first thought, because we have seen the evidence; that the Maldive Islands exist, though we've never seen them; and that pi exists as an abstract reality—but it doesn't really affect us. As Harold Kushner says, "A God who exists but does not matter, who does not make a difference in the way you live, might as well not exist."

What difference does God make in the way we live? Much of our pain stems from being brittle and inflexible in one area, like the O-rings on the space shuttle *Challenger*, exploding lives in the process. To counter this tendency, we must maintain a loving consistency in every area of life. R. C. Sproul contends:

> Social ethics must never be substituted for personal ethics. Crusading can easily become a dodge for facing up to one's lack of personal morality. By the same token, even if I am a model of personal righteousness, that does not excuse my participation in social evil. The man who is faithful to his wife while he exercises bigotry toward his neighbor is no better than the adulterer who crusades for social justice. What God requires is justice both personal and social.

Responsibilities prod us to godliness. For example, being a U.S. senator is an important job, but it's not as important as being a mother, father, child, sibling, or close friend. If something happens to any of those, it matters more to us than all the headlines in the century. God has generously granted to each of us vital positions, more important than we normally think, and our implicit significance changes us. Our stunted, gnarled love gets stretched. We can't be human guinea pigs in a cosmic tragicomedy because the most profound trust imaginable, the creation and nurture of life, is delivered to our care.

We may evade godly responsibilities, of course, while the torpor of luxury entangles us like seaweed wrapped around our souls. Today even spiritual pursuits foster what Becky Pippert terms "self absorption that masquerades as self-improvement."

In the Christian realm, the call for "revival" can lead to self-congratulatory attendance counts and an outbreak of religious enthusiasm that leads to prayer and Bible study that leads to more meetings and more attendance counts. But without the *so that* principle of love, it all leads to "So what?" So what if you fast and pray and see angels and study the Bible and shout "Praise the Lord!" when you skin your knee? The bottom line is, *How do you love?*[8] A revival of

---

8. Tony Campolo says that he can tell the genuineness of mountaintop conversions of youth by how they treat their parents when they get home.

true godliness is seen ultimately in lovers who are risky, inclusive, and life changing. As Barbara Kingsolver notes, we are set on "a path of exploring the great, shifting terrain between righteousness and what's right."

How can we truly know whether we're following God, even with our flaws, or whether we're running a People's Temple course of destruction, even with our good deeds? Ellen White offers a surefire test of discipleship:

> The love of influence and the desire for the esteem of others may produce a well-ordered life. Self-respect may lead us to avoid the appearance of evil. A selfish heart may perform generous actions. By what means, then, shall we determine whose side we are on?
>
> Who has the heart? With whom are our thoughts? Of whom do we love to converse? Who has our warmest affections and our best energies? If we are [God's], our thoughts are with Him, and our sweetest thoughts are of Him.

Sounds like falling in love, doesn't it? On occasion, college students come to me for advice in their romantic life, and though I try to steer clear of matchmaking, I often find myself asking the guy, for instance, one question: "Are you miserable with her, or without her?" The answer might be, "Both," yet some find clarity in considering the question.

Turning the target around, could it be that God is miserable without us? That on us He lavishes His warmest affections and His best energies? Is it conceivable that His sweetest thoughts are of me?

A Lover Who Frees Captives

As Jesus begins His public ministry, He quotes a passage from the prophet Isaiah to announce His mission statement: "The Spirit of the Lord is upon me, because he has anointed me to preach good news to the poor. He has sent me to proclaim release to the captives, and recovering of sight to the blind, to set at liberty those who are oppressed." Those who love God today carry the same mission in their relationships. God's love frees us. Take a quick look at three liberating features of God's love.

Forgiveness. When we've been hurt deeply, it's nightmarishly difficult to forgive, so we might ask, "Is it worth the trouble? Why should I do it? What have I really lost if I don't forgive?" Not forgiving limits us in many ways. An unforgiving spirit saps our creativity, shrivels our sense of humor, and drains our ability to enjoy life. We become languid, irresolute. Unforgiveness weakens our love, even toward people we don't need to forgive. Corrie ten Boom points out the physical consequences of not forgiving:

> I knew forgiving not only as a commandment of God but as a daily experience. Since the end of the war I had had a home in Holland for victims of Nazi brutality. Those who were able to forgive their former enemies were able also to return to the outside world and rebuild their lives, no matter what the physical scars. Those who nursed their bitterness remained invalids. It was as simple and as horrible as that.

We say it's tough to forgive, but it's really much tougher to be restricted in all we do by the heavy chains of guilt and resentment. Forgiving frees us. Forgiving makes life easier, not harder. To forgive doesn't imply that we agree with the wrong that was done, nor does it mean indifference. Forgiving is releasing from our judgment entirely the one who has hurt us, giving that person over to God, and wishing for better things in the future. It may be that we have to forgive over and over for the same offense. Furthermore, we may have to forgive people who are no longer around. An immigrant rabbi made the admission, "Before coming to America, I had to forgive Adolf Hitler. I did not want to bring Hitler inside me to America."

There's another reason that we ought to forgive, one that's emphasized by Jesus repeatedly: "If you forgive others the wrongs they have done, your heavenly Father will also forgive you; but if you do not forgive others, then the wrongs you have done will not be forgiven by your Father." God's forgiveness to us is conditional—on the condition that we forgive others, no matter how spiteful, no matter how undeserving, no matter how often the process is repeated. Why would God demand this? God knows we won't be truly free to love until we forgive.

One noteworthy example of forgiving was shown by Clara Barton, founder of the American Red Cross. A friend of Barton's once reminded her of something especially cruel that someone had done to her years before, but Clara didn't seem to recall it. "Don't you remember it?" her friend asked.

"No," Clara answered, "I distinctly remember forgetting it."

For four years in the 1990s, genocide and war swept through Bosnia. An estimated three hundred thousand people, most of whom were women and children, died. *Childlife* magazine printed words from the surviving children of Bosnia, the wounded sparrows; yet from their mouths waft songs of forgiveness that send the nightingale to shame. "I don't want to call people Muslim or Croat," says Zlatko Sator, eleven. "I want to call them by their names. But other people can call me what they want, as long as they don't kill me."

Semin Cuplov, a fourteen-year-old Muslim boy, fled his hometown after he and his pregnant mother watched his father and grandfather being burned alive. "Don't make a difference between Serb, Croat, and Muslim children here in Bosnia," he entreats, "because I have friends who are Serb and Croat. I don't hate anyone."

"Unless you turn and become like humble children," Jesus promises, "you will never enter the kingdom of heaven."

Acceptance. Charlie Shedd writes often about his wife, Martha, and about their amazingly accepting marriage. One day they had a big argument, and it took some time to heal. The next morning, Charlie found this message on the table.

Dear Charlie:

I hate you.

Love, Martha

Assured of their undeviating acceptance of each other, they could laugh about their differences.

Accepting people doesn't mean agreeing with their ideas or behavior. Rather, accepting is affirming the infinite value of a person, no matter who she is or what he has done. When we judge and label people on the basis of impressions—physical features, clothing, age, mannerisms—we look *at* people instead of *into* them. Nothing is more devastating to love than a critical spirit. Jesus' most scathing attacks were directed at the critics because a critical spirit destroys relationships, and His kingdom is founded on relationships. What's eternally significant is not whether we are right or wrong but how we relate to those we think are wrong. Jesus says, "For if you love only those who love you [who agree with you], what reward have you?" Lovers, pray with King David, "Create in me a clean heart, O God; and renew a right spirit within me."[9]

When I consider acceptance, I think back to Nathan's first big math test in elementary school. He brought home his paper of 100 problems, and there it was, hovering at the top, circled in red: -2. Nathan stood there, all three-feet-ten of him, and said disappointedly, "I missed two." I felt like crying, like someone had kicked me in the stomach and would be kicking my little boy from now on too. At that moment I knew that throughout his education and his life he would be looking at -2 instead of +98.

---

9. Jesus' words are in *Matthew,* chapter 5, and David's are in *Psalm* 51.

We often take a similar approach with people who are physically challenged. "A person who is deaf" is not the same as "a deaf person." Philip Yancey writes:

> I sometimes threaten to produce my own line of get-well cards. I already have an idea for the first one. The cover would read in huge letters, perhaps with fireworks in the background, "CONGRATULATIONS!!!" Then, inside, the message: ". . . to the 98 trillion cells in your body that are still working smoothly and efficiently." I would look for ways to get across the message that a sick person is not a *sick person,* but rather a person of worth and value who happens to have some body parts that are not functioning well.

The Eye of the Storm is the remarkable thirty-minute film about teacher Jane Elliot's lesson on the idiocy of racism. In 1968, Elliot watched in horror TV news reports of the assassination of Martin Luther King Jr. As white male reporters asked, "Who will lead *your* people?" and "How do *your* people feel?" she thought, *This whole thing is so senseless. Children have to find out that this is wrong.* She knew that the next day she would need to discuss the murder with her third-grade class. In Riceville, Iowa, population 898, there were no blacks. "I wanted them to know how it feels to be stepped upon," she later explained.

The experiment is now legendary. After dividing her class into brown-eyed people and blue-eyed people, placing large felt collars on the "inferior" ones, Elliot told her class that brown-eyed people are cleaner, smarter, and more civilized than blue-eyed people.[10] Throughout the first day, brown-eyed children received special privileges and praise, while blue-eyed children received disdainful reprimands and lagged in every area. Elliot recalls in an interview that what had been kind, wonderful children "turned into nasty, vicious, discriminating third graders in the space of fifteen minutes." The first day, brown-eyed children grew haughty as blue-eyed students became miserable, their postures and attitudes slumped in defeat. The next day, the positions were reversed, with brown-eyed children disconsolate and broken. After the experiment ended, Elliot asked students what it felt like to wear the collar. "I didn't even want to try at anything," said one student. "I felt like a dog on a leash," declared another. A boy confessed, "I felt like I was in prison and they threw the key away." When Elliot inquired why the blue-eyed people had done so poorly in

---

10. Any color other than blue was grouped with brown. The children were told ahead of time that this was an experiment.

a phonics game the day before, a girl explained, "We kept thinking about those collars!" Elliot ordered the students to throw the collars away, which they did with relish. The concluding scene showed the class with their arms draped happily around each other, tears of relief glistening in their young eyes.

Fighting prejudice is a critical part of acceptance. In Studs Terkel's *Working*, a police officer has just dredged a drowned boy from a pond and covered him when a woman asks, "What color was he?" The officer answers wearily, "Miss, he's ten years old." His answer echoes those who, when filling out forms requesting "race," choose to write in "human."

Sharing. Yolanda's parents, Richard and Amelia, live in Desert Hot Springs, California, where in the summer at 119 degrees some locals say it isn't hot because it's "a dry heat." That's true to a point, but my body gets fooled into believing it's blazing hot out there. One summer when we were visiting, I left for a late-morning run down the street. As I took off, I felt *good.* The dry heat actually felt invigorating. After more than two miles of virtually effortless gliding, I decided to turn around and head for the house. Perhaps I should mention here that Desert Hot Springs is perched on an incline of about fifteen degrees, and my in-laws' house is near the top. Possibly I should also mention that the sun was climbing a cloudless sky, and I faced more than two miles of uphill running in triple-digit heat. I ran four blocks, walked one; ran two blocks, walked one; ran thirty feet, walked the rest. By the time I lurched through the front door, I was seeing spots.

An hour after hydrating and a cooling shower, I still felt weak. Yolanda and I left for a drive to Palm Springs, but my anxiety heightened as I drove. Everything around me seemed dark. I had never passed out before, and I wondered if I was about to. Was I having a heart attack? An aneurysm? Heat stroke? Glaucoma? My dark thoughts raced with the car for miles as I bravely kept my fears to myself. After ten minutes of agony, however, it was too much. I tried to be delicate in notifying Yolanda of my imminent death.

"Everything's going black!" I whimpered. "I don't know what's happening!"

She took it well. "Oh, yeah," she said, "it's the eclipse."

That's right! Eclipse today. I grinned the confident, secure grin of the resurrected.

Sometimes we go through dark days convulsed with worry and "I trouble," when all we need to do is to share. Communication is sharing ourselves. Sharing takes place in a million forms, from cleaning the kitchen to distributing sacks of dehydrated milk.

Three years ago, Steve was an older theology student at Union College. He and his wife, Melissa, were expecting their fourth child. When complications arose, baby Isaiah Jeremiah was born weeks early. The infant was in critical condition, and the next morning a helicopter flew Isaiah from Lincoln to Omaha's children's hospital, fifty miles away. After Melissa was released, she and Steve rushed home, checked on their other children, packed some clothes, and drove to Omaha. By the time they arrived, their child, nineteen hours old, had died. A nurse handed them their baby. I remember marveling when I heard of this gift of sharing: the nurse had held and rocked the dead baby for an hour until Steve and Melissa could get there.

. . .

God's forgiveness, acceptance, and sharing arrive in one package: Grace. Through His Son's sacrifice, we are forgiven. If you're wondering how this happens, I'll tell you: I don't know. My sense is that nobody knows precisely how forgiveness works here on earth, much less as God is concerned. Forgiveness is an outlandish, mystical gift whenever it occurs. We *do* know that God's forgiving grace heals our infinite wounds and offenses. Forgiving grace says God cares more about our future than He cares about our past.

Accepting grace, as Paul Tillich says in *The Shaking of the Foundations,* is when "a wave of light breaks into our darkness and it is as though a voice were saying: 'You are accepted. You are accepted by that which is greater than you. . . . Do not seek for anything; do not perform anything; do not intend anything. *Simply accept the fact that you are accepted.*'" Accepting grace is a state of unbearable lightness, yet it is solid enough to stand on or swim in.

Sharing grace, we are empowered by God. God shares with us His courage, hope, wisdom, patience, gentleness, joy, peace, and faithfulness so that we may share them with the world. Even with our flaws, God promises, as He did Paul of Tarsus, "My grace is sufficient for you, for My power is made perfect in weakness."[11] In *Parable,* Robert Farrar Capon provides this synopsis:

> Grace is the celebration of life, relentlessly hounding all the non-celebrants in the world. It is a floating, cosmic bash shouting its way through the streets of the universe, flinging the sweetness of its cessations to every window, pounding at every door in a hilarity beyond all liking and happening, until the prodigals come out at last and dance, and the elder brothers finally take their fingers out of their ears.

---

11. *Second Letter to the Corinthians,* chapter 12.

A LOVER WHO GIVES HIS BODY TO HIS BELOVED

As a bridegroom gives his body to his bride, God so loved the world that He gave His only Son's body to the world, for us to do with it as we pleased. After Jesus' tangible body had been mutilated and murdered, another body appeared. The church, Jesus says, is His body, His visible hands, eyes, and feet today. Through the ages, remarkable acts of kindness and cruelty have touched us from this body. The Christian church has given us Albert Schweitzer, Eric Liddell, Martin Luther King Jr., Mother Teresa.

However, the church has also given us the Crusades, the Inquisition, Jim Jones, David Koresh. Can such a malfunctioning body be trusted? G. K. Chesterton contends, "It is no disgrace to Christianity, it is no disgrace to any great religion, that its counsels of perfection have not made every person perfect. If, after centuries, a disparity is still found between its ideal and its followers, it only means that the religion still maintains the ideal, and the followers still need it." Philip Yancey admits, "I rejected the church for a time because I found so little grace there. I returned because I found grace nowhere else."

Certainly Christians are far from having a monopoly on forgiveness, acceptance, and sharing, yet the Bible still declares that those are God's explicit demands of His body of followers. God holds out a challenge for us: "Change the world." You might think He's kidding, but He's not. Not only that, He's already demonstrated how; Jesus landed on our spinning blue ball clutching the same assignment: "Change the world!" How did He do it? He gathered a few men and women, the fringe people in Galilean society, and powerfully, lovingly shared Himself. That's all. No massive P.R. campaign, no political coup, no life-transforming invention, no Yeshua Rabbinical University.

When we speak of greatness, we tend to use terms denoting largeness, but Jesus established an upside-down kingdom. He appeared in a dinky, occupied country. He concentrated His ministry on a small group of followers. His early church met in small groups. He represented salvation in a piece of bread and a cup.

Anyone who has focused the sun's light through a magnifying glass knows why He worked this way: When the circle is smallest, the heat is greatest. God devised the small circle of family for this reason. We cannot generate the heat of godly love without first focusing on specific people, which is why caring for our immediate family comes first.

I stared, disbelieving, when I heard it from my friend Pat. A professional painter was about to paint the inside of her house, including the ceilings, and he hadn't put anything down to cover the floors. Pat hesitated, then asked him if he was going to use a dropcloth. She will never forget what he said: "Ma'am, if you find one drop on your floor, the whole job is free." Some of us may be this careful with our financial investments, cars, or clothes; but are we that full of care in our dealings with people, especially the people closest to us? (The closer we become, the more tactful we must be.) That care and attention is what God asks us to take with one another, so we won't drip hostility or splatter indifference. The whole job depends on it.

God also challenges the church to cross generational, ethnic, and socioeconomic lines to reflect His body's variety. "At its best," Tony Campolo says, "there is no fellowship on earth that is crazier than the church. At its best, the church befriends people we would never get to meet within the sterile confines of our class-structured society. In the church, we are ushered into loving relationships with people who otherwise would be strangers. In the church, Democrats can get to know Republicans, pacifists can get to know soldiers, punk rockers can get to know lovers of Bach."

As life spins faster and faster, like a playground merry-go-round picking up speed, people are dispersing, losing their grip, flying off the edge. The last refuge is in moving toward the center and holding onto each other. As an added benefit, it's only by locking arms around a center that we are forced to look into one another's eyes, and thus catch a vision of ourselves. In *God in the Dock,* C. S. Lewis writes:

> When I first became a Christian, about fourteen years ago, I thought that I could do it on my own, by retiring to my rooms and reading theology, and I wouldn't go to the churches. . . . I disliked very much their hymns, which I considered to be fifth-rate poems set to sixth-rate music. But as I went on I saw the great merit of it. I came up against different people of quite different outlooks and different education, and then gradually my conceit just began peeling off. I realized that the hymns (which were just sixth-rate music) were, nevertheless, being sung with devotion and benefit by an old saint in elastic-side boots in the opposite pew, and then you realize that you aren't fit to clean those boots. It gets you out of your solitary conceit.

Jesus asserts that the gates of hell will not prevail against the church. The church is on the offensive, actively engaging and knocking down hellish barriers. Love and freedom are inextricably entwined, and if freedom is sacred to God, what sort of love does He demand of us? You see, civil rights are not peripheral issues. God's followers stand up for those on the fringes, the disenfranchised, the marginalized, the stepped upon, the ignored. Jesus stood up for them, and stood up and stood up until He stood up on the cross. In the amazing year of 1989, Christian protesters carrying candles, singing hymns, and praying by the millions followed Jesus' mission statement and led Poland, Hungary, East Germany, and Czechoslovakia out from under the crushing weight of oppression.

Jim Wallis relates in *The Soul of Politics* how a young seminarian took scissors and an old Bible and began cutting out every reference to the poor and oppressed. When he was finished, the Bible hung in threads—it was a book full of holes because he had found thousands of references. Wallis writes, "The passion of God for the oppressed of the earth is a secret long hidden from the religious and nonreligious alike. But now the secret is getting out." He goes on to describe the miracle of reconciliation at "gang summits" currently convening in churches, Congressman Tony Hall's spiritual fast for hunger relief, and the communities of hope that are springing up in countless places.

Still, some political activities of the church seem counterproductive. Richard Halverson, recently retired chaplain of the U.S. Senate, responded in an interview in *The Door* about why Christian evangelicals' efforts to influence legislation generate so much animosity. "Because all evangelicals care about is their own agenda," he replied. "They care about abortion and school prayer. They care about them so much that they keep all the phone lines busy, and many of the callers are angry and downright nasty. Yet when it comes to the hundreds of other issues Congress faces, they never hear from evangelicals."

What is a more complete stance? As an example, a consistent pro-life position will recognize the following concerns huddling under its umbrella: the proliferation of weapons around the world, tobacco and alcohol interests,[12] the need to grant asylum to refugees, the death penalty, racism, public school education, poverty, business greed that kills body and soul, child abuse, and yes, those who are most vulnerably exposed on the fringes of life, the elderly and the unborn. While many of these are complex issues, a selective pro-life agenda disgusts. "A saint," observes Paul Sundquist, "is a person who makes goodness attractive."

Rather than swallowing any party line, we all would benefit from a closer examination of what is godly and what is profane. In *Of Fiction and Faith,* Will Campbell gives his perspective on profanities during an interview with W. Dale Brown. Campbell describes what took place when a woman called a radio talk show to ask him a pointed question:

---

12. *Drug Abuse Update* (Summer 1991) reported that "as many college students will die of alcohol-related causes—often based on habits begun in college—as will receive their masters and doctorate degrees."

She said, "Well, what do you think, Reverend Campbell, about Charlie Daniels using bad words on the television?"

"I don't know, ma'am; what did he say?"

"Well, I couldn't repeat that," she answered.

So I offered to call off some bad words and let her just indicate the bad ones with a yes or no. "You don't have to say them," I told her. "Did he say prejudice?"

"No."

"War? Nuclear bomb?"

"Why, no."

"If I don't know what he said and you can't tell me, I can't very well express what I think about it," I finally told her. "Those are the worst words I can think of."

A spiritual, pro-life agenda is also concerned with nourishing and healing the physical body. Freeing others from physical constraints was obviously a huge concern for Jesus, for He was renowned for healing. As physical health affects our thoughts in the mind-body-spirit holistic nature of humanity, health translates to a spiritual concern. Poor physical health is like AIDS of the soul; people don't actually die of AIDS—it weakens their immune system until they succumb to pneumonia or cancer or some other opportunistic disease. Beyond feeding the hungry shines the goal of encouraging optimum health. Too many people are being sugared to death, their vitality and intelligence sapped by debilitating habits.[13] God knows we cannot live as "so that" lovers if we're mired at "so tired" levels.

God's love fits us for eternity and equips us to live together. Cleansed not by the fires of hell but by grace, we receive what Iranaeus calls "grace-healed eyes." What had seemed enormously important is seen as trifling; what had appeared inconsequential is immensely significant.

One of the best-loved converts to the grace-full lifestyle is Ebenezer Scrooge in Charles Dickens's *A Christmas Carol:* "Oh! But he was a tight-fisted hand at the grindstone, Scrooge! A squeezing, wrenching, grasping, scraping, clutching, covetous, old sinner! Hard and sharp as flint, from which no steel had ever struck out generous fire; secret, and self-contained, and solitary as an oyster." Scrooge's former boss, Fezziwig, is a perfect foil—plump with goodwill and

---

13. Weimar Institute created the acronym NEW START for the eight basic laws of physical health: nutrition, exercise, water, sunshine, temperance, air, rest, trust in God.

laughter, he savors life as he enjoys his food, steeped in sage and onions to the eyebrows. As in *Groundhog Day*, a time aberration enables Ebenezer to enjoy a second chance at life. He encounters a rattled Jacob Marley and the Spirits of Christmas, learns the meaning of gratefulness and generosity, and so learns the meaning of joy: "He became as good a friend, as good a master, and as good a man, as the good old city knew, or any other good old city, town, or borough in the good old world." Surely if there is hope for Scrooge, there is hope for you and me, for it is true that God blesses us all, every one.

WANTING TO SEE GOD

Once there were four men who wanted to see God. The men lived day and night in a cold dark room surrounded by thick, towering walls. On the eastern wall, just beneath the ceiling, appeared their one source of hope—a window.

Each day a golden shaft of sunlight lunged through this opening and inched down the western wall. Fascinated, the men watched the light as it moved. They longed to see beyond the window to the true source of warmth; they hungered for a glimpse of the great God of love.

Though the opening was small—too small for a man to fit through—the four men often made heroic attempts to reach it. Each tried running and leaping against the wall, clawing desperately toward the tiny opening, but to no avail. The window was too high.

It became apparent then that the men would have to work together, so they developed a plan. Perhaps by standing one on top of another the person on top might be able to see through the window!

However, the question soon arose: Who will be the one on top? Who will be the one to see God? All realized this was the supreme desire for each man.

And so they sat, wondering.

Presently Rafael stood. "I will support you," he said, and waited for the others.

After a few moments, José slowly pushed himself up. "I will be next," he volunteered. The remaining two sat unmoving, staring at their feet.

At last, with a sigh, Weldon rose. "I will be third," he offered. The three men looked down at Sam. It would be Sam on top.

Rafael went to the eastern wall. He spread his legs, crouched, and pressed his palms against the wall. José placed one foot on Rafael and boosted himself until he stood balancing on Rafael's shoulders. Next Weldon climbed over the straining Rafael, past the struggling José until he could stand, his head just below the window.

Sam wasted no time. He scrambled over Rafael and José and, with help from Weldon, was catapulted to the opening where he thrust his head through . . . ten seconds . . . the men below trembled . . . twenty seconds . . . the column shook . . . twenty-eight seconds . . .

The column collapsed. Arms and legs plummeted to a tangled heap where the men lay moaning, eyes closed, chests heaving. Slowly they untangled and rolled and with painful effort crawled apart to sit. From there the three men eagerly searched Sam's face and waited for the vision.

"I saw through the window," Sam began, "and I saw many things. I saw wispy clouds laced across a bright sky. I watched speckled birds soar and wheel. There were oaks and sycamores on grassy hills and distant snowcapped mountains. I felt the wind slap and heard the rustling of leaves and I smelled smoke in the air.

"I saw many things," he said again, and then he paused, gazing at the window. "But I did not see God."

The men sat huddled in silence, their heads bowed. The air was heavy. The ground seemed unusually cold and hard. Suddenly Rafael spoke.

"*I saw God.*"

The others jerked and stared.

"As I shouldered the weight, the tremendous weight," Rafael continued, "as I staggered and strained under it, my muscles on fire, my eyes stinging, my mind crying out, as I carried it all for as long as I could and then longer—I saw Him."

The others sat, marveling.

"*I saw God, too.*" José's voice shattered the silence. "As I balanced between what was above and what was below, as I felt the soles pushing against my back and head, as I struggled and shifted to keep us steady, to keep us somehow pointing up—I saw Him."

The other sat, thinking.

"*I also saw God.*" Weldon's eyes gleamed.

"As I approached the opening—so near—I wanted to be there myself. But when I stretched out my arms—so far—and lifted a friend, I saw Him."

A Lover Who Shows Up

Gary Swanson's short story "The Woman at the Well" depicts the woman of *John*, chapter 4, flushed with excitement, returning from the well to her lover. "I've seen the Messiah," she breathes, but her companion is dubious. *She goes for water, and she comes back with Messiah?* How does she know He's the Messiah? She explains:

> "It seems He knows us better than we do ourselves. He knows what we
> want—what we really want."
> "What do we really want?"
> "You will know that when you see Him."
> "I am not a religious man . . ."
> She took his hand and led him toward the door. "That is just the part
> that is most thrilling—neither is He."

Jesus is thrilling. Philip Yancey tells how George Buttrick, chaplain at Harvard, disarmed students who came to his office to express their settled unbelief. "I don't believe in God," they'd defiantly declare. Buttrick would say, "Sit down and tell me what kind of God you don't believe in. I probably don't believe in that God either." Then he would talk about Jesus, the remedy for all our ill-conceived notions.

The best way to fall in love with God is to look deeply at Jesus. That look leveled me in my faith quest. I remember reading *Luke* when I first encountered Jesus—small-town carpenter, fearless denunciator of oppression, healer of loathsome disease, warrior of the olive grove, friend of sinners—and I couldn't get enough of Him. Finding any possible opening to bring Him into conversation, I snatched it. He was as sweet as glaze on a hot apple pie, as bright as a welder's arc. About a year later my friend Warren picked up his guitar and started singing a tune I'd never heard: "Let's talk about Jesus, the king of kings is He . . ." That song was living bread to my hungry soul; it sopped up all the thickening soup of my life.

Yancey muses, "*Why am I a Christian?* I sometimes ask myself, and to be perfectly honest the reasons reduce to two: (1) the lack of good alternatives, and (2) Jesus. Brilliant, untamed, tender, creative, slippery, irreducible, paradoxically humble—Jesus stands up to scrutiny."

Christians aren't the only ones who value Jesus. Baha'i adherents honor Him, Muslims view Him as a prophet, and modern Israeli schoolchildren are taught that Jesus was perhaps the greatest Jewish rabbi. Hundreds of thousands of Completed Jews today continue to honor Yeshua as the Messiah of Israel. People hold different views on the person of Jesus of Nazareth. Another avatar. A prophet. A martyr. A good man. But for one pivotal reason we don't want to see Jesus on a Wheaties box.

Forget the feeding of the five thousand, the walking on water, the healings, bringing the dead back to life. Don't bother about them. Really. No big deals. Similar marvels and miracles have occurred throughout history—in fact, Jesus assured His followers that they would do more of these works.

One event in His life stands alone. Don't blink on this one, passing it off as merely a ruse or myth: the Resurrection. Muhammed Ali once confessed that his greatest wish would be to stand at the tomb of Jesus to see if the Resurrection really happened. To dismiss it without honest, thorough, courageous inquiry is to be without intellectual integrity, to bury one's head in the sands of time and ignorance. Grapple with its enormousness. *What would it mean to the world if He had truly risen?* The tomb is empty. Jesus promised He would rise again. Would the snuffling, skeptical disciples have changed—to the point of being stoned, beheaded, crucified, and boiled in oil—for what they knew to be a lie?[14] In his book *Loving God,* Charles Colson reveals what he learned from his experience in the Watergate cover-up:

> With the most powerful office in the world at stake, a small band of handpicked loyalists, no more than ten of us, could not hold a conspiracy together for more than two weeks. . . . No one was in grave danger; *no one's life was at stake.* Yet after just a few weeks the natural human instinct for self-preservation was so overwhelming that the conspirators, one by one, deserted their leader, walked away from their cause. . . .
>
> If one is to assail the historicity of the Resurrection and therefore the deity of Christ, one must conclude that there was a conspiracy—a cover-up if you will—by 11 men with the complicity of up to 500 others. To subscribe to this argument, one must also be ready to believe that each disciple was willing to be ostracized by friends and family, live in daily fear of death, endure prisons, live penniless and hungry, sacrifice family, be tortured without mercy, and ultimately die—all without ever once renouncing that Jesus had risen from the dead. . . .
>
> Take it from one who was inside the Watergate web looking out, who saw firsthand how vulnerable a cover-up is: Nothing less than a witness as awesome as the resurrected Christ could have caused those men to maintain to their dying whispers that Jesus is alive.

---

14. Some of Jim Jones's followers defected. Before the Resurrection, Peter denied his Master, but his loyalty afterward is undeniable.

Being very candid, if I heard that a doornail-dead friend had come back to life, I'd join with the doubting disciples, wouldn't you? I'll believe it when I see it, and maybe not then.[15] Let me poke a finger in His side first. Furthermore, Jesus had to be more than merely *alive* when he exited the tomb, as David Strauss points out: "It is impossible that a being who had stolen half-dead out of the sepulcher, who crept about weak and ill, wanting medical treatment, who required bandaging, strengthening, and indulgence, and who still at last yielded to his sufferings, could have given the disciples the impression that he was a conqueror over death and the grave."

The radical transformation of every disciple is one of the most compelling pieces of evidence for the legitimacy of the Resurrection, for their fearlessness and conviction take root when they see Him. If He wasn't truly dead, His reappearance wouldn't have been a huge issue, but Jesus was dead and is alive, and thus remains most wanted. Because of Him, Christianity is a religion of the Cross, the ancient symbol of death—the firing squad, the gallows, the electric chair, the gas chamber—transformed into a symbol of life and rebirth.

We don't need another good man and great example as much as we need a Savior, a person who can rescue us from meaninglessness and raise our dry bones from the sweating earth. Only one can do that. Only one.

A LOVER WHO EXCHANGES PLACES

"You never know how much you really believe," observes C. S. Lewis, "until its truth or falsehood becomes a matter of life or death to you." It's easy to apply his words to the disciples and to ourselves, but what if we apply the message to God? How much does God really believe in us? After all, we're the ones living and dying here with our beliefs.

In Mark Twain's *The Prince and the Pauper,* Edward Tudor, Prince of Wales, exchanges places with his identical lookalike, Tom Canty, a beggar boy. In the course of the book the Prince of Limitless Plenty and the Prince of Poverty experience what lies on "the other side." Through living the abject life of a pauper, Prince Edward learns how essential and good it is to rule mercifully and justly. When he assumes his rightful throne as king, he is fully persuaded:

---

15. Considering this, Jesus' staying with the disciples forty days beyond the Resurrection makes good sense. His ascending to heaven ten days before the Feast of Harvest, known as Pentecost, also let the young church grapple with its wobbly identity without the training wheels of His visual presence.

More than once when some great dignitary, some gilded vassal of the crown, made argument against his leniency and urged that some law which he was bent upon amending was gentle enough for its purpose and wrought no suffering or oppression which anyone need mightily mind, the young king turned the mournful eloquence of his great compassionate eyes upon him and answered, "What dost *thou* know of suffering and oppression? I and my people know, but not thou."

Though not exact, the parallels are striking. Like the beggar boy, we shall experience a world beyond our imagining where we are treated as children of the King. Like the prince, so it is with Jesus, the Son of Man.[16] He knows suffering. He knows hunger and bone-weariness; He knows ridicule, thirst, and the pain of a close friend's betrayal. He knows about blisters and bugs. He knows the exhaustion of walking miles on dust-caked, grimy legs. He knows the demands and pressures of too little time. He knows the ache of loneliness. He knows the stench of death. He knows fists and kicks and spittle in the eye. He knows the mournful sound of His mother's cries. He knows the taste of His own blood. He knows.

If we consider what we go through on this often dark, demented planet, we know why it was so important for God's Son to become one of us. It's a question of knowledge grounded in experience, a yearning for sympathy, a cause for absolute trust. Like the prince, Jesus of Nazareth "emptied Himself, taking the form of a servant."[17] Like us, He had to rely on faith because He couldn't see with certainty beyond the grave. Incredibly, God emptied and emptied Himself until He became an embryo in the womb of a teenaged girl. The boundless Master of the universe came tethered to an umbilical cord, kicking the walls of a uterus, and emerged a squalling infant smeared with afterbirth and sucking His tiny thumb. Astounding love!

Some gods are idols of menacing demeanor or placid, distant expression. Nothing is less intimidating than a baby. Follow a newborn through a grocery store and watch people perk up with almost magical attention and delight. They're attracted to the little wrapped bundle—defenseless, approachable, innocent, messing diapers, gurgling and cooing. Babies bring people together; we hold babies close. What could God do to more effectively say, "Don't be afraid of me," than to become a baby?

---

16. His preferred designation for Himself.
17. *Letter to the Philippians,* chapter 2.

God is vulnerable.

Writing in *Memoirs of a Lunatic,* the great Russian author Leo Tolstoy (who was also a spiritual mentor of Mahatma Gandhi) recounts how tepid routine destroys our wonder in encountering God's passionate love:

> I well remember the second time madness seized me. It was when Auntie was telling us about Christ. She told her story and got up to leave the room. But we held her back.
>
> "Tell us more about Jesus Christ!" we said.
>
> "I must go," she replied.
>
> "No, tell us more, please," Mitinka insisted, and she repeated all that she had said before. She told us how they crucified Him, how they beat and martyred Him, and how He went on praying and did not blame them.
>
> "Auntie, why did they torture Him?"
>
> "They were wicked."
>
> "But wasn't He God?"
>
> "Be still—it is nine o'clock; don't you hear the clock striking?"
>
> "Why did they beat Him? He had forgiven them. Then why did they hit Him? Did it hurt Him? Auntie, did it hurt?"
>
> "Be quiet, I say, I am going to the dining room to have tea now."
>
> "But perhaps it never happened, perhaps He was not beaten by them."
>
> "I am going!"
>
> "No, Auntie, don't go . . ." And again my madness took possession of me; I sobbed and sobbed, and began knocking my head against the wall.

The picture of little Leo slamming his head against the wall has stuck with me. At times I have felt a similar urge when I've been exposed to responses and broadcasts of amazing gracelessness. Like a small ringbearer at a wedding, we appear fidgety and bored by all the hoopla: "Yes, I've heard about Jesus and all that, (yawn) so . . . what?" As we rush off to tea times and tee times, is God's sacrifice so easy to leave behind?

If it was your earthly father who had been betrayed by a traitor, beaten and bone-whipped to unconsciousness, tortured, tried and found innocent, then spiked to a stake and left to die, and if he did it all *so that you could live,* do you think you would be glibly saying, "Yes, I've heard all that about my father"? Wouldn't you brim with tears each time you thought of him? Could you shrug it off if someone spoke poorly of him, or would you speak up fervently in his defense? Could you forget about him—ever?

Perhaps we've been inoculated with just enough Jesus to become immune. In one of his tales from Lake Wobegon, Garrison Keillor describes an older relative who cried whenever he prayed publicly as he got to the part about Jesus' dying for us. "Everyone else seemed to have gotten over it," Keillor deadpans.

Judging the "so that" spirit of Jesus brings us to the brink of eye-rubbing wonder, enamored not by one who can put the stars in space but by a broken man nailed up outside a city wall. See the greatest lover with crimson flowers in His hands, arms wide enough to embrace the world.

• • •

God, is it possible? Do You love me that much? I pray for forgiveness, God, for numberless thoughts and words and deeds. I pray for graciousness toward every molecule of creation. Let me taste Your Spirit. Inhabit me with unspeakable love. Thank You for Your gifts.

~

The phrases "Jesus saves" or "Jesus is Lord" have been so often used in the absence of any visible historical application that most people simply do not know what the words mean anymore. Perhaps never before has Jesus' name been more frequently mentioned and the content of his life and teachings so thoroughly ignored.

—JIM WALLIS

As many were astonished at him—his appearance was so marred, beyond human semblance, and his form beyond that of the sons of men—so shall he startle many nations.

—ISAIAH, CHAPTER 52

In our world the road to holiness necessarily runs through the world of action.

—DAG HAMMARSKJÖLD

It is only in winter that the pine and the cypress are known to be evergreens.

—CONFUCIUS

Surely he has borne our griefs and carried our sorrows; yet we esteemed him stricken, smitten by God, and afflicted. But he was wounded for our transgressions, he was bruised for our iniquities; upon him was the chastisement that made us whole, and with his stripes we are healed.

—ISAIAH, CHAPTER 53

Eyes and ears are poor witnesses when the soul is barbarous.

—HERACLITIS

And they made his grave with the wicked and with a rich man in his death, although he had done no violence, and there was no deceit in his mouth.

—ISAIAH, CHAPTER 53

Killing Jesus was like trying to destroy a dandelion seed head by blowing on it.

—WALTER WINK

~

7

A Path of Astonishment

THEY HAD COVERED eighty miles. From Nazareth it had taken five days. For most of the miles Mary had walked; the burro jounced too uncomfortably when she rode. Occasionally she mounted it to relieve the pressure in her swollen feet, until the jarring made her moan to stop.

It was odd to see a woman in her ninth month of pregnancy making such a journey, and the trip exacted its toll. Her labor began as they entered Bethlehem. Desperate, Joseph begged for a spare room—anything—for his suffering young wife, but all that was left was a cave where the animals were kept.

They took it. Joseph tied up the burro amid the greasy mud and soupy manure, and in one stall he spread new hay over the ground. Then Mary gripped his hand fiercely and called out: No, there wasn't time to fetch a midwife. Joseph ran trembling for a flask of hot water.

The miles of inhaling dust were over. The frantic searching was past. The agonized cries had ended. Mary gazed at her newborn boy. He lay in a feeding trough cut from a stone shelf. Around them rank animal smells mingled with the sweet odor of old oats and barley. Joseph brought Him to where she lay, and she unwrapped the strips of linen cloth that bound Him and rubbed salt and oil on His tiny squirming body. Binding Him again, she held Him close and kissed Him, then handed Him to Joseph, who gently kissed Him and laid Him back in the trough. Joseph sat down on the hay next to Mary.

"What's wrong?" he asked.

She smiled faintly, that he should know her so well after so short a time. "I thank God for you, and for my Son," she said.

"And . . . ?"

She bit her lower lip. "If only we had traveled faster. We might have gotten a decent room. We might have had time for the midwife . . ."

"We had to rest. You might have given birth on the way," he replied.

She sighed. "I wanted everything to be perfect."

"He's alive and healthy."

"But *here?* With the animals?" Her voice dripped with remorse. "Joseph, *do you know whose Son this is?*"

Joseph held her eyes a long moment. "Yes," he said finally, "I know who He is." He reached over and plucked hay from her hair. "And I know who we are also. We are doing our best."

Mary turned her face away. "Oh, Joseph," she whispered. "What can He possibly do with such a beginning?"

SUNDAY, APRIL 22, A.D. 31

What a celebration! What a party. For more than forty months—three and a half years—His backers have waited and ached for the opportunity. Now the moment is here. Or more precisely, He is here. For on this day He's a different person.[1]

For as long as His followers have known Him He has run a counter campaign. He doesn't pander to public adulation. He tells the truth, no matter how it offends the establishment. Sometimes He avoids the crowds, or He exhausts His time with unsavory individuals. But now, as Passover approaches, with five times the normal population packing the dusty streets of Jerusalem, Jesus seems surprisingly open to the praise. Now's their chance to release the building exhilaration, to trumpet it from the rooftops, to sing it down the narrow streets: "This is Messiah! Messiah is here!"

Jesus asks to borrow a colt to enter the city. Though the disciples are not fully aware of the significance of the request, the five-hundred-year-old prophecy of Zechariah is played out:

> "Rejoice greatly, O Daughter of Zion!
> Shout, daughter of Jerusalem!
> See, your king comes to you,
> righteous and having salvation,
> gentle, and riding on a donkey,
> on a colt, the foal of a donkey."

---

1. The most likely date. The other possible date is Sunday, April 2, A.D. 30. Events described in this chapter are found in *Matthew, Mark, Luke,* and *John.*

No sooner is He seated than a tremendous shout rents the air. "*Hosanna! Hosanna to the Son of David! Blessed is the King who comes in the name of the Lord!*"

It's springtime, with new life budding, and the most unlikely victory parade begins. Unlike processions of other conquering kings, this one carries in its wake no train of manacled captives. Instead, around this King are trophies of His healing. The blind, whom He has delivered from darkness, lead the way. The formerly crippled test footholds and climb trees to break off branches to wave. Hundreds who have listened awestruck to Him, now liberated from fear, superstition, hatred, and hopelessness, line a corridor of joy. Cleansed lepers lay their cloaks before the snorting colt. Lazarus, who recently experienced the full slavery of death, leads the animal on which Jesus rides. Ecstasy bursts from every mouth, as though Jesus has announced, "I accept the nomination!" Palm branches spread before Him like a carpet. Through the sunny streets the crowds surge, filled with singing, laughter, and dancing.

The religious leaders are aroused too. "Look," they gesture wildly, "the world has gone after Him!" Irate, they pace beside Jesus. "Teacher," they shout through the bedlam, "rebuke your disciples!"

Jesus replies, smiling and bouncing along, "I tell you, if they were silent, the very stones would cry out!"

Then, at the crest of a hill overlooking the city, the celebration stops and hushes. All eyes focus on the magnificent temple, gleaming in marble and gold, the pride of the Jewish nation. As reverence descends, a soft gasp escapes, a stifled sob, an anguished cry, and then a torrent of weeping breaks forth. Turning to Jesus, the shocked revelers find Him clutching His breast, rocking in agony on the colt's back. *What in the world?*

Jesus falters through His thoughts. "If you, even you," He chokes out, looking around at the stunned faces, "would know on this day what will bring you peace, but you can't see it. The time will come when your enemies will surround you. They will dash you to the ground, you and your children, and they'll reduce the temple to rubble, because you reject God's offer of peace." Though He knows He will shortly be publicly humiliated and killed, He cries for others, not for Himself. Jesus prophesies and mourns the destruction of Jerusalem forty years in the future, for the proud city that refuses to accept God's leading will refuse to submit to Rome, with horrible results.

The week is wrapped in irony. Today, Jesus' supporters have shown Him their palms. In a few days, Jesus will show them His palms.

MONDAY, APRIL 23, A.D. 31

Jesus and His twelve closest disciples sleep at night this week in Bethany, a town about two miles from Jerusalem. In the morning, on their way to the temple, they pass a fig orchard, and Jesus searches a tree for fruit. Though not fig season, this tree is in full leaf, evidently bearing fruit. After His search uncovers nothing but leaves, a tower of pretentious foliage, Jesus does a strange thing. He curses the tree, saying, "May no one eat fruit from you again." The disciples look at the tree and at one another, raise their eyebrows, and shrug.

As He enters the courtyard of the temple, Jesus surveys the scene before Him. At the beginning of His public ministry He had driven from this spot all the marketers who trespassed on the sacrificial system. Now He finds the temple in even worse condition. The outer court is a vast cattle yard, with pens and cages stacked together, travelers massed in bleating confusion, and money-changers bargaining frantically. The reeking stench of greed fills the air.

Each Passover the blood of thousands of slain animals is poured upon the altar. Over centuries the Jews had lost sight of the reason for the offerings—to prefigure the sacrifice of God's beloved Son, made necessary by the sins of the people. The deaths of innocent animals were meant to symbolize the horror brought about by sin and to bring worshipers to humble repentance. Now the horror lies in the service's casual familiarity, as if God could be honored by callous bloodletting. Jesus knows His blood will be as little appreciated. Seven hundred years earlier the prophet Isaiah had written:

> What to me is the multitude of your sacrifices? says the LORD; I have had enough of burnt offerings of rams and the fat of fed beasts; I do not delight in the blood of bulls, or of lambs, or of he-goats . . . your hands are full of blood. Wash yourselves; make yourselves clean; remove the evil of your doings from before my eyes; cease to do evil, learn to do good; seek justice, correct oppression; defend the fatherless, plead for the widow. Come now, let us reason together, says the LORD: though your sins are like scarlet, they shall be as white as snow.

Suffering travelers arrive at the service in great distress. Many of the sick and diseased must be carried on pallets, and some are too poor to purchase even the smallest offering. They are told they must present a sacrifice to receive forgiveness for the sins that are responsible for their illness, but the exorbitant prices, eventually lining the pockets of the religious leaders, stretch beyond the sufferers' means. Their pleas go unheard, waved away by important hands. Only bribery works in this business environment.

Jesus enters the courtyard with a presence that defies description. A ripple of silence widens until every eye is focused on the Man with the smoldering gaze. Even the animals quiet. The palpable power of God is here. He had cleansed the temple three years earlier. He's back.

"It is written," Jesus announces with volcanic force, "'My house will be called a house of prayer for all nations.' But you have made it a den of robbers." He measures every word. "Take these things *out!*" Overturning the money-changing tables, Jesus rampages through the courtyard. A fearful stampede precedes Him as wide-eyed traders escape with bawling livestock. Coins ring on the marble pavement, but few pause to retrieve them. Jesus bangs cages open, releasing turtledoves into a swirling vortex of winged color. The courtyard is pandemonium. For all those who have been ignored or stomped on, for all the sophisticated posturing, for all the stingy, naked meanness that turns sincere people away His anger moves like a hurricane.

In time, the priests and rulers return to the temple, and there they witness a marvelous sight. Jesus sits with streams of people flowing to His side. The courtyard is filled with the sick and dying and heartbroken, and Jesus is healing them all. Those who are youngest are the most unrestrained and affectionate. After Jesus heals them and their families, they hug Him, kiss Him repeatedly, and sit on His lap. The children begin chanting the praises from the previous day: "Hosanna to the Son of David!"

The chief priests and teachers of the law, standing aloof in their high hats and white robes, are incensed. "Do you hear what these children are saying?" they yelp.

"But of course," Jesus replies with a grin. "Haven't you read, 'Out of the mouths of babes you have brought forth praise'?" The jealous leaders frown. They *must* get rid of Him.

He stays for hours to teach at the temple, and all are astounded by His teaching. Later some Greeks approach the disciple Philip with a request. "Excuse me," one says, "we wish to see Jesus."

When Jesus hears of the request, He grows pensive, His brown eyes roaming the ground. At last He says to those assembled, "The hour has come for the Son of Man to be glorified. I tell you, unless a kernel of wheat falls to the ground and dies, it remains only a single seed. But if it dies, it yields a rich harvest. Anyone who tightly guards his life will lose it, but anyone who loses himself in reckless loving will gain eternal life. Whoever follows me, my Father will honor."

Jesus heaves a sigh and stares into the distance. "Now, my soul is troubled," He confesses. "What shall I say? 'Father, save me from this hour'?" He struggles with the question before the uncomprehending listeners. "No, for this very reason I came to this time." He lifts His eyes to the sky, bright as a blue bowl. "Father," He cries, "glorify Your name!"

A voice booms above, "I have glorified it, and I will glorify it again!"

The people gathered are amazed. They all begin speaking at once about what they've heard, some saying that it thundered, others claiming that an angel spoke.

Jesus is unmoved. He explains, "The voice was for your benefit, not mine. Now is the time for the prince of this world to be unmasked and driven out. But when I am lifted up from the earth, I will draw all people to me."

A man in the crowd remarks, "We have heard from the Torah that the Messiah remains forever. How is it that you say the Son of Man has to be 'lifted up'? Who is this Son of Man?"

Jesus pauses and slowly strokes His beard. His words, spoken so often to so many, have had so little effect. The listeners neither see with their eyes nor understand with their hearts. Some of the religious leaders do believe in Him, but because of the Pharisees, for fear of being banned from the synagogue, they won't admit it. He concludes, "You're going to have the light just a little longer. Walk while you have the light, or darkness will overtake you and you won't know where you're going. Believe in the light, and you will become people of the light."

Then He departs, avoiding the crowds. For now, He needs to be alone.

TUESDAY, APRIL 24, A.D. 31

In the morning, as they walk from Bethany to Jerusalem, Jesus and the disciples again pass the fig orchard. From root to top, the fig tree Jesus had cursed the day before is dead, its leaves brown and drooping. His disciples are dumbstruck. "Teacher, look!" says Peter. "The fig tree you cursed has withered!" The action seems so unlike Jesus, who declared that He came not to condemn the world but to save it. His life is fragrant with life and mercy. Why this?

The barren tree that held pretentious foliage symbolizes any religious body that claims to represent God. Though no other trees in the orchard carried fruit, none gave the appearance of doing so. To pretend to represent God and show none of His generous fruits is especially offensive; hypocrisy is worse than no pretense at all. The withered tree represents magnificent church structures without love inside, high-sounding doctrines not lived, creeds that claim to emancipate but instead enslave, pompous ideologues who speak for the humble Master. At the temple—the resplendent temple housing pompous, pretentious religionists—Jesus will come under attack. The tree will attempt to trip Him up and crush Him.

As He walks through the temple courts teaching the people, the chief priests ask, "By what authority are you doing these things? Who gave you this authority?"

Jesus replies, "Let me first ask you one question. You answer me, and I'll answer you. Here it is: When John the Baptist baptized, did it come from heaven, or was it purely human?"

The priests huddle to discuss how they should answer. "If we say from heaven, He will say, 'Then why didn't you believe him?' But if we say it was purely human, well, we're afraid of what the people will do, for they all believe John was a prophet." Finally reaching a consensus, they tell Jesus: "We don't know."

Jesus cocks His head with interest. "Then I guess," He says, "I won't answer your question either." The crowd buzzes with amusement. "But what do you think about this?" He continues. "There was a man with two sons. The man came to the first son and said, 'Go and work today in the vineyard.' 'No, I won't,' said the son. But afterward he changed his mind and went. When the father approached the other son with the same request, that son said, 'I will, sir,' but he never went. Which of the two did what his father wanted?"

"The first, of course," the priests reply.

"Yes," agrees Jesus, "and I tell you the truth, corrupt tax collectors and prostitutes are entering the kingdom of God ahead of you. For John came telling you to repent and turn toward God, and you didn't believe him, but the tax collectors and prostitutes did. Even when you saw them responding, you refused to believe."

A murmur of approval pulses through the audience. Hearing Jesus put crafty religious leaders in their place fills the commoners with hope. Is it possible that God views the humble believer in a better light than He views men in exalted religious positions? The owlish priests boil with outrage.

But Jesus is not nearly through with them. The consummate storyteller spins two more parables into the warm air. A landowner plants a vineyard and leases it to some tenant farmers, then goes away on a journey. At harvest time the landowner sends servants to collect his share, but the tenants beat up one servant, wound another, and kill a third. He sends more servants, but they're treated the same way. Finally he sends his own son, thinking, *They will respect him.* But the tenants surmise, *This is the future landowner. If we get rid of him, the land will be ours.* So they kill him. "When the landowner himself returns," says Jesus, "what will he do to the tenants?"

Knowing how the parable applies, the crowd responds, "He will give those scoundrels what they deserve and rent the vineyard to other tenants."

Jesus is rolling now. Eyes shining with intensity, He tells how the stone the builders rejected becomes the very cornerstone. Those who fall on the rock are broken, and those who do not are crushed. The chief priests and Pharisees witness in stony silence. Jesus tells a second parable about a wedding banquet prepared by a king for his son. The king sends out invitations, but the people refuse to come. "Everything is ready," says the king. "Whosoever will, come to the wedding banquet!" Eventually all the guests, both good and bad, who are properly dressed for the wedding are admitted.

The Pharisees decide to attack. They set a trap with some of their youngest disciples, whom they suspect Jesus does not know, along with government sympathizers called Herodians. In the tense, occupied atmosphere of Palestine, the Jews chafe under Roman rule. (The Jewish nation has never worn chains well.) But to preach any type of rebellion can lead to death. If pinned down with a well-phrased question, Jesus cannot win; He must alienate one side or another. The spies begin, "Teacher, we know you are a man of integrity. You aren't swayed by anyone's opinion of you, but you speak and teach what is right. Tell us, then, is it right to pay taxes to Caesar? Should we pay, or shouldn't we?"

Jesus has already sniffed them out. "You hypocrites," He says, "why are you trying to trap me? Bring me a coin." Someone hands Him a coin, and He holds it up. "Whose head is this? And whose name is on the inscription?"

"Caesar's," they reply.

"Then pay to Caesar what belongs to Caesar, and to God what belongs to God."

Astonished by His answer, the questioners leave. Later, another Pharisee poses one more question: "Teacher, which is the greatest commandment?"

Jesus says, "Love the Lord your God with all your heart, with all your soul, with all your mind, and with all your strength. This is the greatest and first commandment. The second is like it: Love your neighbor as yourself. On these two commandments everything depends." One cannot be done without doing the other. The first four of the Ten Commandments show how to love God, the last six show how to love others.

"Well said, Teacher," the man replies. "To love like this is more important than all the burnt offerings and sacrifices."

Jesus looks at the man closely and says, "You are not far from the kingdom of God." From that time on no one at the temple tries to trap Him with questions. Jesus swings toward the large crowd that has been listening with delight.

In everything He says they find concepts that are fresh, lucid, and challenging. Now the listeners will hear the strongest cautions in all His teachings.

"Beware of the teachers of the law," He says, "for they don't practice what they preach. Instead they load you with impossible demands that they themselves don't keep. Their whole lives are planned for show—how they dress, where they sit, what they're called. They devour the houses of the poor and then parade their self-righteous prayers. You, however, must not live this way, for all who promote themselves will be humbled, and everyone who practices humility will find promotion.

"But woe to you, scribes and Pharisees, play-actors that you are," He says fearlessly, looking them in the eye on the back row. "You shut the door of heaven in people's faces, neither going in yourselves nor allowing others to go in. Hypocrites! You cross land and sea to make one convert, and when you have him you make him twice as much a child of hell as you are.

"Woe to you, religious leaders, for you tithe down to the last mint leaf in your garden, but you ignore the important things—justice, mercy, and good faith. These are the matters you should practice, without neglecting the tithe. You blind guides: You strain out a gnat and then swallow a camel! You are like white-washed tombs that look good on the outside but inside are full of death and rottenness. You build tombs for the prophets and decorate monuments for heroes, saying, 'If we were alive then, we would never have joined in killing the prophets.' Now you're trying to finish off what your ancestors began. Snakes! How do you think you'll escape the fire of destruction?"

The priests, scribes, and Pharisees are beside themselves. They would arrest Him this instant but they know it would create an uproar.

With tears in His voice, Jesus concludes, "Jerusalem, Jerusalem, you murder the messengers that are sent to you. How often have I longed to gather your children, as a hen gathers her chicks under her wings, and you wouldn't let me. Now all you have is an obsolete temple. You won't see me again until you say, 'Blessed is He who comes in the name of the Lord.'"

Jesus walks away with His disciples; they sit opposite the offering box and watch people put their money into the temple treasury. Some of the rich shake out sacks of money with great clinking fanfare. A poor widow quickly and privately drops in two small copper coins, worth only a fraction of a penny. Jesus says to His disciples loudly enough for her to hear, "Believe me, this poor widow has contributed more than all the others. For they put in what they can easily afford, but she out of her poverty has put in all that she has to live on." Hearing His words, the woman's careworn face glows with peace and gratefulness. She has heard from the Master that motivation matters most. Hers is the greater sacrifice not because of what was given, but because of what was left over. Unselfish acts, often unseen, stand highest in God's sight.

. . .

Every day this week He has taught in the temple, and each evening He has gone to the Mount of Olives to pray. On the Mount this Tuesday evening, four disciples—James, Peter, John, and Andrew—ask Him privately, "When will the temple be reduced to rubble? And what will be the sign of your coming and the end of this world?" Jesus has been waiting for them to ask this. He sits, and they sit around Him, five young men in the mountain twilight. His words will not be forgotten.[2]

The disciples' question is direct: "When will this happen?" Jesus' answer is indirect. He speaks to them first of false messiahs, of end-of-the-world scenarios when "most men's love will grow cold." He tells of the future fall of Jerusalem and of His Second Coming, but He doesn't say precisely when they will take place. "Be ready, be on your guard," He warns them, but He is speaking of spiritual nimbleness rather than military preparedness. He tells them parables. Live vigilantly, live boldly is their theme. Though the discourse began with the disciples asking a chronological question, He answers with ethics: If you live your life loving God and everyone around you, you don't need to know *when* the world will end.

Jesus pauses from His teaching. He reaches down and picks up a blade of grass. "As you know," He says softly, studying the blade, "the Passover Feast is two days away—then the Son of Man will be handed over to be crucified." He has told them before, of course, but their comprehension seems paralyzed. Didn't the triumphal entry two days ago demonstrate that they have little to fear? And who could stand in the way of the passion that cleansed the temple? Isn't this the King of all? The four disciples smile at each other knowingly as if to say, "He's in one of those moods again."

In the palace of the high priest, however, the mood is darker. Caiaphas has assembled elders, teachers of the law, and chief priests to find some way to rid themselves of this pesky Jewish carpenter. An idea, burning like the bite of a red ant, drives them. They plot to stealthily arrest Jesus, and to kill Him. "But not during the Feast," they add, "or the people may riot." They are afraid of the people; they have no fear of God.

---

2. They are found in *Matthew*, chapters 24 and 25; *Mark*, chapter 13; and *Luke*, chapter 21.

Wednesday, April 25, a.d. 31

Jesus and the disciples again stay the night at Bethany, and Jesus spends the day visiting friends Martha, Mary, and Lazarus. Though He has spoken often of the trials before Him, He shares again what lies ahead. His words are dipped in sorrow. Here are friends whose gentle, loyal appreciation buoy His spirit and resolve. He relaxes, spending the day in private prayer and conversation, a respite from the engulfing storm.

In the evening Jesus is the honored guest at the home of a man known as Simon the Leper, whom Jesus had healed.[3] Martha, marvelous hostess, serves the men in one room as Lazarus, the celebrity, reclines at the table with the disciples and other guests. Mary helps a little, but as much as possible she is where she unswervingly chooses to be, near the Master, soaking up His words. The room resounds with animated talk.

Toward the end of the meal, Mary leaves and retrieves an alabaster jar containing a pint of pure nard, an incredibly expensive perfume. Earlier in the day she had observed Jesus' sadness. Grateful that He has pardoned her sins and rescued her brother from death, she purchased the perfume at great personal sacrifice. She moves unnoticed behind Jesus and breaks the jar open. Instantly the fragrance permeates the room, the talking stops, and all eyes rivet on her. Mary pours the perfume on the head and feet of Jesus. Weeping from embarrassment and love, her tears drop like warm rain on His tanned feet. She hurriedly wipes the tears away with her flowing hair.

The awkward silence deepens. The men are offended. In their culture this represents an unseemly public display of intimacy, and her devotion also puts them to shame. One of the twelve disciples, Judas Iscariot, objects harshly. "Why wasn't this perfume sold and the money given to the poor? It's worth more than a year's wages!" Judas is treasurer of the disciples, keeper of the money bag used to support widows, orphans, and the poor.

As the indignation level rises, Jesus notes Mary's distress. She fears that in her extravagant giving she will also be reprimanded by her efficient sister and, possibly, by the Master Himself. It was an impetuous gift.

She attempts a pitiful escape, but Jesus comes to her defense. Lifting His voice above the muttering, He says, "Leave her alone!" The guests quiet. "Why are you bothering her? She's done a beautiful thing to me. You'll always have the

---

3. This feast could have taken place the previous Friday night, six days before Passover, according to *John*. In *Matthew* and *Mark*, the incident appears to have happened Wednesday night.

poor with you, but you will not always have me. When she poured this perfume on my body, she did it to prepare me for burial." Mary looks at Him with stunned adoration. He understands. "I tell you for certain," He continues, "wherever the gospel is preached throughout the world, what she has done will also be told." God prizes courteous gestures of appreciation, particularly when they take place before the funeral.

Judas is furious. How *dare* Jesus rebuke him in front of this company! After all Judas has done for the worthless, ragtag band of believers, this is how he's rewarded? Scorned for the sake of a woman's feelings? Judas bolts from the room. He has endured this long enough. Rumbling the two miles to Jerusalem, he curses under his hot breath.

In the beginning, along with the multitudes, Judas hung enthralled on Jesus' every word. By the lake, in the synagogue, on the Mount of Olives, Judas listened breathlessly to teaching superior to any heard before. "No man ever spoke as this man," he conceded. Moreover, Judas had seen Jesus' power at work. With a word and a touch of His hand, the dying rose to a new future, the blind described rainbows and loved ones, the crippled leaped like gamboling lambs. The man was a walking fountain of exuberant life. Judas united with Jesus in works of mercy and felt his soul stirred with a purity and peace he had never known.

Notwithstanding these positives, however, Judas saw areas of concern. Jesus commented often that His kingdom is not of this world, and after the miracle of the loaves and fishes He actually turned away a call to be king. This was unacceptable. Judas was a shrewd man, worldly wise, and the love of money and power dominated his life. Jesus had placed Judas in charge of the finances so his heart would soften, but Judas instead used the opportunity to help himself to the money whenever possible; the poor would not have seen all of Mary's perfume money, even if she hadn't squandered it. Judas considered himself more far-seeing than the other disciples. If no worldly honors came with being connected to this man, he would watch from a distance—he would not surrender himself fully. A profitable opportunity would pop up somewhere.

And so it has. Judas reports to the chief priests in Jerusalem that he could turn the rabble rouser over to them when no crowds are present for only thirty pieces of silver—the lowest price of a slave. The priests are delighted. Judas doesn't really believe that Jesus will permit Himself to be arrested, for Jesus is the master fox at avoiding traps. Judas will simply teach the Master a valuable lesson, so that in the future he will be treated with more respect. Moreover, he will gain a little pile of money in the deal.

The supper winds down after the scene with Mary. Jesus seems quieter than usual, atypically absorbed. His face is set like flint. It is mid-week, and He is coming at the Cross, coming astonishingly hard.

THURSDAY, APRIL 26, A.D. 31

They appear distracted, too busy to notice, but all know. Mindless chatter can't hide their gnawing uneasiness. At a feast it's customary for a servant to wash the feet of the guests, and while they can see the pitcher of water, the basin, and the towel, no servant appears. The disciples manifest an engaged unconcern, seemingly unaware that anything needs to be done.

Jesus waits, watching. He longs to tell them things that will ease their imminent pain and confusion, but they are not ready, for jealousy and discontent dance feverishly in their eyes. They're still surmising who will be the greatest in the kingdom. Earlier, James and John had asked to sit on either side of Jesus' throne, and now all of them are livid with resentment. John reclines on the left side of Jesus, Judas on the right side. How can Jesus show them that humility constitutes true greatness? How can He kindle their love for each other?

Slowly the Master rises from the table, lays aside His outer garment and wraps the towel around His waist. With shocked interest the disciples look on. Without a word Jesus pours water into the basin and begins washing the disciples' feet. Calmly, purposefully, gently, He moves from man to man. The abashed disciples look away and look within.

When Jesus reaches Judas, He bathes the soiled feet thoroughly and dries them with the towel. With a thrill of sympathy Judas experiences the love this Man holds for him and is tempted to confess his betrayal. But he will not humble himself. His pride is too fierce. Hardening his resolve, he views this act as the cinching piece of evidence that Jesus could never be a ruler. *A king would never debase himself like this. This kingdom is a fraud.* He will never wash another's feet. It is beneath him.

When Peter's turn comes, he exclaims, "Master, are you going to wash my feet?" Jesus' meekness is tearing Peter apart.

Jesus replies, "You don't understand what I'm doing, but later you will understand."

"No," Peter asserts, "you will *never* wash my feet."

Jesus looks into Peter's eyes. "Unless I wash you, you have no part with me."

"Then, Lord, not just my feet," says Peter, "but also my hands and head."

Jesus stifles a smile. "One who has already washed," He says, "needs only to wash his feet." After washing each disciple's feet, Jesus comments, "Now, you are clean." His gaze travels around the circle until He stops at Judas. "Though not every one of you."

Two weapons for a conqueror: a basin and a towel. The disciples are now teachable, ready to be filled. All but one. Their Passover feast begins: lamb, bitter herbs, unleavened bread, wine, dried figs, grapes, and dates. Jesus speaks of His example, that hereafter they should wash one another's feet, and that the greatest among them will be the one who serves. Then He looks down, biting His lip. "I tell you for certain, one of you is going to betray me, and it would be better for him if he had never been born."

His disciples stare at one another in disbelief. One by one they ask Him, "Is it I?" Peter motions to John and mouths, *"Ask Him which one."*

John leans toward Jesus. "Lord, who is it?"

Jesus whispers, "The one I give this piece of bread to when I have dipped it in the dish." Dipping the bread, He gives it to Judas Iscariot.

Feigning innocence, Judas responds, "Surely not I, Teacher."

Jesus regards him sadly. "You have said so. What you are about to do, do quickly." No one else understands what is happening. Since Judas is in charge of the money, some assume Jesus is telling him to buy what's needed to eat or to give something to the poor. Judas enters the night.

The company is lost in thought. Passover beautifully memorializes the miracle in Egypt when death passed over every house marked with blood from a faultless lamb. Recounting the Egyptian miracle, Jesus then breaks with tradition. He lifts a loaf of unleavened bread, signifying absence from the leaven of sin, thanks the Father, and breaks off pieces for His followers, saying, "Take, eat. This is my body given for you. Do this in remembrance of me." He holds the cup of wine, gives thanks, and offers it to them, saying, "Drink from it, all of you. This cup is the new covenant of my blood, which is poured out for many. I will not drink again of the fruit of the vine until I drink it with you in my Father's kingdom."

The disciples look puzzled. *He won't drink again until . . . when?* Jesus reads their thoughts. "My children, I will be with you only a little longer," He says. "You will look for me, but where I am going you cannot come. A new command I give you: Love one another. As I have loved you, you must love each other. This is the one true sign that you are my disciples."

Simon Peter asks, "Master, where are You going?"

"Where I'm going, you cannot follow," Jesus replies, "but you will follow later."

"Lord, why can't I follow you now? I will lay down my life for you."

Jesus looks at Peter. "Will you, really? This very night you will all desert me, as it's written, 'I will strike the shepherd, and the sheep of the flock will be scattered.' But after I have risen, I'll go ahead of you into Galilee."

Peter declares, "Even if all the others desert you, *I* never will."

Jesus examines Peter sorrowfully. "Simon, Simon, Satan wants to sift you like wheat. But I've prayed for you that you won't lose your faith. And once you have recovered, you must strengthen your brothers."

"Lord, I am ready to go with you to prison and to death!"

"I tell you, Peter," returns Jesus with a piercing gaze, "today—yes, tonight—before the rooster crows twice you will deny three times that you know me."

"Never!" Peter insists. "Even if I have to die with you, I'll never disown you." All the disciples say the same.

Jesus lets it alone. The time is coming soon enough. They will need words of hope to remember, to guide them through the choking blackness ahead. He scans the anxious faces of the men He has gathered to Himself and feels compassion for them. "Don't be troubled," He assures them. "Just believe in me." He says that He's going to prepare a place for them, and that in seeing Him they have seen the Father. Furthermore, if they love Him they will keep His commandments and abide in Him—no casual, off-and-on connection, for they are branches of the living vine. In every difficulty they are to see a call to prayer. He will leave them another counselor, the Holy Spirit, to be with them and teach them forever.[4] They sing a hymn, the Passover *hallel*, their deep voices interweaving in joyful strains. Jesus prays a passionate plea for unity, purity, and involvement in the world. When He finishes, they leave for a nearby olive grove called Gethsemane, which means "oil press." A full moon creates stark shadows. As they near the grove, Jesus grows strangely quiet. His breath arrives in short gasps. He says to His disciples, "Sit here, while I go and pray. Pray for yourselves, that you won't yield to temptation." He takes Peter, James, and John with Him.

Jesus is faltering. He stumbles and groans. His labored breathing stalls, and He steadies Himself on the others.

"Master, are you all right?" In the darkness the three men look into a face they have never seen before. It is the face of death. Upon Him who knows no guilt the sins of fallen humanity are tumbling. So dreadful does sin appear, so blameworthy for the world's infinite suffering, that Jesus is tempted to believe it will shut Him out forever from His Father.

---

4. See *John*, chapters 14 to 17.

He exclaims, "My soul is sorrowful! I'm so depressed I could die. Oh, stay here. Oh, stay awake with me." He trudges a short distance from them, but not so far that they can't see and hear. He falls full on the earth, His body writhing in agony. A breeze blows the trees' arms high above the shivering grass. Jesus feels the gulf of separation—so broad, so dark, so deep. Clawing at the cold ground, He pulls Himself close, as if to prevent Himself from being drawn farther from God.

"Abba! Daddy!" He whispers. Pale lips issue the plea, "Everything is possible for you, Abba. Please let this cup pass from me." He strains to form the words. "Yet," he adds, "yet not my will, but yours." He remains fetally curled for a long time. The three disciples don't know how to help. They sense that they cannot interfere. In dread and denial they succumb to full stomachs and a longing to escape. Eventually, staggering up, Jesus lunges toward His friends. Surely they will have some comfort and assurance for Him! He finds them sleeping.

"Simon," He says painfully, "couldn't you stay awake with me one hour? Watch and pray that you don't fall into temptation. The spirit is willing, but the flesh is weak." In His hour of greatest suffering, He cares for others.

Jesus returns to His place. Again He groans, "Oh . . . oh, God . . ." His suffering crashes in waves, more powerful than before. He pounds and kicks the earth. His sweat droplets become blood exuding through His pores, a condition known as haematidrosis, caused by massive fear and suffering. As He wrestles alone with the powers of evil, the brutal features of the situation press upon Him. What will be gained by His sacrifice? God's chosen people will reject Him. His own disciple will betray Him. One of His closest followers will deny Him. All will forsake Him. The hopelessness overwhelms Him.

"Father, please, please, take this cup of hell from me. Take away this death and damnation. Abba, Abba!" The words strangle in His throat. "Nevertheless," He whispers hoarsely, "not what I want, but what you want."

He longs for companionship, and again He goes to the three disciples. They remain heavy-lidded, exhausted from sorrow. His arrival awakens them. Speechless, they stare in horror. His anguish has so altered His appearance that they hardly recognize Him.

Jesus stumbles back. He prays not for His disciples now but for His own soul. Grimacing, He crashes to the ground. His entire being convulses. He is tasting the sufferings of every person's death. The awful moment has come—that moment which decides the destiny of the world. Will the innocent Son of God take upon Himself the curse of sin? Will He drink the cup of humiliation and agony, of separation from the Father? He struggles to His hands and knees, rocking with the ache. He knows that, if left to itself, humankind will perish. But the awesome power of sin stuns Him. "O My Father," He says a third time, "if possible, let this cup pass from me." He pauses, and eternity hangs in the balance. All of heaven is watching. Angels behold the scene in silent wonder. His eyes are shut, his breathing sharp against His teeth. "But," He exhales, "if this cup will not pass from me except I drink it," He struggles to finish the thought, "Your will be done, Father. *Your will be done.*" The choice is made. He will save humanity at any cost to Himself, that through Him billions may gain the loving freedom of eternal life.

He falls dying. A blinding light suddenly appears, and a comforting angel, sent by the Father, supports Jesus' head. The angel assures Him of the Father's love and confirms that Jesus' sacrifice will indeed overthrow the powers of evil, that His kingdom will know no end, and that His followers will thank Him forever. He will see the human race saved. Though still in agony, Jesus' discouragement is lifted. Peace settles on Him. He has endured the unendurable. The disciples see the angel, note that their Master is once more in the hands of God, and again give in to weariness.

A serpent of torches slithers uphill. Jesus rises to meet it. He returns to His disciples a third time and finds them slumped together. "Still sleeping?" He says. "It's time. The Son of Man is betrayed. Get up; let's be going. See," He gestures toward the bobbing flares, "my betrayer approaches."

Judas has often been here to pray with Jesus. This time, though, a pack of soldiers and religious officials wielding weapons and cords trails him. Their eyes glow orange in the night.

"Greetings, Master!" Judas announces and kisses Him on the cheek. The other disciples rise and walk slowly toward the commotion, rubbing their eyes.

Jesus fixes him with a stare. "Judas, do you betray me—with a kiss?" Judas slinks back into shadows. Jesus addresses the mob. "Who is it you want?" He asks with quiet dignity.

"Jesus of Nazareth!" they reply.

"I am He," Jesus announces, and as He speaks a divine light flashes from His face. The rabble stagger back, falling to the ground, covering their eyes. Though Jesus could easily make His escape, He stands serene and self-possessed. Again He asks them, "Who is it you want?"

Scrambling to their feet, embarrassed, they answer, "Jesus of Nazareth."

"I told you that I am He. Let these others go."

The serpent coils quickly around its prey. Soldiers step forward and grab

Jesus. The disciples are astonished and angry at Jesus' rough handling. Lithe as a great cat, Simon Peter springs at the captors, sword held high, and with a wild cry he swings for the head of Malchus, the high priest's servant. The servant dodges, the blade slices off his right ear. Malchus screams in pain, clutching a bloody stump.

"Enough of this!" Jesus commands. Though held firmly, He releases His hands and touches the man's wound. Instantly the ear is made whole. "Put your sword away!"

Peter appears confused and drops his sword. Jesus says in a magisterial voice, "All who live by the sword shall die by the sword. Do you think I can't call on my Father to send for me more than twelve legions of angels? But how then would the Scriptures be fulfilled? The cup my Father has given me, shall I not drink it?"

He turns to the crowd and searches their faces. "You come at me with swords and clubs? Every day when I was with you in the temple courts, you didn't lay a hand on me. But this is your hour, when darkness reigns." Emboldened, the soldiers and religious officials seize Him again and arrest Him. They run an iron rod behind His back through the crooks in His elbows, tie the rod and His hands together, and push Him forward. His pride wounded, Peter suggests that the disciples save themselves, and they all flee. Jesus watches behind Him as their retreating forms disappear.

FRIDAY, APRIL 27, A.D. 31

Past olive groves, over the Kidron, and through the sleeping city's streets the mob takes Jesus to the palace of the ex-high priest, Annas. As patriarch of the priestly family, Annas commands respect, and in the early morning hours Caiaphas, the present high priest, is busy summoning select members of the Sanhedrin council. Two charges will be brought against Jesus. For the religious court, the crime of blasphemy will suffice, but in their occupied state, the Jews cannot lawfully execute a prisoner. For the Romans, the crime of sedition hangs Him.

When Annas eventually appears, he questions Jesus concerning His doctrines and doings, attempting to draw out the nature of the secret society Jesus has established. Why did they meet in private? To plot their insurrection?

Jesus hides no secrets. "I've spoken openly to the world," He counters. "I've always taught in synagogues or at the temple where people gather. I don't speak in secret. Why do you ask me, anyway? Ask these here who have heard me. Obviously they know what I said."

Annas knows what Jesus means. For years the priests have sent spies to report on Jesus' words, and Annas would just as soon keep this aspect of the priests' activities under cover. In fact, they are the ones with the secrets. One of the religious officials, frustrated at seeing Annas silenced, slaps Jesus in the face, saying, "Is that the way to answer the high priest?"

Jesus replies, unperturbed, "If there is something wrong in what I've said, tell me what it is. If what I said is true, why do you strike me?" Annas perceives that nothing more will be gained. He sends Jesus, with His hands still tied, across to wait for Caiaphas.

A strange drama plays while Jesus is being questioned. After the arrest at Gethsemane, two of the disciples, Peter and John, follow the mob from a distance. When John arrives at the council hall, he's admitted as a well-known disciple, for the priests want him to witness the humiliation of his leader, but Peter is forced to wait outside, feeling sorrier and sorrier for himself. Soon John comes back and persuades the woman at door duty to let Peter in.

John draws as near to the proceedings as possible. Peter determines to stay clear; he overhears the taunts and jokes of the onlookers and he feels ashamed and alone. It's cold at three in the morning, so the servants have started a charcoal fire in the middle of the courtyard and are warming themselves. Peter stands with them to get warm. By mingling, he means to give the impression that he's with those who arrested Jesus. He's also a bit on edge, hoping he won't see Malchus.

When the woman at the door receives a break from her duty, she also approaches the fire. She recognizes Peter as the one who had entered with John. Peter looks so dejected that she asks him, "Are you one of this man's disciples?" Suddenly the conversation stops, and all eyes turn on Peter. He pretends not to understand what she's saying, but she persists.

At last he flushes and barks, "No, I'm not! Woman, I don't know what you're talking about." Shaking his head, he walks to the entryway. His first denial. A rooster crows.

Meanwhile, with many of the Sanhedrin assembled (without suspected sympathizers, such as Joseph of Arimathea, Simon of Bethany, and Nicodemus), Caiaphas assumes his seat on the throne as presiding officer. He is barefoot and wears a dark blue headdress. His white robe is covered by a shorter dark blue robe fringed with pomegranates and golden bells and a vestlike *ephod* embroidered with purple, scarlet, and gold. In the center of the *ephod* sits a golden square inset with twelve gemstones, representing the twelve tribes of Israel.

On either side of him stand more than fifty people, the council, witnesses, a small gallery, and Roman soldiers. The crowded room smells of men who have been hastily wakened. Normally the crime is private and the trial is public, but with Jesus everything will be reversed. The yellow flames of two oil lights form changing shadows. In the middle of the room stands the prisoner. Caiaphas has been looking forward to this confrontation. The trial begins.

Witnesses come forward to tell what Jesus has done that is worthy of death. One by one they present their evidence, and one by one they return to their places. Caiaphas is growing annoyed. *Can't these idiots get their stories straight?* The "evidence" is so conflicting as to be inadmissible. He drums his fingers on a gilded armrest, staring angrily at the other members of the council. They know what they want. They've paid these people money. Why is this so hard? Jesus gazes straight at Caiaphas.

Two miserable witnesses step forth. "Well, He . . . I heard Him say He'd destroy the temple and rebuild it in three days," says one.

"And . . . and that He would build another one not made by man," adds the other, licking his lips. His eyes move from Caiaphas to the council members to the guards.

"When did this happen?" asks Caiaphas, leaning forward.

"About three days ago—"

"About three years ago."

The witnesses look at each other.

"Well," thunders Caiaphas, "which was it?"

"It was . . . three years ago that He talked about the three days," explains one.

"And where did He say this?" prompts Caiaphas.

"In the temple court—"

"In Galilee,"

The room crackles with tension. Caiaphas snarls at the two, dismissing them. Gathering up his robes, he takes the floor himself. For a few moments he paces before Jesus, who stands erect, hands bound in front of Him, waiting.

Suddenly the high priest stops. "Have you nothing to say? What about all this evidence against you?"

Jesus gazes at him steadfastly and remains silent. This infuriates Caiaphas further. "Tell us, then," he shouts, "are you Messiah, the Son of the Blessed One? I charge you by the living God," his voice rises, "tell us whether you are the Messiah, the Son of God!"

Jesus knows that to reply now will mean certain death, yet this is the one question He will answer. Every head is bent to listen. The courtroom is still in the flickering light.

"I am," says Jesus. He looks around the room with penetrating eyes. "And I tell all of you, in the future you will see the Son of Man seated at the right hand of Power, and coming in the clouds of heaven."

Caiaphas freezes. Everyone freezes. The vision of a future reality paralyzes them. Then, gathering himself, Caiaphas screams, "Blasphemy!" He turns to the council members. "Blasphemy!" A maniacal grimace contorts his face, and taking up the hem of his outer robe in two hands, he rips the fabric. "Why do we still need witnesses?" he rages. "You heard the blasphemy. What is your finding?"

The room erupts in shouts. The verdict is unanimous. Death.

Jesus is dragged and pushed by the guards, who enter fully into the spirit. "Is this the Messiah, then?" They crack blows between His shoulder blades and punch His kidneys. Everyone takes a shot. One man spits in His face then knees Him in the stomach. Even the council members spit on Him and slap at His head. Someone produces a rag and blindfolds Him. The crowd pummels Him with fists, rocking His head until blood flows freely and welts appear. "Prophesy to us, bastard! Who struck you?" Kicks and abuse rain on Him with satanic fury. His noble innocence fills them with hatred. They kick and shove Him out of the room and around the upper courtyard. In the courtyard below, the fireside crowd joins in the abuse.

During Jesus' trial by Caiaphas, Peter had attempted to join in the crowd's jests, but his commentary lacked feeling. Even in his act he occasionally could not restrain his sorrow and dismay at the turn of events. Hearing one of his comments, another perceptive servant woman said to those standing at the fire, "This fellow is one of them. He was with this Jesus of Nazareth."

A man asked, "Are you one of His disciples?"

Peter denied it with an oath. "By the God above, I am not," he protested angrily. "*I don't know the man!*" He looked stricken. This was his second denial. Peter could stand up to the point of a sword, but he could not bear the point of a finger.

Now, the farce of a trial has ended and a verdict reached; Jesus is being mauled. Peter watches from below. He can't believe what's happening and shouts out in alarm in spite of himself. Those standing around him hear the words. "You're one of them. You're Galilean," says one man. "Your accent gives you away."

Tearing his eyes from Jesus, Peter replies, "Man, I don't know what you're talking about!"

Another servant, a relative of Malchus, challenges him further. "Didn't I see you with Him in the olive grove?"

Out of fear, shame, and exasperation, Peter begins to curse. The disciples are known for their purity, so to justify his assumed character he roars and swears. In summary he bellows, "I don't know the man!" As he does so, the rooster shrilly crows. At that moment a path appears to the face of Jesus, who turns and looks at Peter. Peter's eyes meet Jesus'. In the Master's face, Peter reads deep pity, sorrow, and forgiveness, but no anger.

That look awakens Peter's memory. He recalls his boast that he would gladly go to prison and to death for his Lord. He remembers Jesus saying that Peter would deny Him three times that very night. The Master's strength and gentleness; His miracles of mercy; His patience with His thin-skinned, thickheaded disciples; His promise to pray for Peter so that he wouldn't be "sifted like wheat"—these memories crash upon him in an avalanche of emotion. As Peter looks, a fist smashes Jesus in the face and He crumples, reeling. Unable to stomach it any longer, Peter runs wildly into the darkness. Blinded by tears, lurching through the streets, he doesn't know or care where he's headed. He wanders until he finds himself in Gethsemane, where just a few hours earlier he had slept while his Master suffered. Now it is Peter who suffers. Crying bitterly, he falls on the spot where Jesus agonized and wishes he might die.

At sunrise the Sanhedrin reconvenes officially. The entire council hadn't been present at the night trial, and trials lawfully must be conducted during the day. Jesus has been kept in a holding cell where he's endured more insults and physical abuse from the guards. Now He is brought before the Sanhedrin again. They hope to hear some pronouncements that will be construed by the Romans as a serious political threat. Members ply Him with questions, but He remains silent.

"If you're the Messiah," they conclude, "tell us."

Jesus answers, "If I tell you, you won't believe me, and if I ask you a question, you won't answer me. But in the future, the Son of Man will sit beside almighty God,"

"So you are the Son of God?" they ask.

"As you say," He answers.

The trial is over. Again declared guilty, Jesus is being sentenced to death when a hoarse voice cries out, sending a thrill of terror to every onlooker. "He is innocent! Spare Him, O Caiaphas!" Through the startled throng presses a haggard, guilt-riddled Judas Iscariot. Rushing to the front, he wails, "I have sinned, for I have betrayed innocent blood." It's evident that the priests have bribed the disciple. The priests are embarrassed by this revelation; they pretend not to know the man.

"And what does that have to do with us?" one responds, attempting to divert the blame. "That's *your* problem."

Judas turns to Jesus, clutches His legs, and in torment begs Him to deliver Himself. Jesus' face is a grisly mass of purplish bruises, cuts, dried spittle, and blood. Jagged scratches line His neck. He looks down at Judas with love and sadness and says through swollen, bloody lips, "This is why I came into the world." A whisper of surprise runs through the assembly. The conviction takes hold of some that this man is more than mortal. *But if He's the Son of God, why doesn't He free Himself?*

Shrinking into himself, Judas appears to grow old before their eyes. Then, springing to his feet, he flings the thirty silver pieces on the floor in front of Caiaphas and sprints from the room. His despicable treachery leers at him in every face he sees. With dawning recognition of what he's done, he goes out and hangs himself—forever marked as one of history's most tragic stories.

After subjecting Him to more spitting and hitting, the officials propel Jesus to Pontius Pilate, the Roman governor in the district. Pilate has been sent an urgent early morning message that the Jewish leaders have seized a dangerous insurrectionist. The crowd stops outside the palace because they will not go in and be ceremonially defiled; entering a pagan house would preclude them from observing Passover. Flanked by two soldiers, the prisoner stands before the crowd with His back to it. Pilate comes out to them and asks, "What charges are you bringing against this man?"

The leaders realize that they can't substantiate the charges against Jesus. "If He weren't a criminal," they answer, "we would not be handing Him over to you." They hope that their importance will bring about a quick judgment.

But Pilate is in no mood for trifling. He has been called out early in the morning to meet with these people who won't enter his palace because he is "unclean." He declares, "Take Him yourselves and judge Him by your own law."

Sensing their disadvantage, the leaders change their approach. "As you know, we have no right to execute anyone. We found this man inciting our people to revolt, telling them that it's wrong to pay taxes to Caesar, and claiming to be Messiah, a king."

Pilate searches Jesus' face. As governor and judge, he has dealt with all types of criminals, but this one is different. Pilate finds no trace of guilt, no fear, no defiance. He recalls stories he has heard of miracles performed by a Jewish prophet and, his curiosity aroused, he asks Jesus, "Are you the king of the Jews?"

"Yes, it's as you say," Jesus replies.

Hearing these words, the mob screams more accusations, their fists raised in frenzied rage. The uproar is deafening.

"Aren't you going to respond to their charges?" Pilate shouts to Jesus. Jesus makes no reply. Pilate is astonished. Though waves of fury beat against this man, he stands unmoved. His whole being radiates tranquil innocence. Pilate enters the palace to escape the tumult, then summons Jesus for a private meeting.

"Now, the question again," says Pilate. "Are you the king of the Jews?"

Jesus searches Pilate's eyes. "Are you asking this for yourself, or because others have spoken to you about me?"

Pilate stiffens. "Am I a Jew?" he sneers. "It's your own people and the chief priests who have handed you over to me." He bends closer. "What have you done, anyway?"

"My kingdom is not of this world," Jesus states impassively. "If my kingdom were of this world, my followers would have fought to the death to prevent my arrest. But my kingdom is not of this kind."

"So you are a king."

"The reason for my coming into the world is to witness to the truth. Everyone who is of the truth hears my voice."

Pilate takes a step back. "What is truth?" he asks. He doesn't wait for an answer. The crowd is clamoring for him. Stepping outside, he raises his hands and announces, "I find no case against Him."

This infuriates the crowd. They threaten to report Pilate to the Roman government. "This man has stirred up people from Galilee to this place!" they yell. When Pilate hears that Jesus is from Galilee, he sends Jesus to Herod Antipas, the ruler of that province, who is staying in Jerusalem. Though Pilate and Herod have been enemies, after this day they become reconciled. The soldiers lead Jesus to Herod's judgment hall. With each transfer the eager crowd expands.

. . .

Herod is pleased to see Jesus; he has wanted to meet Him and see a miracle. *Oh, this will be good entertainment,* Herod thinks. He begins by asking Jesus some questions, but Jesus gives no answers. Taking advantage of the silence, the priests vehemently accuse Him. Herod charges them to be quiet and orders a few diseased and maimed people to be brought before the miracle worker. The priests shout, "No! He works miracles by Beelzebub!" They have plotted too many nights and waited too long for Him to go free now. The room is utter bedlam. "He's a traitor!" "He's a blasphemer!"

Turning to Jesus, Herod threatens, "I can have you killed, you know. Work for us a miracle, and then we'll believe." Jesus stands silent, ignoring the request. God doesn't perform for the sake of curiosity; He knows that shallow belief is short-lived. Sensationalism sells tickets but saves no souls. Besides, any healing now would be interpreted as merely an effort to save His own life. Jesus' refusal irritates Herod, and again he threatens Him: Herod had ordered John the Baptist's execution—he could order another. Jesus maintains His profound silence.

"Enough!" Herod says, turning angrily to the crowd. "He's an *imposter!* He deserves whatever He has coming." Herod pauses a moment, considering. "And because some think He should be king, let's dress Him as a king should look." Herod will have his entertainment, after all. An elegant robe is brought out and placed on Jesus' shoulders. Abuse rains on Him again as the crowd, bowing in mockery, spits in His face, spewing insults and curses. The soldiers and Herod join the sport. Jesus makes no complaint. Herod, who had wrestled with his conscience over John's death, sends the prisoner back to Pilate.

Pilate is not pleased to see Jesus again. The judge's seat has been moved outside the palace to a place called the Pavement, and from it Pilate speaks to the throbbing crowd. "You brought me this man as a political agitator, and I want you all to know that I have examined Him thoroughly on this point and I find Him innocent. Obviously Herod came to the same conclusion, since he sent Him back to us." The crowd begins screaming for Jesus' death. "As you can see, He's done nothing to deserve death!" Pilate responds. He's weighing his political alternatives. Palestine is a mere frontier province, a sandy patch on the eastern shore of the Mediterranean, and he has loftier aims. These religionists could make a promotion difficult if he doesn't grant a concession. "I will therefore have Him flogged," he says, "and let Him go."

Like chunks of meat to a school of piranha, his words madden the mob. Sensing the weakness of a judge who would whip an innocent man, they press their will upon Pilate, touching him on his most vulnerable spot: "This man wants to overthrow Caesar!" "You are no friend of Caesar's!" "Crucify Him!"

At that moment a servant hands Pilate a message from his wife. Pilate's face clouds with concern. The note reads, "Have nothing to do with that innocent man, for I have suffered a great deal today in a dream because of him." Her warning confuses him, as he yearns to take the expedient path. Looking at the battered Jew in a kingly robe, Pilate believes his wife. But the crowd hungers for this man's blood. Then Pilate is reminded of a custom at Passover for the governor to release one prisoner chosen by the people. Awaiting execution is Barabbas (literally, "son of the father"), who had been imprisoned for insurrection and murder. Believing the charges against Jesus baseless and spawned from envy, Pilate is confident that the crowd wouldn't choose to release the cruel criminal Barabbas. "Which one do you want me to release to you," Pilate asks, "Barabbas, or Jesus, who is called Messiah?"

With one voice the crowd roars, "Barabbas!"

Thinking they haven't understood the question, Pilate repeats, "Do you want me to release 'the king of the Jews'?"

"No!" hollers the pack. "Give us *Barabbas!*"

"What shall I do, then, with the one called Jesus?"

"Crucify Him!"

"Why? What crime has He committed?"

But they shout all the louder, "Crucify Him!" and continue chanting, "Crucify Him! *Crucify Him!*"

Pilate asks a third time, "Why? What evil has this man done? I haven't found anything that deserves death. I'll have Him flogged and then let Him go."

Louder and louder swells the chant, "Crucify Him!"

When Pilate sees that he's getting nowhere and that a riot is brewing, he commands that a basin of water be brought to him. In response to the death demands, Pilate publicly washes his hands, holds them up, dripping, and declares, "I am innocent of this man's blood. The responsibility is yours."

The mob yells back, "His blood will be on us and on our children!" The ill-fated response will be tragically misapplied for centuries to come.

Frustrated, Pilate orders his guards, "Release Barabbas to them."

Jesus is led away to be flogged. In a Roman flogging, a soldier grips a flagellum of braided leather thongs with metal balls woven into them. Pieces of sharp bone are tied at the end of each piece of leather. After the victim is stripped, the soldier whips him with fantastic torque, hitting the shoulders, the buttocks, and the backs of the legs. As the metal balls strike, they produce deep bruises that break open with repeated blows. The bone fragments shred skin, muscles, and ligaments until sinews and even the spine may lie exposed. Some strokes curl around the side of the torso and rip up the chest. The sufferer is sliced to quivering ribbons of bleeding flesh.

Jesus is taken to the Praetorium, an enclosed courtyard, where all the soldiers of the Syrian garrison are called together and the crime announced: "He says He's the king of the Jews!" Raucous laughter resounds through the courtyard. The king of the Jews is Caesar Tiberius, after all. Insults and jokes fly at this ragged king. A few soldiers hatch an idea to have more fun with this and receive permission to leave the premises. Jesus is untied from the rod and ropes and stripped of the mocking robe and all His clothes. A short stone column, about three feet tall, stands in the center of the courtyard with two large iron rings embedded in its base. Two soldiers bend Jesus naked over the top of the column and tie His wrists to the iron rings on the far side.

A heavily muscled soldier brandishing the flagellum stands motionless behind Jesus. Rising on his toes, the soldier brings the instrument down with whistling velocity. Metal and bone smash against the back and ribcage, and an involuntary moan escapes Jesus. Aiming a little lower, the soldier recoils and strikes again. He will put on a show for the admiring soldiers. The bone shards rip through skin and pull out bits of flesh. Jesus' lips move as though in prayer. Again and again the grunting soldier brings down the weapon with exacting force. After a few minutes the tribune steps in to check on the prisoner, making certain He isn't dead. Jesus is unconscious, so the two soldiers untie Him and another soldier tosses a bucket of cold water on Him to revive Him. The two soldiers pull Jesus to a rubbery-legged stance.

As He regains consciousness, trembling in spasms of fatigue and pain, Jesus squints into the sun. His clothes are returned and he is dressed. Those soldiers who had left earlier have returned with a purple cloak, a heavy reed stick, and a ringlet of woven thorns. They drape the cloak over His bleeding shoulders, place the stick scepter in His shivering hand, and crown Him with the dead thorns, which are usually stacked in piles and used for starting fires. After stepping back carefully to make certain their creation is "just right," the soldiers kneel, bow their heads, and shout, "Hail, king of the Jews! His majesty, the king of the Jews!" The laughing soldiers then step forward and spit in Jesus' face. One grabs the stick and taps down on the thorns until blood runs down Jesus' cheeks and catches in His beard. Jesus says nothing. Other soldiers on the perimeter begin taunting Jesus, sadistically slapping Him, backhanding Him, boxing Him, breaking the stick over His head. Jesus eventually sinks to His knees. The tribune calls for the fun to stop.

Though the soldiers block the view, the slowness of the returning procession indicates that the hunched prisoner is in poor condition. Pilate announces, "See, I'm bringing Him out to you now, but understand that I find no fault in Him." When the prisoner's contingent arrives, Pilate's face registers shock. He orders the soldiers to turn the prisoner around.

The crowd sucks in its collective breath. Jesus' features are almost indistinguishable. His face is a suffering mask. His eyes are nearly swollen shut, nose smashed, puffy cheeks mottled with welts, distended lips crusted with oozing blood. The purple robe and crown of thorns provide a grotesque contrast to His appearance. Some in the throng turn away from the revolting sight.

Hoping to appeal to their pity, Pilate says, "Behold the man!"

But the chief priests and religious officials are dead to pity. They pick up the chant again, "Crucify! Crucify!"

Pilate is incredulous. "You take Him and crucify Him, then! He's not guilty in my eyes."

One of the leaders insists, "We have a law, and according to that law He must die, because He claims to be the Son of God." When Pilate hears this, he blanches. *The Son of God?* Retreating inside the palace, he beckons the soldiers to bring the teetering prisoner to him.

"Where do you come from?" Pilate asks. Jesus looks straight ahead without responding. This both baffles and vexes Pilate. "Are you refusing to speak to me?" he exclaims. "Don't you realize that I have the power to set you free, and I have the power to crucify you?"

With effort Jesus moves His lips. "You would have no power over me except as it is handed to you from heaven. The one who delivered me to you carries the deeper guilt." Caiaphas is a representative of God and has received greater spiritual light—he should know better, as should all the religious leaders.

The crowd calls for Pilate. They distrust anyone's standing too long in the presence of Jesus. As Pilate steps into the warm sunlight, someone shouts, "If you let this man go, you are no friend of Caesar's! Anyone who claims to be a king is against Caesar!" This could be the fateful message that reaches Rome, Pilate knows. Sitting on the judge's seat, he brings Jesus out.

"Here is your king!" Pilate says to the people.

But the multitude howls, "Away with Him! Crucify Him!"

"Shall I crucify your king?"

Among the hubbub of voices the chief priests give a frightful answer: "We have no king but Caesar!"

Pilate looks at Jesus. In the vast, roiling sea of faces, His alone is peaceful. Again Pilate weighs his options, whether to follow his conscience or drift with the current of opinion, adhere to principle or cling to self-interest. He orders Jesus to be crucified. Jesus will die on Barabbas's cross. Pilate specifies a placard drawn up of Jesus' crime, written in Aramaic, Latin, and Greek, to be hung around the neck of the prisoner. The sign reads, "Jesus of Nazareth, the King of the Jews." Two convicted robbers are brought out of prison to join Jesus, whose robe is removed. The rods are removed from all three, but their hands are still tied. Each robber has his crime printed on a sign and hung around his neck. Two dozen soldiers surround them.

. . .

Wooden beams fall upon the three prisoners. Each beam makes up a horizontal crosspiece and is about six feet long; three upright poles stand embedded at the crucifixion site. The two robbers shoulder their beams and begin trudging through the narrow streets of Jerusalem toward Golgotha, the place of the skull. Weakened by His struggle in Gethsemane and the hours of abuse, His back unbendable and His shoulders a field of bloody furrows, Jesus shuffles slowly, pulling and dragging the heavy beam, bumping over the stones. Past houses and shops with entrances crammed with curious onlookers, the sorry spectacle proceeds. News of the trials and conviction of Jesus has spread throughout the city. A jeering crowd trails Jesus as He staggers along.

"He can bring back the dead and preach about His kingdom, but He can't lift a cross!"

"Maybe that cross *is* His kingdom!"

"Can you recognize your father in this crowd? It could be any one of us."

Jesus' slow progress irritates the soldiers, and they continually shove Him forward. A Roman centurion riding a horse keeps an eye on the straggler. As officer in charge, he must not allow the prisoner to die too soon. It isn't long, however, until the beam catches on a stone, a soldier shoves, and Jesus enters hypovolemic shock. He has lost too much blood. His eyes roll back in His head, and He collapses.

The centurion, realizing that this man cannot carry the beam farther, scans the people beyond the square of spears. No Jew will carry the defiling burden during Passover, but a non-Jew coming in from the fields, Simon, from North African Cyrene, has paused among the bystanders. The centurion points to him.

"You! Pick it up."

Simon looks around to see whom the officer is addressing. When Jesus revives, Simon is forced to shoulder the cross. He will later become a Christian, as will his sons. In the large crowd behind Jesus, along with the venomous rabble, a clot of women mourn for Him. They are not followers of His but are moved from human compassion. After a time, Jesus turns and says tenderly, "Women of Jerusalem, don't weep for me, but for you and your children. For the days are coming when you'll say, 'Lucky the women who never conceived, the wombs that never gave birth, the breasts that never produced milk.' People will plead with the mountains to fall on them and the hills to bury them. Because if this is what men do when the wood is green, what will they do when it is dry and fit for kindling?"

The crowd silences, sobered by the thought. In the throes of His misery Jesus continues to think of others. The centurion marvels. He has watched Jesus comport Himself with courage for hours, and now His love blooms like a blossom of sky-blue flax in the dead of winter. *What is it about this man?*

When the prisoners arrive at Golgotha they are offered wine with gall in it. Jesus tastes the bitter drink, often used as a sedative, and refuses it. He will need all His faculties in the journey ahead. A soldier leans a ladder against the middle pole and hammers at the top the sign defining Jesus' crime. The Jewish leaders who have trailed the death march glimpse the sign for the first time, fixed for the world to see. Offended, they dispatch a cadre of representatives for an immediate audience with Pilate.

"Don't write 'The King of the Jews,'" they protest, "but 'This man claimed to be King of the Jews.'"

Pilate is weary of their machinations, and he despises his own weakness in this matter. Clenching his jaw, he says, "What I have written, I have written."

The prisoners are stripped naked, their clothes tossed in front of the poles on which they will be crucified. Jesus' tunic is stiff with blood. His thorns have fallen off along the way. Each upright is eight feet high with a slanted notch at six feet for the crossbeam, enough room to accommodate any man whose legs are bent. Often criminals of the state are left on the wood to rot after death, their lower legs devoured by dogs and their bones picked clean by carrion birds. This day Jewish leaders don't want the desecrating corpses left up over the Passover Sabbath, especially as Jesus is a Jew.

Simon has dropped the beam. Soldiers fling the carpenter down against the rough wood, and two soldiers hold each of His arms flat. Jesus doesn't struggle. Instead He prays aloud, "Father, forgive them. They don't know what they're doing." The centurion hears the prayer and wonders again what manner of man this is. A fifth soldier holds a six-inch long square iron nail over the upper wrist, considered part of the hand (a nail in the palm would tear away). He hammers the heavy nail through Jesus' wrist deep into the wood, crushing His median nerve. Jesus cries out and writhes in agony.

Quickly the soldier drives a second spike through the other wrist. The beam is raised a few feet and a soldier lashes both arms tightly with a rope so the wrists can't pull through the nails. Four soldiers pick up the crossbeam and jam it into the notch of the upright. Jesus groans with the impact, and as His legs dangle the weight adds fire to His arms. Then the soldiers attend to the feet.

Crucifixions vary. In some crucifixions a type of seat is added to furnish a resting spot and thus lengthen the suffering, but the urgency lies now in quickening the process. Sometimes feet are nailed through the heels, with each foot on either side of the pole or turned sideways on top of each other.

After soldiers lift and hold Jesus' knees, the nailer presses the right foot over the left and drives a longer nail through both arches, anchoring the feet. Again

Jesus cries out and thrashes His head in distress. The torment of crucifixion has begun. As He slowly sags with more weight on His wrists, merciless arrows of pain shoot along the median nerve from the fingers through the arms. To relieve the anguish, He pushes Himself up, grating His raw back against the wood and placing full weight on the nail in His feet, feeling the searing of foot nerves and muscles being torn. Eventually the arms and legs tire and cramp in ferocious knots. With the cramps comes the inability to push Himself upward to breathe. The crucifixion position so stresses the diaphragm that He is in a constant position of inhaling. His lungs can't exhale. Jesus is drowning, suffocating. He fights to push Himself up again to draw a shuddering breath. This relentless cycle may continue for days, minute by endless minute. One word describes the pain: *excruciating*—literally, "out of the cross."

The four soldiers who held down His arms divide Jesus' pile of clothes among themselves. An undergarment is left over, a bit of a novelty in that it is seamless, woven in a single piece. "Don't tear it up," they agree. "Let's cast lots to see who wins it." As they have to wait anyway, they sit and throw dice for the undergarment. With the game of chance, another centuries-old prophecy of Scripture is confirmed, "They divided my garments among them, and for my clothes they cast lots."[5]

In front of the nailed, naked Jesus stands a mixed multitude of enemies and friends, priests and Zealots and pilgrims, the idle and the morbidly curious, His mother and other relatives, and His disciples. Some of them are crying, shaking their heads at the hideous injustice. Others, intoxicated with hate, shake their heads for a different reason.

"My, my. So! You can destroy the temple and build it in three days, can you? All right, step on down here and get started, Son of God. You're already dressed for work. Come on, come on, we don't have all day. Well, maybe you do . . ."

"This is interesting," the chief priests, scribes, and elders muse aloud. "He can save others, but He can't save Himself. Pitiful, isn't it? Here's the deal, King of Israel, come down now and we'll believe in you. Promise! If you're the Messiah, the chosen one of God, let God rescue you. Now, where is that faith of yours?"

The soldiers join in the harassment, strutting up and offering Him sour wine, saying, "If you're the king of the Jews, come have a drink with us. Save yourself. You can do it. Just try *real hard*."

One of the criminals, frantic with unendurable pain, heckles Him. "Aren't you the Messiah? Set yourself and us free, you God-forsaken worm."

---

5. See *Psalm* 22, verse 18.

The other thief had also maligned Jesus in the beginning, but as time wears on he sees the divine imprint on this man. After the angry robber hurls an insult, the other thief says, "Don't you fear God? You're getting the same thing He is, but we deserve it—He did nothing to deserve this." He pushes off his nail and sucks in a ragged breath to plead, "Jesus, remember me when you come into your kingdom!"

In the midst of His pain here's a gleam of consolation for Jesus—the first product of His sacrifice. Jesus pushes off His own nail and answers decisively, "Truly, I tell you today, you will be with me in paradise."

Near the cross stands His mother. She has suckled Him, cleaned Him, tickled and laughed with Him, taught Him, and watched Him grow into a man. God's man. Though she hasn't always understood Him, He's been an unfailing comfort and joy to her. Now, she's watching and enduring the most ruthless, humiliating ordeal imaginable, aimed at her boy. Yet not her boy. God's Son. She has known this might happen, as if she were the only one who heard when He spoke of His impending death. This scene is too horrible to believe, though. *If there's one person who doesn't deserve this . . .*

Jesus reads His mother's posture—downcast, in tears, bereft of hope, the light in her eye extinguished. He notes her standing next to John, His most trustworthy disciple. Fixing His sight on His mother, Jesus says, "Dear woman, there is your son." To John: "Here is your mother." A gift from the cross. In time she will know one more.

Grimacing, He pushes off again, bleeding and naked, arms stretched out like wings to the open air. *What manner of God is this?* He moans as His shoulders dislocate. ("My bones are out of joint," says the psalm.) His aching lungs steal another breath.

At noon a phalanx of leaden clouds scud across the land. An eerie mantle of darkness, murky as midnight, descends on Jerusalem, cloaking the disgrace of the Son. The darkness lasts three hours—the crowd thins considerably. At the center of the solid darkness the sin-bearer cannot sense His Father's presence. Pinned under humanity's free choice to separate from God, Jesus experiences the ultimate separation, the second death, the void of eternal nothingness. For three hours He strains desperately to see through the palpable darkness. Raising His battered, puffy face, He screams, "My God, My God, why have you forsaken Me?" There is no response.

Jesus must endure two more intolerable afflictions. As the pericardium slowly fills with serum and compresses the heart, a crushing pain squeezes His chest. With the loss of tissue fluids His heart struggles to pump heavy, thick, sluggish blood. Jesus tastes blood in His breath, on His tongue, in His nose. He knows now that He is mortally wounded. A death chill creeps through His body. His throat is dry, thistled and burred—He can't swallow. As He craves fluids to replace the lost blood volume, Jesus blurts, "I'm thirsty!" One of the soldiers sticks a sponge on a stalk of hyssop and dips into a deep jar filled with *posca,* a drink of sour wine, water, and beaten eggs. He lifts the dripping sponge to Jesus' cracked lips, then retreats to sit and wait.

A window opens in the dense, black clouds, and a brilliant shaft of sunlight illuminates Jesus. He feels an erratic hammering in His chest, a pounding tympani gone mad. His diaphragm is paralyzed, starving for oxygen, the effect of respiratory acidosis. The end is here. Quivering leg muscles strain to push off, to stand up on the brutal nail again—once more—and with His last breath He shouts: "*It is finished!* Father, into your hands I commit my spirit." And then, He dies.

The bruised, lacerated, swollen body sags on the cross. There will be no more pushes.

Darkness again envelops the scene. A low rumble builds to a wailing roar, wind screeches, thunder booms, lightning bolts lash. With the middle cross at the epicenter, a rock-splitting earthquake shakes the cowering spectators into heaps. Creation seems to be disintegrating. At this precise moment at the temple the innocent lamb representing the Messiah is before a priest for the evening sacrifice. As the priest raises his knife to slay the lamb, the temple quakes and his knife drops to the heaving floor. Suddenly the broad inner veil of the most holy place is torn with unimaginable force from top to bottom, exposing the secret space where the Shekinah glory of God has dwelt. Once a year the high priest enters this compartment to make atonement for the sins of the people. Now laid open to view, the space's sacred significance is annulled. No earthly power could rip the curtain from top to bottom. In the rumbling confusion the lamb escapes. The true sacrifice is already accomplished.

. . .

After the earthquake and the tempest are stilled at the crucifixion site and the sunlight returns, a remarkable admission surfaces. The centurion, having witnessed Jesus' patience, mercy, and authority, His shout of victory and the phenomena attending His death, stares at the supple form on the cross and announces, "Surely this righteous man was the Son of God!" Those words accompany the somber crowd that departs the scene. Not a few who had brayed, "Crucify Him!"—swept up with the bloodthirsty horde—walk home slowly, stinging with remorse.

An hour earlier, with the city steeped in darkness, a delegation of Jewish dignitaries had approached Pilate. They had asked for his consent to have the legs of the criminals broken to hasten their deaths, so their bodies could be taken down before Sabbath. Pilate had assented. He wanted the reminder of his cowardice buried as soon as possible. Two guards bring the order to the centurion.

The centurion passes along the order. A soldier picks up a stout board much like a bat. Positioning himself in a batting stance, he delivers a cracking blow at both of the shins of the first prisoner, who cries out and collapses in the throes of suffocating death, unable to raise himself. The soldier moves to the body of Jesus but doesn't swing at the legs. That one's already dead. He moves to the third prisoner, who watches in unspeakable horror. Professional soldiers recognize death, but the priests must make absolutely certain. They ask another soldier to deliver an undeniable death thrust to the one on the middle cross. Taking a step back, the soldier grips his spear with two hands and rams the point through the ribcage and lung, stopping in the heart. When the soldier pulls the spear away, clear pleural and pericardial effusion and blood flow out, indicating Jesus died of heart failure. Now the priests are satisfied. The troublemaker is forever silenced. Jesus fulfills prophesies even after His death, however. The Scriptures say of the Passover lamb, "They shall leave none of it until the morning, nor break a bone of it," and, "They shall look on Him whom they have pierced."[6]

As Sabbath approaches, the city quickly picks up after the earthquake. Joseph of Arimathea, a rich, prominent member of the Sanhedrin and a secret follower of Jesus, goes boldly before Pilate to ask for Jesus' body. Pilate is shocked to hear that the prisoner was dead before His legs were broken and summons the centurion to verify the report.

"He's dead, already?" Pilate asks.

The centurion looks stricken. "Yes," he replies, "it's true." Pilate studies the soldier. The centurion has never reacted like this before.

Pilate orders that the body be given to Joseph. On the way back to Golgotha, Joseph buys some linen cloths and meets up with Nicodemus, whose servants carry about seventy-five pounds of costly spices for the embalming. No one in Jerusalem could be shown more respect.

By the time the two arrive, the disciples have left the crucifixion scene. They couldn't watch anymore. John alone stands with Jesus' mother, Mary

---

6. *Numbers,* chapter 9, verse 12; *Exodus,* chapter 12, verse 46; *Psalms,* chapter 34, verse 20; and *Zachariah,* chapter 12, verse 10.

Magdalene, and other women who care for their lifeless Master. None of Jesus' relatives is in a position to claim His body for burial, for they are all Galileans and own no tombs in Jerusalem. They are astonished to see the two respected leaders, a Sadducee and a Pharisee, ministering to Jesus. Joseph tells them that he has a newly hewn tomb nearby, carved out of rock for him and his family, and that the body will be laid there. He is family.

The bodies of the two thieves have been taken down by the soldiers and transported to an unmarked burial ground. Joseph unrolls the linen shroud and spreads it on the ground while Nicodemus props the ladder against the spine of the cross. John supports the Master's mother, fragile in her grief. Nicodemus climbs, iron claw in hand, and uses the claw to untie the rope binding the arms. Then he wraps the rope around Jesus' chest, beneath the armpits and over the beam. He tosses the loose ends down to Joseph, who pulls them taut. Nicodemus climbs down the ladder and stands before the cross. Purchasing leverage on the crossbeam, with sudden, wrenching movements he applies the claw to pry a nail loose. The mutilated body of Jesus swings away and hangs from one arm. Another abrupt pull on the other side and the body slumps against the rope, supported by Joseph. It is gruesome work. The eyes are vacant, sightless. Nicodemus kneels under a curtain of hair matted with blood and frees the feet. The legs drop, and Nicodemus braces them with his left arm. John moves to help him.

"Okay," Nicodemus says at last, "lower Him."

As Joseph inches forward, the body descends. John cradles the torso, its arms flopping about his shoulders. The two men carry the corpse awkwardly to the shroud and lay Him down. They fold the unhinged arms across His chest. The skin is cold as clay. His thickening blood is rigid in the extremities. Some of the women help wash as much of the blood off the body as possible. Weeping in sympathy, they scrape wet cloths over His torn and crusted frame—temples, chest, arms, side, feet, back—and distribute Nicodemus' spices among the linens while assuring one another through tears that, yes, they will do even more for Him after Sabbath.

Joseph ties a strip of linen around the battered head, closing the mouth and lightly covering the eyes. The remainder of the face is left unwrapped for identification purposes. With the body bound and tucked for transfer to the nearby crypt, the three men hoist and carry the corpse, shuffling under the weight. Nicodemus and John bear on their robes the smeared blood of Jesus. Joseph, carrying the legs, crouches and enters the low tomb backward. They place the body gently on a stone shelf and straighten the limbs.

After the men exit, the women come in. The room smells of death. While the other women tenderly console and embrace her, His mother gazes at her child with inexpressible grief. *Is this His end? If only He hadn't come to Jerusalem.*

Outside, a large millstone rests in an inclined groove by the entrance. Once the women are out, Joseph rolls the stone downhill until it rocks into a notch to cover the opening. Removing the stone will require pushing it out of the notch, uphill—not an easy task. John prepares to take His mother home but first stops before Joseph and Nicodemus.

"Thank you," he says.

The two avert their eyes and nod. They will be with John much more in the future. For now, they have done what they can. After the others have left, Mary Magdalene and another Mary, sit down and stare numbly at the stone. Eventually they also get up in the gathering dusk and walk despondently to their homes, leaving the Master behind in the silent tomb.

It's been a long day. A very long day.

SATURDAY, APRIL 28, A.D. 31

On Sabbath, the chief priests and Pharisees pay Pontius Pilate another visit. Word has reached them that Nicodemus and Joseph are now with the disciples, to the point of placing the carpenter in Joseph's own crypt. The religious leaders are tired of surprises.

"Sir," they state respectfully, "we remember that when that imposter was alive He said, 'After three days I will rise again.' So give the order for the tomb to be closely guarded until the third day. Otherwise His disciples may come and steal the body and tell the people that He's been raised from the dead. Then we would be faced with a worse fraud than the first one."

"You have your own temple police," Pilate reminds them. "Go and make it as safe as you think necessary." Across the millstone at the tomb, the temple guards place cords, securing the ends to solid rock and sealing them with wax and the Roman seal. The stone can't be moved without breaking the seal. A guard of many soldiers is stationed to protect the grave from intruders. No possibility exists for anyone to steal the body now.

The disciples plod through the day in numbed shock—their hopes pulverized, their best friend gone. At the beginning of the week, they believed that He would ascend His throne. Now, He is dead? Dead. They carry no appetite for food or conversation. Peter in particular stays to himself. Swollen-eyed, heads down, they meet in the upper room where the Passover Feast had been held

Thursday night, hiding from the religious leaders, yet not caring whether they live or die. The Life has already left them. They wrap their arms around each other but remain inconsolable.

That day many who had traveled great distances arrive at the temple for an audience with the man who reportedly heals on Sabbath. The feeble and ailing inquire, "Who can tell us? Where is Jesus of Nazareth?" When told of the previous day's events, they are stupefied. *Could such a thing happen?* The priests turn back the lepers, their mournful cries of "Unclean, unclean!" resounding through Jerusalem. The deaf cannot hear their warnings. The lame hobble away. Families who have brought their dying sink under their disappointment. "Where is the light of the world?" ask the blind on this darkest of all days. There is no physician like the one who lies in Joseph's tomb.

The name of Jesus and the strange events of the past day are on the lips of thousands in the city. Reports of His mock trial and the inhumanity of His treatment circulate everywhere. Some recall the prophecies that point to the Messiah's suffering and death. Examining the sacrificial system and the sanctuary, they will be convinced that the actual Passover lamb has been sacrificed and prophecies fulfilled. Months ahead, on the day of Pentecost, thousands of believing unbelievers will decide to follow Jesus.

After sunset, Mary Magdalene, Mary the mother of James, and Salome buy and prepare spices and perfumes to anoint Jesus' body. That night all rest, except for the guards.

SUNDAY, APRIL 29, A.D. 31

The darkest hour is just before daybreak. In the stillness the soldiers' senses are bared and every sound magnified. They have talked through the night of the absurdity of this assignment, the overkill of it all, but as professionals they do their job. There comes the merest pop. Pebbles roll downhill. Limbs snap. The soldiers stand with weapons drawn, peeling back the darkness, ready for anything. The violence intensifies—jarring, reverberating, crashing, an earthquake knocks the men to their knees, where with inarticulate amazement they witness the appearance of a being unlike any they have seen. His countenance is like lightning, and his clothes glow with an unearthly light. The being exudes infinite power. This is no mortal warrior. The normally brave soldiers fall to the ground, chins scraping dirt. Cowering, they peer through trembling fingers as the drama unfolds.

The heavenly angel slides aside the sealing stone as if it were a leaf. With a voice like a hundred trumpets, he commands, "Son of God, come forth! Your Father calls you." The angel stands aside.

Out of the tomb steps Jesus. No crown of thorns punctures His head. No mocking robe covers His shoulders. No spikes pin His hands and feet. The man whom soldiers derided, slapped, whipped, and speared steps forth glorified, victorious over the last great enemy, death. The angel bows in adoration, and a choir of unseen voices bursts into rapturous singing. Jesus proclaims, "*I am the resurrection and the life!*" Then He walks out of sight.

The angel hops up on the stone and sits. This is their chance. The soldiers stagger to their feet and run, running to get away, running to find someone to tell, running until the feeling comes back. *What just happened?* They babble to one another. *Did you see . . . ?* Because they failed miserably at their assignment, some soldiers dread facing Caiaphas, but others see this as their only hope of avoiding punishment, possibly execution. The soldiers tell all, just as they experienced it, to the Hebrew leaders. "You felt the earthquake? We saw Him *alive!*" they exclaim. "It *was* the Son of God!"

The priests freeze in shock. Caiaphas tries to speak. His lips move, but he makes no sound. Their worst fears have come to pass. The impossible has happened. When they regain their composure, the priests and elders tell the soldiers to wait while they convene in another room.

"We cannot let this get out!" they fume. "What can we say?"

Evil never gives up. They decide that the best recourse is to pay the soldiers a bribe to circulate an implausible story. Meeting again with the soldiers, they say, "Hear this, now. You tell people, 'His disciples took Him during the night while we were asleep.' If your story reaches the governor, we'll cover for you to keep you out of trouble." Thinking they have little choice (who would believe the truth?), the soldiers gladly take the money to spread the lie. But the memory of that night will haunt them the rest of their lives.

However, by this time they are not the only ones who know. While it was still dark, Mary Magdalene had walked to the tomb to meet the other women and prepare Jesus' body. Feeling the earth shift, Mary braced herself against a tree and continued toward the grave. When she arrived, she saw that the stone had already been removed. Surprised, she looked into the tomb. It was empty. Leaving her spices, she ran off to tell the disciples the bad news.

The other women are walking toward the grave site from a different direction. Carrying the aromatic spices and perfumes, they leave just after sunrise. On the way they wonder, "Who will roll the stone from the entrance?" Arriving, they find spices lying by the entrance and the stone rolled away. Bending down, they step through the opening. The Master's body is gone. Instantly two angels, gleaming with blinding intensity, stand beside them. The terrified women fall to their knees, hiding their faces.

One of the angels says, "Don't be afraid." The women peek up. "You're looking for Jesus, who was crucified," the angel continues. "Why do you look for the living among the dead? He isn't here. He has risen! Remember what He said to you, that the Son of Man will be betrayed into the hands of sinful men, be crucified, and rise on the third day." Yes. They remember now. "Go quickly and tell the disciples—and Peter." The angels disappear. Shaken and bewildered, the women hurry from the tomb, afraid yet exploding with joy, and race to tell the disciples.

Meanwhile, Mary has located Peter and John, informing them of the grave robbery. The two abruptly take off running, with Mary following. John outsprints Peter to the tomb and stops at the entrance, puffing. He notices the burial linen lying on the floor. Peter rushes past John, ducking inside. Along with the linen shroud, the cloth strip that had been tied around Jesus' head is folded neatly in a corner. John steps in. They aren't certain what to make of it. Puzzled, dazed, and sweating, they leave, passing Mary standing mutely outside.

Mary is beside herself with grief. Sobbing, she leans against the tomb, her soul empty and aching. After weeping for a time, she stoops to look into the tomb. Where Jesus' body had been, one at the head and the other at the foot, sit two angels in white. One asks her, "Why are you crying?"

Seeing angels would normally give her pause, but Mary's anguish overwhelms her. "They took my Lord away," she chokes out, "and I don't know where they put Him." If this rich man's tomb is too honorable a burial site for Jesus, she will find another place for Him. She senses a presence and, glancing behind her, sees someone standing, waiting. Blinded by tears and hiccuping gasps, Mary assumes it must be the gardener.

"Why are you crying?" the man asks. "Who are you looking for?"

"Sir, if you have carried Him away, please tell me where you have put Him, and I'll take Him."

He utters her name. "Mary."

She turns and calls out, "Master!" Falling at His feet, she clutches Jesus as if He were a dream.

"Don't detain me now," He says gently, "for I haven't ascended to the Father." Jesus has lingered to stay with His friends, to watch the disciples running back and forth, and to see them react to the good news. Now He will go to the Father, for the Son wants to be certain that His sacrifice is accepted, that His forgiveness covers all. He sends Mary back to the others with the wondrous, astounding report that He's alive.

When Mary returns to the disciples, her face is radiant. "I have seen the Lord!" she exclaims. The other women are already at the house. They too have seen Him, as He appeared to them on the way back. Animated talk and laughter bubble over into happy squeals and hugs. The disciples witness the scene with sulking skepticism. Would the Master show Himself to women and not to them? A woman's testimony is not even acceptable in a court of law. The disciples know He was dead. Dead. They can't believe these women. This is ludicrous.

Later that day, two believers walking the seven miles from Jerusalem to the town of Emmaus discuss the events surrounding the weekend. A stranger joins them, but somehow they are kept from recognizing Him. When Jesus inquires about the topic, the two believers stand still, their eyes brimming with sadness. One of them, named Cleopas, says, "You must be the only person staying in Jerusalem who doesn't know what has happened there."

"What has happened?" asks Jesus.

They relate to the stranger the catastrophe of the past three days, of the death of the one they had hoped would be the redeemer of Israel and the curious emptiness at the tomb. Jesus listens patiently and then, instead of revealing Himself dramatically, explains how all the events fulfilled what Moses and the prophets had spoken in the Scriptures. The Teacher is interested in converting minds. Words of life and good sense and assurance flow from Him. He asks, "Didn't Messiah have to suffer all this before He entered His glory?"

As they approach Emmaus, the stranger appears to be continuing on His way, but the two travelers urge Him to lodge with them. "It's nearly evening," they point out. "Stay here." He accepts their friendly invitation. Jesus never forces His company on anyone; if they hadn't asked, the two would have missed His further companionship. At the table, Jesus takes the seat of honor reserved for guests, blesses and breaks the bread, and hands it to the two believers. Immediately Cleopas and his friend recognize the hands, those extraordinary hands, and their eyes are opened.

"Master!" they exclaim, and He vanishes. The two stare at each other in speechless wonder. Once they recover sufficiently, they compare impressions: "What about you? Did you feel your heart on fire when He was on the road explaining the Scriptures to us?" Then, bursting to tell what they've seen, who they've seen, they retrace the miles to Jerusalem. This time they make their way in the darkness by the rising moon, with steps so light the journey seems but a short hop.

For fear of the Jewish leaders, the doors of the house are locked. When the two are finally let in and the door barred behind them, they find the disciples gathered with other Jewish friends and believers. All are eating fish and bread and talking excitedly. "The Lord has risen indeed!" they tell the two. "He even appeared to Peter!" The two panting travelers turn to Peter, who nods, beaming.

"He appeared to us also!" they declare. The room hushes as they relate what happened on the road and how they recognized Him in the blessing of the bread. Suddenly, Jesus Himself appears among them. Startled cries erupt and many move back, eyes wide, believing they see a spirit.

Jesus says calmly, "Peace be with you." He realizes, though, that they are anything but peaceful. "Why are you frightened, and why do questions rise in your minds? Look at my hands and feet. It is I myself! Go ahead, touch me, for a spirit doesn't have flesh and bones." He shakes His head. "You are so slow to comprehend. The priests and rulers remembered that I said I would rise on the third day, but you wouldn't believe the women even when they saw me. You want more proof? Here." He shows exquisite hands, feet, and side. The former wounds are visible but completely healed on a body that glows with vitality. *He's incredibly alive.* Not a limp or bruise afflicts Him. While they're all staring, disbelieving for joy, He inquires with a mischievous smile, "Do you have anything here to eat?" Someone gives Him a piece of broiled fish and He eats it, watching the disciples and licking the tips of His fingers in delight.

The disciples stand around grinning like fools. They can't take their eyes off Him. *Who would have thought?*

God is surprising.

. . .

Yes, Jesus, yes. I am surprised also, and I find myself falling in love with You, who can neither stop living nor giving. Resurrect my hope. Burst the tawdry shackles of my near-life experience. Heal me, too. Send me forth with radiant joy. Astonish me with Your presence this moment.

~

Surely I would sooner have one say there was no such man as Plutarch than that there was one Plutarch who would eat his children as soon as they were born.

—PLUTARCH

It's easier to believe a lie that one has heard a thousand times than to believe a fact that no one has heard before.

—UNKNOWN

At the service tonight, the sermon topic will be, "What is hell?" Come early and listen to our choir practice.

—CHURCH BULLETIN ANNOUNCEMENT

I don't like being afraid. It scares me.

—MARGARET HOULIHAN, *M*A*S*H*

Death is just nature's way of telling you, "Hey, you're not alive anymore."

—BULL, *NIGHT COURT*

I'm not afraid of dying. I just don't want to be there when it happens.

—WOODY ALLEN

He was so grateful, and said I was the best friend old Jim ever had in the world, and the only one he's got now; and then I happened to look around and see that paper.

It was a close place. I took it up, and held it in my hand. I was a-trembling, because I'd got to decide, forever, betwixt two things, and I knowed it. I studied a minute, sort of holding my breath, and then says to myself:

"All right, then, I'll go to hell"—and tore it up.

—HUCKLEBERRY FINN

Death ends a life. But it doesn't end a relationship.

—HAL HOLBROOK

God loves each one of us, as if there was only one of us.

—AUGUSTINE

No longer do I call you servants, for the servant does not know what his master is doing; but I have called you friends.

—JESUS

~

8

THE WORST LIE EVER TOLD

AS A PLAYER on the Cal Poly San Luis Obispo basketball team, I survived numerous road trips in a long van nicknamed "the gray ghost." The hours traveling could have dragged, but bantering laughter and occasional actual conversations made the trips a welcome respite from college classes. For one away game my freshman year I sat in the back with Mike Record, a teammate who would later stand as a groomsman at my wedding.

Mike and I both came from homes with Christian traditions, though we weren't what we would call "believers." Immediately we delved into discussing life, lurching with the "ghost" over pertinent and impertinent terrain. What stands out twenty-eight years later is a complaint Mike voiced that day.

"You know," he said, "I don't think I could ever become a Christian. There's too much stuff that I can't really buy into."

"Yeah? Like what?" I prompted.

"Like hell. My sister woke up with nightmares after hearing about burning forever in hell. She screamed every night for two weeks. She couldn't go back to sleep, and I couldn't either. What good is that? I'm not interested in anything that's going to scare me that bad."

I agreed. Mike's comments remind me of Jonathan Edwards's Puritan classic, "Sinners in the Hands of an Angry God." This 1741 sermon provoked his listeners to weeping, shrieks, and groans. Edwards certainly had a flair for flaring imagery:

> The God that holds you over the pit of hell, much as one holds a spider or some loathsome insect over the fire, abhors you, and is dreadfully provoked: His wrath toward you burns like fire; He looks upon you as worthy of nothing else but to be cast into the fire. . . .
>
> O sinner! consider the fearful danger you are in; it is a great furnace of wrath, a wide and bottomless pit, full of the fire of wrath, that you are held over in the hand of that God, whose wrath is provoked and incensed as much against you, as against many of the damned in hell; you hang by a slender thread, with the flames of divine wrath flashing about it and ready every

moment to singe it and burn it asunder; and you have no interest in any Mediator, and nothing to lay hold of to save yourself, nothing to keep off the flames of wrath, nothing of your own, nothing that you have ever done, nothing that you can do, to induce God to spare you one moment.

Throughout the sermon God is pictured as a psychotic sadist who takes immense delight in torturing us forever. Edwards concludes with an appeal to "awake and fly from the wrath to come." Many listeners converted on the spot to receive the benefits of eternal fire insurance.[1]

Puritan children endured frightful blasts of hellish rhetoric as well. A collection called "Divine Songs for Children" contains the bleak lyrics, "There is a dreadful Hell/And everlasting Pains,/There Sinners must with Devils dwell/In Darkness, Fire, and Chains." Hardly a soothing lullaby.

My earliest memories are of receiving burns, once from an iron on my palm, and again from a floor heater on a bare sole. A serious burn sears my threshold like no other pain. In my spiritual journey, I reached the conclusion that if God would fry people forever, keeping them alive to sauté without hope or relief, while His chosen children enjoy the blissful pleasures of paradise, I'd have nothing to do with that God. I wouldn't fry an earthworm for a week. But God would preserve people—grandmothers and grandfathers, Aunt Sophie and Uncle Mel, brothers and sisters—to suffer infinite billions of eons of unbelievable agony? And, in a hideous twist, He does it out of *love*.

No, thanks, I decided. If that's God, I won't serve Him. If that's love, I don't want it. I still feel that way.

So I stayed clear of Christianity, believing in "Jesus" but not really "believing" in the Bible. Today I see God was exhorting me during my time of unbelief, "Good for you, Chris. Reject the lie. Now keep searching, keep longing, keep listening for me."

Of all the evil people in history—King Ahaz, Herodias, Genghis Khan, Josef Stalin, Idi Amin, Pol Pot—none is *nearly* as brutal and inhumane as God the Father, if we believe the scenario painted by many Christians. While Stalin and Pol Pot were satisfied with the deaths of their enemies, God has, it seems, tortured millions of people for thousands of years in the liquid fires of hell, hurling new victims daily into the cauldron of no escape. Moreover, God rewards Satan by hiring him as head chef in charge of the cooking. Incredibly, *Christians* are spreading this most heinous lie about God that can be conceived. How did this happen?

---

1. Of Edwards's nearly five hundred published sermons, only one deals with this fearsome hell.

From our cradles we reach upward yearning for fairness, rooting for the underdog, cheering with the final payback. But this life is unfair; some people obviously get away with too much. Thus cultures throughout history have developed systems of reward and punishment in afterlife. According to the ancient Greeks, the damned spend eternity facedown in a swamp of mud and frogs. For Jewish believers, Sheol is a dark underworld, and Gehenna is named for a garbage dump outside Jerusalem where trash and animal carcasses were flung into fires. One medieval Catholic order called the Redemptorists describes hell dwellers "swimming in fire like a fish in water." Puritans fanned images of hell to white heat. During the 1700s scientists theorized that hell is located on the sun or aboard a comet.

A story circulating in churches during the 1980s reported that "scientists" looking for oil in Siberia drilled down nine miles and broke through the earth's crust into a place that is 2,000° F. Lowering microphones into the hole, they heard human voices wailing in hell.[2] Charles Spurgeon alleges, "A lie travels around the world while Truth is putting on her boots." I'm reminded of the tale of two men meeting at a bank.

"I heard you won $40,000 in the oil business," one fellow exclaims. "Congratulations!"

The other man regards him balefully. "It was $20,000. It was in gold. It wasn't me—it was my brother. And he lost it."

"Oh, well," shrugs the first man. "Close enough."

The false dogma of everlasting suffering in hell has produced millions of honest skeptics and unbelievers. This one tenet has dissuaded more people from loving God than any other teaching. In his autobiography, Charles Darwin reflects that he was "very unwilling to give up" his hold on Christianity, but disbelief crept over him. He warrants, "I can hardly see how anyone ought to wish Christianity to be true; for, if so, the plain language of the text seems to show that the men who do not believe—and this would include my father, brother, and almost all my best friends—will be everlastingly punished. And this is a damnable doctrine."

THE LIMITS OF FEAR

Motive matters. I like the story of a man who meets an angel walking down a road. The angel carries a bucket of water in one hand and a torch in the other.

---

2. Never mind how a microphone could withstand that heat, or where you could locate an extension cord nine miles long. The story was consequently exposed as a hoax.

"Why are you carrying that torch and water?" the man inquires.

The angel replies, "The water is to put out the flames of hell, and the torch is to burn down the castles of heaven. Then we'll see who really loves God."

Fear *is* an effective short-term motivator, as we can all attest. We don't get into trouble in school if we're afraid of what will happen at home as a result. As we grow older, we react less to parents and more to law enforcement officers and employers, fearing our freedoms will be curtailed, our reputations sullied, our paychecks stopped.

What fear lacks is staying power. As a long-term motivator, fear is impotent. Once we believe we won't get caught, or we don't care if we do, our loyalty and obedience evaporate. Rebellion takes root like a ropy weed. When Mom and Dad are out of sight, the kids light up cigarettes behind the fence. Adults turn to more sophisticated evasions—we falsify tax figures and call in "sick." At any age, people lie to avoid facing the feared music.

A crisis of fear enlightened me during my drivers' education class at Chaffey High School in Ontario, California. As a scared young driver under the guidance of our instructor, Mr. Heald, I was steering down Mt. Baldy and braking cautiously with every curve. Eventually Mr. Heald advised, "You don't have to brake in this section. Just let the car go."

I'm driving with a madman, I thought, and I continued braking. After all, the lives of two fellow students grimly clutching their knees in the backseat mattered to me. I felt responsible. I was also mindful of careening through the guardrail and sailing over the cliff. Following two more brake taps, Mr. Heald calmly spoke again.

"If you touch the brake again before I say you can, I'm going to flunk you."

Ahhh! We're all gonna die! I clutched the wheel in a death grip and focused all my energies on the pavement, preparing to negotiate turns at 90 miles an hour. I really didn't want to die, but at that time in earth's history, flunking was worse than death. *Farewell, world . . .*

We glided through the next six curves. I barely had to budge the wheel. "Okay," Mr. Heald said as we approached a steeper section, "you can brake now."

After that I braked only when necessary. Many times since, when following a fitful braker down a mountain, have I wished that Mr. Heald and his absolutes could sit in the front seat with everyone. For all its "educational" benefits, fear is irrational. Mark Twain points out that a cat will never sit twice on a hot stove, but it will also never again sit on a cold one.

Fear can also create unnecessary pain. One week before his seventh birthday, Geoffrey wanted to learn how to dive off the diving board at Uncle Marty's pool. I explained that he should first curl into a ball and roll in. Time and again Geoff poised with toes dripping off the edge of the board, crouched, leaned toward the water, and opened like a jack-knife to splat on his belly. It couldn't have felt good.

"Geoff, you're opening up," I explained. "Just roll in. It won't hurt as much, either."

Lean. *Splat.* Lean. *Splat.* Seventeen or more tries later, we decided to wait for another day. He couldn't bring himself to stop "braking."[3] In life, whether meeting new people or engaging new ideas, we must work from a platform of trust and confidence. Otherwise, as Dr. Robert Anthony contends, "the thing we run from is the thing we run to," and we live our lives landing directly on our worst fears.

Parenting provides such profound insights into God's dealings with us. We have to wonder when we hear of the lie of eternal torture whether we believe God is a worse parent than we are. Would you have your children be afraid of you?

What happens when we fear God? Compliance that arises from terror will not, cannot last. We'll live cautious, resentful lives, hiding behind fences and braking with every curve, belly flopping on dives and wondering all the while, *Why does God make this so difficult?* When the Bible says, "The fear of the Lord is the beginning of wisdom," it speaks of the healthy respect we extend to any terrific power, be it electricity, a lioness, or a locomotive. God deserves this respect. But note that this respect is the *beginning* of wisdom. *Beyond* respect extends the infinite reaches of trusting love—wisdom's destination.

One constant appears whenever God through His angels or the Son approaches humankind. We find it in Luke's account of the birth of the Christ child as the angel says, "Do not be afraid, Mary." Zechariah, father of John the Baptist, is startled by an angel, who then urges, "Do not be afraid." An angel calms the shepherds: "Be not afraid, for I bring you good news of a great joy."

Jesus Himself assures, "Let not your hearts be troubled, neither let them be afraid." As He walks on the water toward the disciples (a fearful sight!), He affirms, "It is I; do not be afraid." Elsewhere He comforts, "Fear not, little flock, for it is your Father's good pleasure to give you the kingdom." After His resurrection, an angel says to the women seeking Jesus' body, "Do not be afraid," and Jesus appears and reassures, "Do not be afraid." When He materializes in the disciples' midst, he twice declares, "Peace be with you."

Friendship without fear is a maturing theme in interacting with God.

---

3. The following day he dove successfully without his all-important teacher.

Apparently God desires personal, authentic interaction, as does any sincere friend. God's *best* friends fearlessly ask Him hard questions. Abraham asks God hard questions about Sodom's fate. Moses inquires about God's fickle people. Job buzzes like an angry hornet with questions. David in the psalms rants and wonders about God's justice. After their brother dies, Martha and Mary, two of Jesus' closest friends, question why He did not arrive sooner to save Lazarus. Christ's disciples continually question Him, sometimes to exasperating lengths. On the cross Jesus Himself, astounded by the enormity of sin, asks of the Father, "Why have you forsaken me?" The God who created in us a spirit of inquiry welcomes our questions.

Respect is, of course, the basis for any friendship, and friendship based on trust is strongest. Yet we can trust others to act consistently and still despise them. Even cosmic terrorism that is dependable will not elicit love. God seems to desire to woo us fearlessly to His side. Paul of Tarsus speaks to this with his question to the Romans, "Do you not know that God's kindness is meant to lead you to repentance?"[4] (They didn't, apparently.) Jesus died to "deliver all those who through fear of death were subject to lifelong bondage."[5] John concludes in his first biblical letter, "There is no fear in love, but perfect love casts out fear."

THE BIBLE AND HELL

Imagine that you're looking through the owner's manual of your car for information on how to drive. You decide to flip through the pages, gleaning information from selected passages. Here's what you learn from your spotty search:[6]

- Keep your foot on the brake pedal
- The most important thing to remember is to avoid pressing down on the accelerator
- If you do, the tires may explode and injure a passenger or bystander

Obviously, you conclude, this car a deathtrap, and the car's designers are morons. Why would anyone want to drive a car like this? You decide to sell it for scrap metal.

---

4. *Romans,* Chapter 2.
5. *Hebrews,* chapter 2.
6. These quotes are from our car's owner's manual.

Unfortunately, this is how many people read the Bible; here a little, there a little, until at last from force of "logic" they're led to scrap this nonsensical, dangerous Christianity. "It just doesn't work." Like any owner's manual, the Bible is written for mature readers. The *context* of the manual's statements provides a fuller, clearer view.

"After you start the engine, let it idle for a few seconds. *Keep your foot on the brake pedal* and put the gearshift lever in gear. . . .

"When starting your vehicle's fuel-injected engine, *the most important thing to remember is to avoid pressing down on the accelerator.* Use the accelerator only when you have problems getting your vehicle started. . . .

"Extreme acceleration [on slick roads] can cause the front wheels to spin. Do not spin the wheels at over 35 mph. *If you do, the tires may explode and injure a passenger or bystander.*"[7]

With selective editing, it's possible to make anything and anyone look foolish. Making nearly anything look *good* is also achievable. After watching an awful movie, I've sometimes wondered if the reviewers' raves could have been taken out of context:

"Magnificent!" ["What a magnificent waste of money this is!"]

"Deeply moving." ["As my feet slid along the slimy floor under my seat, I found my legs deeply moving during much of the film."]

"One of the year's best!" ["Looking for a sleep enhancer? This is one of the year's best!"]

"Two thumbs up!" ["The best way to experience this movie is to put two thumbs up, stick them in your ears, and cover your eyes with your fingers!"]

Whenever we examine any advice or description, we do well to consider its context. An erratic search is not good enough, especially when reading the library of the Bible, though some have resorted to this approach to find evidence for eternal torture. Here are the most common references and their contexts.

1. *The parable of the rich man and Lazarus.* The kernel of this account lies in the description of a rich man who died and "in Hades, being in torment, he lifted up his eyes, and saw Abraham far off and Lazarus in his bosom. And he called out, 'Father Abraham, have mercy upon me, and send Lazarus to dip the end of his finger in water and cool my tongue; for I am in anguish in this flame.'"[8]

---

7. This one I still wonder about.
8. *Luke,* chapter 16.

Taking this parable literally produces a number of problems. Are the "dead in hell" really able to communicate with those in heaven? Wouldn't that remove more than a smidgen of the peace from paradise? Is Abraham (or anyone else) able to assist the damned?

Jesus uses a well-known story to illustrate a point. This story was circulating among the Pharisees at that time, as recorded in *Josephus' Discourses to the Greeks Concerning Hades*. Using their own imagery, Jesus warns the Pharisees that misusing wealth should bring forth true repentance and concludes that signs and wonders are not enough to cause people to change their lives, because "if they do not hear Moses and the prophets, neither will they be convinced if some one should rise from the dead." By brilliant design Jesus ends with this line, for both He and a friend named Lazarus would later do just that—rise from the dead—with foreseeable results.

2. *Unquenchable fire.* This expression is found twice in the Bible and refers to the fact that no one will be able to put out the fire. *The fire will run its course.* Firefighters today come up against unquenchable fires—too hot to douse—which they must let consume the building or forest. But these unquenchable fires are out once the fuel has burned.

3. *Eternal fire.* The New Testament book of *Jude* describes the ancient cities of Sodom and Gomorrah and surrounding cities, as receiving a "punishment of eternal fire."[9] Sodom and Gomorrah were burned to the ground thousands of years ago. Do these cities continue to burn today? No. Peter's second letter in the Bible points out that the cities turned "to ashes." "Eternal fire" refers to the *effect* of the fire. The effect lasts for eternity.

4. *Everlasting punishment.*[10] Notice that this phrase is not "everlasting punish*ing*." What possible purpose would be served by unending torment? The punishment—separation from God—lasts forever. It is a done deal. No second chances.

5. *For ever and ever.* King David says, "The LORD God of Israel chose me from all my father's house to be king over Israel for ever." In many instances of the Bible, "for ever" means "as long as life shall last."[11] Jonah depicts himself as being swallowed "for ever," which amounted to three

---

9. Often overlooked by evangelicals is the Bible's appraisal of a primary sin of Sodom, that "she and her daughters had pride, surfeit of food, and prosperous ease, but did not aid the poor and needy" (*Ezekiel*, chapter 16, verse 49).

10. Or "everlasting destruction."

11. *Revelation* describes smoke that goes up "forever and ever." How else can you illustrate "permanence" in vision?

days and three nights. The word *forever* is used fifty-six times in connection with things that have already ended.

The words "eternal torment" do not appear in the Bible. Keeping people alive to suffer for eternity would require a vicious, constant miracle from God, one that is totally incompatible with His character.

THE GRATEFUL DEAD

A basic problem with many ideas of hell arises from perceptions of what happens when we die. Knowing our flickering mortality can be snuffed out at any second does create an awareness of beyond, of fleeting being. A professional football lineman, a massive mountain of a man, out mowing his front yard one summer afternoon, dies instantly when a car swerves through a hedge and across the freshly mown lawn. Or we hear of a rogue fire, a gas leak, a cancerous cell gone mad. A princess crushed. Open any major newspaper and you will likely find at least twenty people surprised by death. We wonder why and how we should perform our own parts before the play is canceled. We are as curious as the boy who wrote, "Dear God: What is it like when you die? Nobody will tell me. I just want to know. I don't want to do it. Your friend, Mike."

At this point I ask you to consider some concepts that generate wide division even among Christians. In a sense, the question of what happens to people after they die is an impractical concern in this life. What will happen will happen. However, as it affects our view of God, the concern grows in importance. If our beliefs about afterlife lead us to hate the Creator, to distrust Him as arbitrary, severe, or undependable, we enter a perilous country.

One basis for the traditional view of the nature of hell is the commonly held assumption that our souls are separate from our bodies and are naturally immortal.[12] If this is true, then these souls have to go *somewhere* at death. Belief in immortality of the soul is understandable, essentially because we want to be in control of eternity. In *Four Views on Hell,* Clark Pinnock writes, "Immortality is a gift God offers us in the gospel, not an inalienable possession. The soul is not an immortal substance that has to be placed somewhere if it rejects God."

I don't know how to enter this discussion any other way than by looking at the Bible to unveil the nature of life and death. Most people miss the alternatives in the most famous verse of the New Testament: "God so loved the world

---

12. Often this is the only view heard. It is at least time for a fresh look at the issue.

that he gave his only Son, that whoever believes in him should not perish but have everlasting life." Notice the choices: *perish* or *live*. This is a matter of life or death, not life or agony. The Bible says that the wages of sin is death, not pain.

The view of an eternal soul, separate from the body, did not derive from a biblical tradition. The Hebrews did not espouse it.[13] The Greeks viewed the soul as indestructible; in classic Greek thought, the spiritual realm is superior to the physical realm. In *Phaedo*, Plato reports Socrates as reasoning that "when death attacks a man, the mortal portion of him may be supposed to die, but the immortal goes out of the way of death and is preserved safe and sound." Herodotus writes that the Egyptians were the first "to teach that the human soul is immortal." Actually, the earliest recorded instance is in Satan's first earthly lie hissed through the serpent to Eve: "You will not die."

Genesis records that God "formed man of dust from the ground, and breathed into his nostrils the breath of life; and man became a living being." In the Bible, dust and breath equals life; body plus breath equals a soul. The soul does not exist apart from the body. The word *being* is *nephesh*, also translated in the Bible as "soul," a breathing creature. Richard J. Foster comments, "I do not have a spirit: I am a spirit. Likewise, I do not have a body: I am a body." Nearly 1,700 times in the Bible we can find the word for "soul" or "spirit." Never is the word *immortal* attached to it. This we find puzzling, of course. "When I erase a word, where does it go?" asks comedian Stephen Wright. When we turn off a light bulb, where does the light go? They don't go to heaven or hell. They simply cease to exist.

Seeing people as breathing souls enables us to treat everyone with dignity and respect, whether we regard them as lazy, arrogant, racist, or insane. With this understanding, we view persons of the opposite sex, no matter how scantily clad or physically alluring, as *human souls*—beings of infinite value—never as objects or body parts to be used. Employers who treat employees like machines are engaging in a soul-destroying practice. Subjecting our bodies to unhealthy habits—whether to stress, chemicals, or gossip—affects our souls. It may be argued that the false dichotomy of "secular and sacred" comes from the misunderstanding of the holistic nature of body and soul, for all of life is sacred.

What happens when life ends? It's customary to speak of people after they die as being in "a better place now." After an important victory for his team, a famous sports figure said of his recently departed father, "I know he's looking down on me and smiling." While the sentiment is sincere, popular, and appro-

---

13. The rich man and Lazarus parable and a few obscure texts do not establish an ample rationale.

priately unchallenged at the time spoken, we need to ask some hard questions about this view. Is he also "looking down on you" when you're depressed? Is he watching you when you struggle and fall and cry hot tears of shame? Does he see his grandchildren go through the agonies of growing up? Does he "look down" on all those who suffer in quiet despair? What about the two million child prostitutes around the globe being tortured? And the thirty-three children who will starve to death in the next minute—can he see them also? I suppose we could say, "Oh, he sees only the good things." But might he ever *wonder* about what he's not seeing? Might he worry some? Or does God perform a celestial operation to make us selectively blind and deaf? Is this way better than no consciousness until the Resurrection?

When Mother Teresa died, I mourned a holy presence gone from our world. On TV news an acquaintance of hers said, "She can rest now." Less than a minute later a local priest appeared on the screen to lament her death and to point out the "bright side" of her passing. "We have her now in heaven," he said, "to intercede in our behalf." When I heard that, I thought, *That's not much of a rest, is it?* Not only does Mother Teresa have to "intercede" for us, but she also must witness anew the brutalities and sufferings that broke her heart on earth, apparently without a respite.

God's way is much better. Mother Teresa rests in her grave, awaiting the Resurrection. She exists in the memory of God, and she will awake to a world liberated from the plague of lingering death. The hands that cradled the leprous heads of Calcutta's poorest will still serve others, but in the light of everlasting joy and peace. I look forward to personally saying "Thank you" to her. She has cradled my head as well, and the beaten, bleeding head of my Master.

Death is often referred to in the Bible as a sleep.[14] In one of the great passages of literature, Paul of Tarsus writes to the church in Corinth:

> Lo! I tell you a mystery. We shall not all sleep, but we shall all be changed, in a moment, in the twinkling of an eye, at the last trumpet. For the trumpet will sound, and the dead will be raised imperishable, and we shall be changed. For this perishable nature must put on the imperishable, and this mortal nature must put on immortality. When the perishable puts on the imperishable, and the mortal puts on immortality, then shall come to pass the saying that is written:

---

14. The doctrine discussed here is often dismissed under the label "soul sleep." Unfortunately, labeling can keep us from looking more deeply into any matter.

"Death is swallowed up in victory."
"O death, where is thy victory?
O death, where is thy sting?"

Note that our nature is called "this mortal nature." See also that the dead are raised, not lowered from heaven. Elsewhere Paul asserts that "since we believe that Jesus died and rose again, even so, through Jesus, God will bring with him those who have fallen asleep." When His close friend Lazarus dies, Jesus speaks to His disciples: "'Our friend Lazarus has fallen asleep, but I go to awake him out of sleep.' The disciples said to him, 'Lord, if he has fallen asleep, he will recover.' Now Jesus had spoken of his death, but they thought that he meant taking rest in sleep. Then Jesus told them plainly, 'Lazarus is dead.'"

Just before He raises Lazarus, Jesus says, "I am the resurrection and the life; he who believes in me, though he die, yet shall he live." Everyone, believers too, dies a biological death. The book of *Acts* states that the patriarch David "both died and was buried," but that "David did not ascend into the heavens."[15] Later, the Bible describes God as the one "who alone has immortality."[16]

Death is like a deep, dreamless sleep. When we awaken, we think, *Has time passed? It seems only a moment ago.* Even for insomniacs, there's no escaping this sleep. Harry Houdini, the great escape artist, couldn't do it. Evangelist Aimee Semple McPherson was buried with a connected, live telephone in her coffin, but no one has received a call from her—not even "collect."

Yet we know this sleep is the enemy. We do not "go gently into that good night," because that "good night" was never meant to darken our lives. The dead are neither in heaven, nor wandering the earth, nor agonizing in flames. When Jesus raised Lazarus after he was dead and stinking four days, Lazarus did not emerge bubbling about the wonders of heaven. Solomon concluded, "The living know that they will die, but the dead know nothing."[17]

At the Crucifixion, to the dying thief who says, "Jesus, remember me when you come into your kingdom," Jesus promises, "Truly, I say to you today, you will be with me in Paradise." In the original Bible text, there was no punctuation between words. Some English translations place a comma before "today," but this couldn't be the case. Christ didn't go to heaven on the day He died; on Sunday morning, days later, He asks Mary not to detain Him "for I have not

---

15. The Bible records that Moses and Elijah were taken up to heaven in their physical bodies.

16. *First Letter to Timothy,* chapter 6.

17. *Ecclesiastes,* chapter 9. The *Psalms* state, "The dead do not praise the LORD, nor do any that go down into silence," and "When his breath departs he returns to his earth; on that very day his plans perish" (115 and 146).

yet ascended to the Father." Jesus proclaims on *this* day, when I seem to be nothing, I say to you that we will be in Paradise together. That's also why Jesus says, "I will come again and will take you to myself, that where I am you may be also."

The question of the nearness of that Second Coming has perplexed more than a few seekers. Jesus says three times in the final Bible chapter, "Behold, I am coming soon," but those words were written 1,900 years ago—at least sixty generations ago. Somehow that doesn't sound *soon* to me. I've heard people say that it's soon in the context of eternity, but any length of time is soon in that context. Common wisdom dictates, "How long a minute is depends on which side of the bathroom door you're on." Does a similar relativity hold true for heaven's door?

Everyone understands the proximity and suddenness of death. *Soon* is the beat after my next heartbeat. If we understand the concept, after a person dies Christ comes a blink—"a twinkling of an eye"—later. Soon enough. Paul of Tarsus reminds us, "The Lord is not slow about his promise as some count slowness, but is forbearing toward you, not wishing that any should perish, but that all should reach repentance. But the day of the Lord will come like a thief, and then the heavens will pass away with a loud noise, and the elements will be dissolved with fire, and the earth and the works that are upon it will be burned up."

This fire is kindled by the brightness of His coming, and people perish "because they refused to love the truth and so be saved."[18] The saved are raised "incorruptible," materializing from their graves or the briny depths of the ocean, or from where they were incinerated to shadows by nuclear winds. For now they are held in the mind of God. Otherwise, we are left with a raft of unanswerable questions: Why should the dead have to deal with knowledge of the sufferings on earth? Why would God send people back to be raised again? And why will God have a Resurrection?

Again, whether after death people rest in the grave or go someplace else is not a major matter–unless some must then go to shrieking, unending torment. That is a major matter.

GOD'S WRATH

Giving up the lie of never-ending torture also brings up a potential danger. In finding our God approachable, we run the risk of worshiping a kind of namby-pamby Being, a simpering God who wheedles and whines, God Lite with no

---

18. *Second Letter to the Thessalonians*, chapter 2, verse 10.

sharp edges and less accountability.[19] An Eternal Doormat does not rouse respect nor beckon lasting love. By contrast, in *The Silver Chair,* C. S. Lewis's Aslan the Lion represents another God:

> "Are you not thirsty?" said the Lion.
>
> "I'm dying of thirst," said Jill.
>
> "Then drink," said the Lion.
>
> "May I—could I—would you mind going away while I do?" said Jill.
>
> The Lion answered this only by a look and a very low growl. . . .
>
> "I daren't come and drink," said Jill.
>
> "Then you will die of thirst," said the Lion.
>
> "Oh dear!" said Jill, coming another step nearer. "I suppose I must go and look for another stream then."
>
> "There is no other stream," said the Lion.

God cares enough to mean business. Life matters. Peace matters. Love matters. When we read in the Bible of God's wrath, we must put it into context as well. There is a righteous wrath of God.

God gets wrathful over what angers all rational beings—dying children, selfish cruelty, hopeless injustice. The difference with God is that He knows the underlying cause: separation from Him. God longs to heal us, and like any competent doctor He refuses to treat solely the symptoms. A heart attack isn't treated with antiseptic spray and bandages. When a heart is consumed by disease—arteries blocked, atrium leaking, valves corroded—a complete heart transplant is needed.

The first chapter of *Romans* explains what God does when He is wrathful, "For the wrath of God is revealed from heaven against all ungodliness and wickedness of men who by their wickedness suppress the truth." How is the wrath revealed?

"God gave them up in the lusts of their hearts to impurity" (v. 24).

"God gave them up to dishonorable passions" (v. 26).

"God gave them up to a base mind and to improper conduct. They were filled with all manner of wickedness, evil, covetousness, malice. Full of envy, murder, strife, deceit . . . foolish, faithless, heartless, ruthless" (v. 28).

The wrath of God the Father is seen most clearly against His Son on the

---

19. Robert Godfrey finds one result of this in the "God is my girlfriend" songs of contemporary Christianity.

cross, where Jesus carried the sins of the world. How did God treat the Sinbearer? *God gave Him up.* God, the ultimate and only realist, allows "natural consequences" to run their course. Because freedom is sacred to God, He permits nature—even evil nature—to carry on. God doesn't miraculously keep people alive forever to torture them. The worst thing and the best thing God can do to us is to let us have our way. After teaching us, disciplining us, warning us, pleading with us, encouraging us, and continuing to love us ("How can I give you up?" He says),[20] God allows us to "sleep in the beds we've made." Any good parent would do the same.

Though admittedly uncertain about its physical nature, C. S. Lewis often writes about hell, including this selection from *The Problem of Pain:* "In the long run the answer to all those who object to the doctrine of hell is itself a question: 'What are you asking God to do?' To wipe out their past sins and, at all costs, to give them a fresh start, smoothing every difficulty and offering every miraculous help? But He has done so, on Calvary. To forgive them? They will not be forgiven. To leave them alone? Alas, I am afraid that is what He does."

Lewis sees in the lost (those who "reject everything that is not simply themselves") an overwhelming arrogance and desire for control. They do not wish the universe to be free. Instead, as he declares in *The Great Divorce,* "the demand of the loveless and the self-imprisoned [is] that they should be allowed to blackmail the universe: that till they consent to be happy (on their own terms) no one else shall taste joy: that theirs should be the final power; that Hell should be able to *veto* Heaven." The universe would never be safe.

The Associated Press reported in 1996 that a Church of England commission formally rejected the idea of hell as a place of unending agony. According to the commission, "Christians have professed appalling theologies which made God into a sadistic monster and left searing psychological scars on many." The report says belief in everlasting punishment has lost much of its medieval momentum for many reasons and that among them "have been the moral protest from both within and without the Christian faith against a religion of fear, and a growing sense that the picture of a God who consigned millions to eternal torment was far removed from the revelation of God's love in Christ." It's about time.

---

20. *Hosea,* chapter 11.

How It Matters

Does it make a tangible difference what we believe about God? Our perceptions of God and life are the fuel that drives us wherever we go, so if a Mercedes designed for unleaded gasoline receives instead curdled goat's milk, sputterings should not shock us. Every relationship suffers when we view God as an enemy. Ali ibn abu-Talib writes, "He who has a thousand friends has not a friend to spare, and he who has one enemy will meet him everywhere." This is particularly true when the one enemy is God.

History demonstrates that in a desperate effort to keep others from suffering eternal torture, any device appears acceptable and warranted, from the iron rack of Inquisition to the syrupy lie of bad evangelism. In the shadows cast by the everlasting flames, every excess, all acts of coercion and deception, are understandable. To save others from God, we become Satan. Jesus details the real effects of misinterpreting God's character: "Indeed, the hour is coming when whoever kills you will think he is offering service to God. And they will do this because they have not known the Father, nor me."[21]

During a heated debate in the U.S. Senate, one senator told another to "go to hell." The offended senator appealed to Calvin Coolidge, presiding vice president, concerning the appropriateness of the comment. After leafing through some pages, Coolidge looked up and declared dryly, "I've been going through the rule book. You don't have to go."

We have the final choice in eternal life because the last judgment is actually about our judging God. Could I truly love this God? Many check on the divine invitation ❏ *Will not attend.* Though everyone is invited—the Bible says, "whosoever will"—we decide whether we will get up and get there. God provides the clothes, food, and transportation. Do we want to live forever with Him? The judgment of God is precisely that.

No belief is more important than the belief that hell is an end to all suffering. If we're wrong here, all is lost, all is fear. Fear and hellfire are two reasons even those who love Jesus can't bring themselves to love the Father. (How many "Honk if you love God the Father" bumper stickers have you ever seen?) After all, *Jesus* wouldn't burn people in hell for eternity. Most people make a distinction between the character of the Father and the Son. But Jesus doesn't. Jesus insists, "If you've seen me, you've seen the Father," and, "I and the Father are one." Good news.

---

21. *John,* chapter 16.

Brennan Manning comments, "So many Christians I know stop at Jesus. They remain on the Way without going where the Way leads them—to the Father." Among the many reasons Jesus came to earth was to reveal the Father. Just prior to His torture and death, Jesus explains to His disciples, "The hour is coming when I shall no longer speak to you in figures but tell you plainly of the Father. In that day you will ask in my name; and I do not say to you that I shall pray the Father for you; for the Father himself loves you."

God yearns to have us living with Him, as seen in the parable of the Prodigal Son, in reality the parable of the forgiving father, the waiting father, the I'm-so-laugh-out-loud-glad-you're-home father.[22] When he spots the object of his affections headed his way, even from a distance, the father actually *runs* with flapping robes to greet his wayward child. He doesn't sit back and wait until the child is sufficiently repentant. And when they meet, he hugs and kisses the child with wild abandon. The child protests ("I am not worthy of this"), but the father shushes him and spares no expense to honor him—the most extravagant robe, ring, shoes, food, and party hats. With all of the "lost" parables—the lost sheep (knowing it was lost but not knowing how to get home), the lost coin (not knowing it was lost), and the lost child (knowing he was lost and knowing how to get home, but not caring)—God's response is the same: "The lost has been found. Come! *Celebrate* with me!" Joyous relief floods each reunion. In the same way, Someone beyond is also eagerly waiting for us.

In his short story "God Is Barefoot," Joe Daniels details how, as a nine-year-old child of alcoholic parents, he grows accustomed to living on the receiving end of rage, though "half the time I was never sure why Dad was mad at me or at Mom or my brothers." He just knows something bad is in store for him, so he is constantly waiting for what his parents call "the other shoe to drop."

Joe's friend is Dick, another nine-year-old with alcoholic parents. Joe likes Dick because he is always barefoot and because he asks "about stuff that nobody else would. Like did my dad yell like that all the time? Or how did I really get that burn on my arm?" One sweltering July day Joe mentions to Dick that he is waiting for the other shoe to drop again. Suddenly Dick suggests they visit the inside of St. Leonard's Church, across the street. "You gotta see this," he urges.

Creeping inside the side door, the boys enter a huge sanctuary. Joe stays close to the door "in case some grown-up saw me and yelled at me, so I could make a run for it. That's the way the world worked—grown-ups yelled at you and you

---

22. See *Luke,* chapter 15.

ran." Joe slowly walks in farther, past candles burning in red glasses before a statue of a man wearing a brown robe—Dick figures it is St. Leonard—and past the reds and blues of stained-glass windows. What Joe feels most is the silence.

> Silence at home was when you woke up in the middle of the night, took the pillow off your head, and knew that Mom and Dad must have stopped fighting and gone to bed. Silence was when you got out of bed in the morning and tried not to step on the creaky floorboards on your way to the bathroom if your parents were still sleeping. But this was a different silence. It was a silence you could wear like a winter coat—heavy and warm and kind of comforting.

Dick sits on a front pew, swinging his bare feet, looking up at the big Jesus on a cross hanging from the ceiling. Joe joins him uneasily, and they sit quietly for a long time. When they leave, Joe is glad to get outside, until Dick peppers him with questions.

> "Didja see it?" Dick asked.
> "See what?"
> "That's God up in the front there, right?"
> "Jesus? I guess so."
> "So you saw it, right?"
> "Saw what? What was I supposed to see?"
> "He doesn't wear shoes either! God is barefoot. Go back and look if you don't believe me."
> Go back in there? My heart was still pounding like crazy. "So what does *that* mean?" I asked.
> "If God doesn't wear any shoes, He can't drop any."
> As glad as I was to have gotten out of that church, a part of me wanted to do just what Dick said, to go back and look. I went back to the door, opened it, and looked inside.
> God was barefoot.

By the time Joe closes the door, Dick is gone. Joe sits on the hot concrete church steps and tries to figure out what it all means. He needs to figure out a lot of things on his own because he can't talk to anyone in his family—they don't talk to each other about anything. Though he doesn't think much about it, he thinks of God pretty much as he thinks of his dad: He does what his dad says and tries to stay out of his way so he won't say or do the wrong thing and "get creamed." And he spends a lot of time waiting for the other shoe to drop, for something bad to happen. "But if God didn't wear shoes," he muses, "there was no other shoe to drop. That meant that maybe I didn't have to be afraid of God. That maybe He was someone I could like! That was something I'd never thought of before."

Joe gets up, considers going back inside the church for another look, chickens out, and heads slowly across the street toward his house. Then he stops.

> Something was different now. I mean, my parents would still fight, and the drinking wouldn't stop. All those outside things would be the same as before Dick talked me into going inside that church.

> But now something was different on the inside. And it was going to be better.

Joe had made an unimaginable discovery, one that forever changed his life. God is friendly.

. . .

God, thank You for being more than good. Forgive me for leaning away from Your reach out of my fears, false though they be. Enable me to fight the lie of endless torture wherever it rears its head and to trust you, to let Your unbearable light chase the shadows from my heart, and to see that You are truly running to meet me with an eternal welcome.

~

What does it profit a man, to gain the whole world and lose his own soul?

—JESUS

The sacred trinity of feeling good, looking good, and making good are very good goods, but they make very bad gods.

—LEWIS SMEDES

You can't have everything. Where would you put it?

—STEPHEN WRIGHT

Don't bustle me. Don't now-then me.

—EEYORE

Time is that elusive quality of nature which keeps events from happening all at once. Lately, it doesn't seem to be working.

—DOUGLAS ADAMS

People who claw their way to the top are not likely to find very much wrong with the system that enabled them to rise.

—ARTHUR SCHLESINGER JR.

It is an old and ironic habit of human beings to run faster when we have lost our way.

—ROLLO MAY

Undoubtedly we have improved means—but unfortunately, we have not improved ends. We have better ways of getting there, but no better places to go. We can save more time, but we are not making any better use of the time we save.

—PETER MARSHALL

I wouldn't give a fig for the kind of simplicity which exists on this side of complexity, but I would give the whole world for the simplicity that exists on the other side of complexity.

—OLIVER WENDELL HOLMES

Where your treasure is, there will your heart be also.

—JESUS

~

9

"I Got No Time for God"

It's the morning of March 3, 1991, and a United Airlines Boeing 737 powers up from Stapleton Airport in Denver. Flight 585 typically requires thirty minutes to reach Colorado Springs. Three miles short of the Colorado Springs runway, the plane suddenly rolls over, nosedives toward the earth, and buries itself fifteen feet into a community park. The plane disintegrates in a massive fireball, instantly killing twenty passengers and five crew members.

That day, that hour, I also flew out of Stapleton on a United Airlines plane. After landing in Washington, D.C., I listened on the car radio to the news of the crash and thought, *That could have been me.*

On August 8, an eight hundred-page National Transportation Safety Board report provided no conclusions on the cause of the tragedy. The voice recorder transcript, however, did record the last words of pilot Captain Harold L. Green and copilot Patricia Eidson, according to the Associated Press "both competent pilots with no record of on-the-job problems or serious personal difficulties":

At 9:42:29, after the final descent checklist was completed, Eidson noted a 10-knot fluctuation in airspeed and Green responded, "Yeah, I know . . . awful lot of power to hold that . . . airspeed."

Eidson mentioned another 10-knot gain in speed and then issued a muffled "Wow." That is followed by the apparent sound of engine power reduction and Eidson's statement the plane is at 1,000 feet.

"Oh God," she exclaimed at 9:43:32.

Green said: "15 flaps"—flaps at 15 degrees—and then he, too, yelled "Oh" and Eidson swore.

9:43:36.5—Green: No [very loud].

9:43:37.4—Click sound similar to flap lever actuation.

9:43:37.5—Eidson: Oh [expletive].

9:43:38.2—Green: Oh [expletive].

9:43:38.4—Eidson: Oh my God! [unidentifiable click sound]. Oh my God! [a scream].

9:43:40.5—Green: Oh no [expletive]!
9:43:41.5—Sound of impact.

Mr. Green and Ms. Eidson had no idea you would be reading their last words right now. They also weren't worrying about checking the oil in the car, making more money on a part-time job, or getting that C+ in British literature.

What would be on your mind if you had ten seconds while going down? Besides the delirium of *I'm gonna die!* you'd probably turn your thoughts to the most important things in your life. For most of us those would be matters of transcendent love—family, close friends, God. Those few moments crystallize the essence of life.

Though we're aware of this "higher plane," we have to admit that too often in daily living the important gets squeezed out by the urgent. Unfortunately, the urgent is seldom important, and the important is rarely urgent. We can come to believe, as I overheard someone say, "I got no time for God. I'm too busy trying to survive." Somehow our priorities drift, and we get swept into the muddled mind-set described by Gordon Dahl: "Most middle-class Americans tend to worship their work, work at their play, and play at their worship." Our lives become uneasy, rushed, shallow; we carry no steadying, calming purpose. Much of this drift from God can be accounted to three areas: money, amusements, and time.

One of the longest laughs on record involves money. It happened on Jack Benny's radio show, as Benny is accosted by an armed robber.

"Your money or your life!" the robber demands.

A pause ensues. A *long* pause . . . fifteen seconds . . . thirty seconds . . . forty-five seconds. . . . The audience screeches, their laughter building, knowing the agony of loveable, cheapskate Jack.

"Well?" the robber asks impatiently.

"Don't rush me," Benny replies. "I'm thinking about it." Another long pause, filled with laughter. Finally, Benny relents, "Oh, all *right*. Here's the money."

To some, money is life itself. Money clings to us until we come to believe we are worth what we earn, and purchase. Net worth equals self-worth. But even a brief look at the rampant alcoholism and drug abuse, divorces, and teenage suicides in affluent homes is enough to give us pause. At the height of her popularity, "material girl" Madonna complained to *Rolling Stone*, "Is anyone really happy? I don't know anybody who is." A life built primarily on acquisitions scuttles on spindly, brittle legs. The view that financial prosperity brings contentment is a shimmering mirage.

On October 19, 1987, Wall Street suddenly rolled over and plummeted, screaming toward earth. What astounded people then—and what will astound people when it happens again—is that none of the business whizzes, investment gurus, and economic genies of the financial world could figure out what happened. "I don't understand it," conceded the president of AT&T. The chief financial officer of United Technologies Corporation admitted, "We don't know how to interpret it." In *The Hunger for More*, Laurence Shames documents the prologue and the aftermath of Meltdown Monday.

That day the Dow Jones Industrial Average lost "22.6 percent of its remaining value, or almost double the proportionate decline of Black Tuesday, 1929." The *New York Times* called it "the end of business as usual." More important, the drop signaled the end of the eighties-style era, a period of self-interest and status symbols when luxuries and necessities merged, and "success" meant purely, "How much is in my paycheck?" Merrill Lynch produced one of the hallmark ad campaigns of the decade: "Your World Should Know No Boundaries." That was before "the day after," as Shames details it:

> With head-spinning suddenness, the habits, patterns, and expectations formed during the truncated decade came to seem outdated and, even worse, naive. Advertisements, college curricula, career paths, lives—suddenly everything seemed due for a revision. . . . If you were the Harvard Business School, what did you say to your students that day? If you were the account exec on BMW or Rolex watches, what clever notions did you have as to how to move your product? . . .
>
> Eighties values, dubious in the best of economic times, now seemed downright embarrassing. Not only were they narrow, selfish, fogeyish—it turned out they didn't even work. Delirious greed and runaway careerism had seemed amusing for a while, but October 19 killed that mood as fast as turning the lights up at a bar.

What makes this book especially remarkable is the ending. Those materialistic days, Shames asserts, are now behind us. We are "finally addressing the often-asked, always-shrugged-off question, *What is all that money for?*" In ringing tones he concludes, "More money, more tokens of success—there will always be people for whom those are adequate goals, but those people are no longer setting the tone for all of us."

Remarkable, because more than a decade after Meltdown Monday we're at it again, even more in the grasp of greed, more enchanted with the rocketing

Dow, more driven by our next Lexus—more *more* than before. A few years ago my thirteen-year-old son received notice that he had "won" ten million dollars—"$27,770.00 every month!" Toward what noble aims did the contest benefactors direct my son's new wealth?

> You could choose a car one month and a diamond ring another. Or you could string a few monthly payments together and put together a down payment on a really big ticket item (a Rolls . . . a Ranch . . . a Yacht!). All the while that your old friends and neighbors were struggling to balance their monthly budgets, the **Blakes** would be living in the lap of luxury.

Perhaps we haven't learned at all.

AMUSING OURSELVES TO DEATH

When Alvin Toffler published *Future Shock* in 1970, he proposed that human beings are increasingly prone to information overload, decision stress, and sensory overstimulation. Today, "knowledge" mounts geometrically, the average U.S. home accumulates more than one thousand unsolicited pieces of mail a year, and virtual reality rocks our living rooms. The shocking future is present. As a result, we may find ourselves incapable of sorting through the avalanche to make even vital decisions. This could explain why 23 percent of U.S. men deal with depression by trying to sort out their problems, while 35 percent deal with depression by watching television.[1]

In 1985, Neil Postman published *Amusing Ourselves to Death* to denounce the decline of the Age of Typography and the ascent of the Age of Television. The book's foreword contrasts two negative utopias, the dark vistas of George Orwell's *1984* and Aldous Huxley's *Brave New World*. While many view the books as parallel creations by British contemporaries, notable differences arise:

Orwell's *1984* Fears	Huxley's *Brave New World* Fears
1. Externally imposed oppression	1. Internally imposed oppression[2]
2. Books banned	2. No reason to ban a book
3. Deprived of information	3. So much information that we are reduced to passivity and egoism

---

1. From *What Counts: The Complete Harper's Index* (New York, NY: Holt, 1991), p. 98.
2. We come to "adore the technologies that undo [our] capacities to think."

4. Truth concealed	4. Truth drowned in a sea of irrelevance
5. A captive culture	5. A trivial culture
6. Controlled by pain	6. Controlled by pleasure
7. What we hate will ruin us	7. What we love will ruin us

It's now evident who was more correct. Even in formerly totalitarian societies, the Huxley vision prevails. In *Give War a Chance*, P. J. O'Rourke observes that seventy-two years of communist bullhorns were "drowned out by a three-ounce Sony Walkman." In 1991, *Harper's* index reported that the United States had 4,532 movie theaters; the former Soviet Union had 150,000. What we love will rule us. That's why loving God supremely is so basic, so indispensable.

Amusement loosely translates to *a*, meaning "without," and *muse*, meaning "thought." At times we savor giving thought a rest (some claim that I've rested for months at a time), but as with anything, amusements can be overdone. I knew someone who always had to have a radio or television blaring. A moment's silence meant for him an unthinkable, hellish interlude.

When Neil Postman refers to the Age of Television, he has ample reason. More than 95 million people in the United States watch television each night. Across the world 250,000 TV sets are produced every day, one for every child born. Television (including videos) is a medium of bursts of disconnected images, "fragments of events." Postman terms the result *disinformation*, entertainment-saturated information—particularly in TV news—that "creates the illusion of knowing something but which in fact leads one away from knowing." He goes on to lament the death of meaningful discourse: "In courtrooms, classrooms, operating rooms, board rooms, churches and even airplanes, Americans no longer talk to each other, they entertain each other. They do not exchange ideas; they exchange images. They do not argue with propositions; they argue with good looks, celebrities, and commercials."

As a consequence, many opinions are actually emotions—"being offended" is the lowest blow. We become so enamored by seamless, exciting, horrifying presentations that a simple truth gets buried. A pure love is passed over. While we sit on the couch, our principles are snatched up and swallowed; we are willing food for the Cyclops.

The overstimulation of future shock combined with the Age of Television has created other unforeseen effects. On a flight in the early 1990s I sat next to a child psychologist. I was editing a youth magazine then, so my interest piqued when he told me of the types of cases he treated. Eventually I inquired, "What are you seeing more of now than before?"

"Self-mutilation," he said.

Somewhat stunned, I asked, "Why do they do it?"

"Because they have lost the ability to feel," he replied sadly. "They have been so overstimulated by Nintendo and Walkmans and MTV that the only way they can feel anything is to carve themselves up."

Time After Time

A New York City subway token booth attendant spends most of her day watching the passengers: "They like to run," she says. "They don't feel right if they don't run. This is what I watch—the rat race. I watch them run to work, and I watch them run home."

"The trouble with the rat race," Lily Tomlin quips, "is that even if you win, you're still a rat."

We pay for plastic utensils and pizza delivery, drive while chatting on a cellular phone, listen to Mannheim Steamroller as we exercise, and can now purchase throwaway underwear ("Save time" the package proclaims. "No laundry"). Yet we feel rushed, irritable, exhausted. I occasionally ask audiences when I speak, "How many of you are too busy?" Invariably more than 90 percent raise their hands. "It is ironic," writes Jeremy Rifkin in *Time Wars,* "that in a culture so committed to saving time we feel increasingly deprived of the very thing we value."

Sue Monk Kidd tags us "quickaholics." We want food. Quickly. We want entertainment. Quickly. We want to finish this book. Quickly. A home loan can be approved within twenty-four hours, microwaved water boils in sixty seconds, my computer rarely makes me wait more than five seconds. I realize that your reading this book is a concession of time for you. Our time is the ultimate sacrifice, the most valuable thing we share—beyond money, possessions, and wisdom.

The story is told of a man phoning an airline and asking, "How long does it take to fly from Montreal to Vancouver?"

"Just a minute," the clerk replied.

"Thank you," said the man, and hung up.

We're concerned with saving time but we don't know why we're doing it. "I'm running," a close friend confided in me. "I know what from, but I don't know what to."

One image surfaces when I think of the effects of money, amusements, and time on modern society. Locusts. For centuries nobody knew where locusts came from. As Annie Dillard recounts in *Pilgrim at Tinker Creek*, though locust plagues are well documented—they can blacken a sky for nine hours as they pass—no one understood how or where they originated. The millions of ravenous, rasping creatures could denude entire countries. Entomologists would see them laying eggs, would label specimens, but find none the next year. Then mysteriously, years later, they appeared again.

The mystery was solved in 1921 by a Russian naturalist named Uvarov. He determined that locusts are ordinary grasshoppers "gone berserk." Placed in crowded glass jars, grasshoppers become locusts, a process Dillard describes:

> They literally and physically change from Jekyll to Hyde before your eyes. They will even change, all alone in their jars, if you stimulate them by a rapid succession of artificial touches. Imperceptibly at first, their wings and wing-covers elongate. Their drab color heightens, then saturates more and more, until it locks at the hysterical locust yellows and pinks. Stripes and dots appear on the wing-covers; these deepen to a glittering black. They lay more egg-pods than grasshoppers. They are restless, excitable, voracious. You now have jars full of plague.

Has there ever been a better description of people "stimulated by a succession of artificial touches"? The artificial touches of caffeine, Fox TV, fluorescent lights, adrenaline addiction, computers, telephones, bump and scurry make us restless, excitable, voracious; we metamorphose into people plague.

Amid the Madness

A direct relationship exists between busyness and spiritual dryness. We have crowded God out of our lives—there's no space left for Him on our "things to do" list. No energy. No time. No room at the inn. What comes as a startling revelation is that God has anticipated this and made a weekly provision for us, a relief package. Sabbath.

In the Bible's Ten Commandments in chapter 20 of *Exodus,* the Sabbath commandment surfaces as a timely bridge between the first four (how to love God) and the last six (how to love people):[3]

---

3. The Sabbath was being honored before the Ten Commandments, as seen in the threefold miracle of *Exodus,* chapter 16. Though it's brimming with conflicts over change, the New Testament records no battles about changing something as fundamental as Sabbath observance.

> Remember the Sabbath day, to keep it holy. Six days you shall labor, and do all your work; but the seventh day is a Sabbath to the Lord your God; in it you shall not do any work, you, or your son, or your daughter, your manservant, or your maidservant, or your cattle, or the sojourner who is within your gates; for in six days the Lord made heaven and earth, the sea, and all that is in them, and rested the seventh day; therefore the Lord blessed the Sabbath day and hallowed it.

God reminds His people of the importance of Sabbaths when He says to Moses "Say to the people of Israel, 'You shall keep my Sabbaths, for this is a sign between me and you throughout your generations, that you may know that I, the Lord, sanctify you.'" Sabbath is God's marriage covenant of trust.

When Jesus appears on the scene, the Sabbath receives fresh emphasis. Jesus Himself keeps the Sabbath (*Luke,* chapter 4) and fights to preserve it from being trampled by the Pharisees, whose main contention is whether Sabbath healing should be considered desecrating "work." He concludes, "It is lawful to do good on the Sabbath."

Through Jesus, God models how to remain unaffected by encompassing madness. As J. B. Phillips relates: "It is refreshing and salutary to study the poise and quietness of Christ. His task and responsibility might well have driven a man out of his mind. But He was never in a hurry, never impressed with numbers, never a slave of the clock." Along with prayer and willing obedience, Sabbaths helped the carpenter remain on God's timetable.

Whether God's followers should honor the Sabbath is never an issue. In fact, Jesus' followers honor the Sabbath during His life on earth, at His death when He is buried between Good Friday and Resurrection Sunday, and years after His Resurrection.[4] In *Matthew,* chapter 24, Jesus describes the destruction of Jerusalem four decades after His death, and urges, "Pray that your flight may not be in winter or on a Sabbath." He also asserts, "If you love me, you will keep my commandments."

The Book of *Revelation* portrays an end-time scenario with the central question, as always, "Who is God?" *Revelation* broadcasts an end-time call for creatures to worship the Creator "who made heaven and earth." God's followers are those "who keep the commandments of God and the faith of Jesus." In an age that believes humans somehow developed from primeval slime to unfathomable complexity, Sabbath is the only commandment that points back to God as our

---

4. See *Acts,* chapters 13 through 18.

Creator, worthy of genuine awe, loyalty, and love. Sabbath affirms that we breathe and move with transcending purpose—we are not random collections of molecules. Our lives matter. At the conclusion of *Revelation's* fourth chapter, God's seeking followers cast their symbolic crowns before God's throne and sing:

> You are worthy, our Lord and God,
> to receive glory and honor and power,
> for you created all things,
> and by your will they were created,
> and have their being.

With their allegiance, they receive from God all that He imparts. Each Sabbath bears the imprint of God's signature. In recent years millions of people have discovered the beauty of the Sabbath. In place of nonstop sprinting, Sabbath provides a calm place, a warm place, a wise place. A time for all time, just in time.

REST—A CALM PLACE

My favorite button on the TV remote is labeled "MUTE." In our house we honor a rule that whenever a commercial appears, we MUTE it. Though we spend less time than the average family in front of the flickering blue light, we still see too many ads, but the MUTE softens their intrusive, insistent edge. We are in control, after all.

I also like to watch sports, such as pro football, and press MUTE. On occasion I put on a melodic CD like Vivaldi's "Four Seasons" or Handel's "Water Music Suites." While players crash and crush, their concussive sounds are lost to me. The commentators are precisely as I enjoy them. Silent. No hyped build-up. No babbling analysis. Football is actually a soothing sport.

Observing Sabbath is pressing MUTE on the world. Screaming newspaper headlines? MUTE. Bills in the mail? MUTE. Homework and housework? MUTE. They're still there, but we pay no attention—we give them a rest. For twenty-four hours we are not under the tyranny of the urgent. We are in control, after all.

On Sabbath we rest from *hurry*, because we are drunk with hurrying. My unabridged dictionary lists 172 different definitions—no word carries more—for *run*. We skim across our lives in hyper living—rarely dipping beneath the surface, unless we crash. That stops us. Hospital waiting rooms become our churches because we pause there to contemplate life and eternity.

When I was about twelve, I spent an agitated night in a camper at an unfamiliar campsite. Around midnight I heard footsteps nearby, but when I lifted my head to look out the window, the footsteps stopped, and I saw no one. I tried to keep completely still, and then looked *quickly* to catch the intruder, but somehow he (I figured) saw me in time. This peeping game continued for about an hour, until I realized that in the echo chamber of my pillow I had been hearing my own heartbeat thumping out its frightened cadence. Each time I raised my head, the "footsteps" ceased. I cannot remember a time my hearing was more acute. We must be remarkably still to hear the heartbeat of God. What a giant step it is not to move.

Doctors can determine how old a fetus is by the rate of its heartbeat. As we grow older our heartbeats slow, but pressures make them skitter. For some of us it's the stabbing of sales quotas and the maelstrom of early morning traffic. For others it's cramming for a test or the whiff of a full diaper. For still others it's a noisome tenement and the dread of a hopeless future.

Have you ever shopped for a vast variety of different people? Think of it: *What could God have given everyone that would be just right?* He chose the perfect gift of time, a buried treasure in our sand-blown age. A sanctuary in the week. A slowing of our hearts, that we might hear His.

A Sabbath rest from hurry does not mean mere inactivity. On Sabbath we rest from the *sameness* of the week. The banker cooped up all week in an office should get outdoors; a highway construction worker might sit in an easy chair and read a deepening book. An elementary teacher may prefer to be with adults; an accountant could choose to direct a children's choir. Furthermore, our needs and yearnings change from week to week.

Rarely do we admit the poverty of too much. But as Abraham Heschel reports, the Sabbath is "a realm of time where the goal is not to have but to be, not to own but to give, not to control but to share, not to subdue but to be in accord. Life goes wrong when the control of space, the acquisition of things of space, becomes our sole concern."

Sabbath is others-centered, an antidote to self-addiction. We make time for family, close friends, God. We connect with transcendent matters. Resting from ourselves, we become ourselves again. This is the rest depicted by Tilden Edwards in *Sabbath Time:*

> Full rest involves all that we are: our bodies need to participate from head to toe, inside and out. Our minds and our prayers need to relax their frequent weekday grasping, striving, judging, fearing. *Full* rest is full openness.

Full openness is God's image revealed in us: wherein all possibility, perspective, loving is obscurely realized.

The wonder is that even Christians miss this Sabbath rest. They don't realize the gift Jesus intends when He promises, "Come unto me, all who labor and are heavy laden, and I will give you rest." On this day our thoughts lift above the mundane; we are changed, rising to new life with the Master. The following lines, engraved on the doors of some old churches of the Church of England, apply to each Sabbath:

> Enter this door
> As if the floor
> Within were gold,
> And every wall
> Of jewels all
> Of wealth untold;
> As if a choir
> In robes of fire
> Were singing here
> Nor shout, nor rush,
> But hush . . .
> For God is here.

ASSURANCE—A WARM PLACE

The comic character Pogo the 'possum complains, "We are confronted with insurmountable opportunities." Daily we see added things to do, find more insider tips to "get ahead." We can't stand the thought of letting the newspaper go unread or allowing a bargain sale to slide by without developing anxiety.[5] Tilden Edwards claims that "stopping work tests our trust: will the world and I fall apart if I stop making things happen for a while?" In *My Fair Lady*, Eliza Doolittle accents an apt response: "Without your twirling it the earth still spins, without your pulling it the tide rolls in, without your pushing them the clouds roll by." Edwards suggests how the Sabbath leads us to deeper levels:

The different dimensions of Sabbath rest . . . involve two stages. The first is simply *letting go*, renouncing our normal routines and work. . . . The second

---

5. "Progress," notes e. e. cummings, "is a comfortable disease."

stage moves beyond this negative freedom to a positive internal response. It involves letting ourselves *be* in that fresh space in such away that we realize appreciatively and joyfully our holy connectedness.

After being calmed, we are filled. As Mother Teresa says, "We must free ourselves to be filled by God. Even God cannot fill what is full." And so we find ourselves filled with four Sabbath joys: grace, delight, rhythm, and peace.

The Sabbath presents to us our intrinsic worth apart from profession, past, or appearance. It is a day of grace. At the end of a consuming week, Sabbath disengages us from the belittling belief that we are worth what we earn and produce and look like. We're reminded again that God loves and appreciates us because of who we *are*—His children.

"I gave them my Sabbaths," God says in *Ezekiel,* chapter 20, "as a sign between us, so they would know that I the Lord made them holy." God assures us that the way to achieve holiness—wholeness—is to celebrate not our creations but His creations.

In this context Sabbath creates a counterpoint to legalism, the foundation for most of the world's religions. Legalism teaches that we can somehow earn our way to salvation (or nirvana, paradise, enlightenment, harmony) by what we do. Unfortunately, legalism lies at the base of pride, the root of our separation from God and from each other; hence our need of "connectedness."

God in effect assures us every Sabbath, "You are a human being, not a human doing or a human done. You are valued, even if you produce nothing—you are worth an infinite amount. You are priceless because I have paid infinity for you. You are my child. 'I will never forget you. Your name is graven on the palms of my hands.'"[6]

The Sabbath is also a day of delight, as defined in chapter 58 of *Isaiah:*

> If you turn back your foot from the Sabbath,
> from doing your [business] on my holy day,
> and call the Sabbath a delight
> and the holy day of the Lord honorable;
> if you honor it, not going your own ways,
> or [pursuing your own business], or talking idly;
> then you shall take delight in the Lord,
> and I will make you ride upon the heights of the earth.

---

6. See *Isaiah,* chapter 49, verses 15 and 16.

Finding Sabbath delightful is difficult if we're pushing papers at an office, or even if we're watching television, the epitome of "talking idly." Ashley Montagu concludes that "television is the principal contributor to loneliness. What happens is that the family 'gets together' alone." We watch with rapt disinterest as humanity is exploited and degraded. In contrast, the psalmist in Psalm 101 resolves, "I will walk with integrity of heart within my house; I will not set before my eyes anything that is base."

Saving extraordinary surprises for the seventh day enhances how we view it: a longed-for book, a luscious raspberry dessert, the company of a close friend, or a hike to wild alpine forget-me-nots. Jesus pronounces, "The Sabbath was made for people, not people for the Sabbath." However we choose to rejoice each Sabbath, we honor it first when we delight in it.

Life is full of rhythms, from the sun's rising to the night's dreaming, and like adding seasoning to sauce, meaningful traditions help flavor those rhythms. Traditions for candled birthdays, costumed holidays, and red-petaled anniversaries sculpt memories and strengthen relationships. Children especially (we're all children) enjoy stories, safe places, and unpredictable predictability.

Sabbath traditions have been around since the beginning: "So God blessed the seventh day and hallowed it, because on it God rested from all his work which he had done in creation." To commemorate His creation, God hallows— sets aside for a particular purpose—the seventh day. As far back as human history can be traced, historians find the seven-day week as we know it. This discovery appears as a curiosity because the seven-day cycle is the only major means of marking time that does not depend on a visible, natural process, unlike days, months, and years. Followers of Judaism still honor the Sabbath as Joseph, Jesus, and Paul of Tarsus kept it. Why don't most Christians keep this Sabbath?[7] Perhaps they misunderstand that Jesus was contesting *how* the Sabbath is kept, not *if* it should be kept. Others associate Sabbath with the joyless, juiceless routines of the Puritans.

Our family has developed its own Sabbath traditions and rhythms.[8] For a

---

7. Most worship on Sunday because Jesus rose on that day. The change to Sunday worship came about gradually, originating not in the Jerusalem community but in the second-century Roman church. Musician Michael Card, along with millions of others, is now keeping the biblical Sabbath. "We started out of this desire for simplicity and this appreciation for rest," he explains. "But I think, really, the thing that pushed me over the edge was a Seventh-day Adventist brother who said, 'God didn't change any of the other commandments, so he hasn't changed that one.' The rationale behind that argument, I thought, was pretty airtight."

8. Presented here as one example. Please adapt Sabbath traditions to your circumstances, tastes, and needs.

typical Sabbath (this past one, as I write) on Friday afternoon Nathan empties trash baskets and Geoffrey roars about the house with a vacuum cleaner, reserving the thirteen carpeted steps for Dad, the stair master. Yolanda lights candles—in bathrooms, on the kitchen counter, and the coffee table—and prepares homemade potato soup and pineapple muffins. I mix a pitcher of grape juice. Geoffrey and Nathan choose midnight blue place mats, plates, cloth napkins, and slender glasses to set the table while I prime CDs of Handel's *Messiah* and Take 6. Lifting down the Sabbath candle, Geoffrey sets it in the middle of the dining table and strikes a match. I watch the light dance in his eyes. This same flame has danced in the Sabbath eyes of Sarah and Abraham, Miriam and Moses, Jesus and Paul. We're following a three thousand-year-old tradition.

When seated, we join hands and sing. Our song is "Family," and it ends with, "I'm so glad He's brought us all together. And I'm so glad that the Father is our God." If any of us is absent, we skip the song. I pray a prayer of gratefulness, pledging to God our open lives and total loyalty, anticipating the hours of intimate friendship ahead. During the meal our custom is to share what we're thankful for from the past week.[9] Geoffrey swallows a few mouthfuls of steaming soup and begins, "I'm thankful this week that I got an A on my history test."

After a pause, Yolanda says, "I'm thankful that I feel better after being sick Tuesday."

"I'm thankful that my classes went well this week," I offer.

Nathan has already downed the soup and two muffins when he declares, "This week I'm thankful that I got to eat out at the Olive Garden."

After we clear the table, it's my turn for family worship, so I ask three questions: "When was a time that you were really scared? What scares you now? How do we get over our fears?" Our answers range from getting lost at the mall to nearly plummeting down a cliff face. Hearing present fears gives glimpses into my family and myself that I would not have guessed. We share practical helps we have used, heard, and read. I conclude, reading aloud the end of chapter 8 in *Romans:* "I am sure that neither death, nor life, nor angels, nor principalities, nor things present, nor things to come, nor powers, nor height, nor depth, nor anything else in all creation, will be able to separate us from the love of God in Christ Jesus our Lord."

Because sunset differs every Friday, we choose how we will spend the time after worship, whether playing board games, groaning at my home videos, or

---

9. In her delightful book *Traveling Mercies,* Anne Lamott writes, "Here are the two best prayers I know: 'Help me, help me, help me,' and 'Thank you, thank you, thank you.'"

attending a program at church. Tonight we talk, and laughter fills our halls.

Saturday morning we go to different Sabbath school classes; Yolanda and I attend a class called "Something Else," a gathering of about sixty people—ages twenty to seventy—that uses as its mission statement, "The kingdom of God consists not in talk but in power."[10]

Initially we listen to each other's concerns and thanks. We pray for each other as a roll of names grows on a white board: Amy and Nick (newlyweds), Bill (a member's father, dying from prostate cancer), Josh (a son, in remission from leukemia), Cindy (found a house to move to). Cindy is asked if she needs help, and soon a crew of eight volunteers agrees to meet the next morning. For twenty-five minutes we listen to and pray for each other. Life's heights and depths bolster and batter us during this time each week—we fluctuate often between laughter and sorrow.

Paul stands up and says, "This week our money ministry project is for a single mother who can't pay a phone bill. She needs some help to start fresh." We pass around an envelope that typically brings in $120 a week to fund special projects, about sixteen per year. The class also operates a soup kitchen—buying food, cooking, serving, cleaning up—one Sabbath a month. We're reminded each week that a healing community can help more people than we ever could as individuals. Then we turn toward discussing matters of the deeper life. Mark leads a lesson on loving the unlovely. We call out traits that truly bother us.

"Meanness."

"Arrogance."

"Clipping fingernails in church."

Mark asks, "How should we treat these people? If they are hurting others, are we doing them or anybody a favor by just ignoring them? When should you step in?" We break into smaller groups. Lively, respectful discussion ensues. I hear snatches of conversations.

"Sometimes I'm the most annoying person I know . . ."

"We should act right even if we don't think we'll have any effect . . ."

"Thomas Kelly said, 'We cannot die on every cross.' . . ."

"Being annoying isn't a reason. I'm sure Jesus was seen as annoying sometimes . . ."

We look at what the Bible has to say on the subject. Sometimes we're left figuratively scratching our heads, at other times we wonder at the transcendent insights. The words of Jesus especially provide challenge and assurance. We finish

---

10. *First Letter to the Corinthians*, chapter 4.

as a large group, summarizing what we can agree upon. In conclusion, two old friends finally agree that they find each other incredibly annoying, and the class erupts in glee.

Following Sabbath school comes a church worship service where we sing, pray, reflect, laugh, listen, read the Bible, and renew our love for God and for each other. Jesus is lifted up as the center of our lives.

This Sabbath afternoon we "potluck" at a park, combining food with five other families. We can spend the afternoon talking, throwing an aerobie, hiking, reading, or getting involved in some type of volunteer service. One humid summer afternoon we set up a "free lemonade" stand for bewildered passersby on a bike path. Saturday evening we worship again to close the Sabbath, singing with Nathan's piano, focusing on what we especially enjoyed about the day.

Each Sabbath is atypical. You can find as many Sabbath-keeping variations and rhythms as there are Sabbath keepers, all savoring a day of delight, a creative, right-brain day with our right-brained God. Does every Sabbath run smoothly? Not in our lives. We still battle against our culture's squeezing and sly demands at the hands of the clock. C. S. Lewis speculates that the human race struggles with time because we were originally created for timelessness— for eternity. Yet it does seem that if our bodies can remember chicken pox thirty-five years later, we can remember to celebrate what is truly important from week to week and establish a rhythm of godly searching and celebrating.

The "world," of course, will break into this rhythm if we allow it. Eugene Peterson writes:

> The "world" is sometimes our friends, sometimes our families, sometimes our employers—they want us to work for them, not waste time with God, not be our original selves. If the world can get rid of Sabbath, it has us to itself. What it does with us when it gets us is not very attractive: after a few years of Sabbath breaking we are passive consumers of expensive trash, and anxious hurriers after fantasy pleasures. We lose our God and our dignity at about the same time.

An art contest was once held with the object being to depict *peace.* Entries poured in, paintings of mist-veiled waterfalls, barefoot lovers strolling along endless sand, sublime sunsets, suckling babies, azure mountain lakes mirroring snow-capped peaks. But the winner was none of these.

The winning entry depicted a terrific storm at sea. Rain like liquid bullets fell in torrents. Ferocious winds whipped towering waves. Dark, heavy clouds pressed down while lightning stabbed the sky. In the midst of this turmoil, along the curl of a wave, a sea gull glided serenely.

The gull's progress did not require tranquil surroundings. Its happiness wasn't dependent on circumstances. It was at peace.

Through grace, delight, rhythm, and peace, amid the world's blistering furies and icy fears, the Sabbath assurance of a warm place next to God's heart brings fulfillment.

CLARITY—A WISE PLACE

A young fighter pilot once maintained that he didn't really require an oxygen mask up to twenty thousand feet. He could function fine without it, thank you. His superiors, deciding to *show* him, placed him in a low-oxygen chamber that simulated air at twenty thousand feet and asked him, after a few minutes, to write on a pad of paper his full name, address, family's names, social security number, and phone number.

Upon exiting, the pilot grinned. He felt fine—no problem. Then he looked at what he had written and stared slack-jawed. The last three items were total gibberish, incomprehensible scrawling. He hadn't known his state at all. Like the pilot, we function each week in rarefied, depleted air. The life-giving oxygen masks of prayer, the Bible, and Sabbath enable us to legibly live God's love.

Modern society suffers from acrophobia—a fear of high ideals and lofty thoughts. Bombarded by amusements, we lose time for thoughtful reflection. In a famous passage, Henry David Thoreau writes, "I went to the woods because I wished to live deliberately, to front only the essential facts of life, and see if I could not learn what it has to teach, and not, when I came to die, discover that I had not lived." Admirable and virtuous, surely, but realistically, with our responsibilities, can we leave and do what Thoreau did?

Sabbath is our woods, our Walden Pond. Each week Sabbath engages us and lifts our sights. And as with my childhood terror in the camper, each time we raise our heads the "footsteps"—those dreadful ones in the darkness—cease. If our thoughts never rise above the level of humanity, if we never contemplate infinite wisdom and love, we will sink lower and lower.

God proclaims Sabbath a day of liberation. In *Genesis* the Sabbath is tied to Creation, but in *Deuteronomy* God connects Sabbath to freedom: "Remember that you were slaves in Egypt, and that the LORD your God brought you out of there with a mighty hand and an outstretched arm. Therefore the LORD your God has commanded you to observe the Sabbath day."[11]

Jesus goes out of His way to liberate on the Sabbath. On one Sabbath He heals "a man blind from his birth," and a few Pharisees denounce Him, saying, "This man is not from God, for he does not keep the Sabbath." Jesus pays them no heed.

On other occasions, He responds directly. Walking through a wheat field, He confronts His inquisitors, the traveling truth squad. "Had you known what this means, 'I desire mercy, and not sacrifice,' you would not have condemned the guiltless. For the Son of man is lord of the Sabbath." Sabbath—the Lord's day—is for mercifully setting people free. Jesus makes His point even more decisively another Sabbath. He approaches a painfully hunched woman—for eighteen years she has been unable to stand straight—suffering probably from rheumatoid arthritis, and says, "Woman, you are freed from your infirmity." He touches her. "Immediately she is made straight, and she praises God."

The ruler of the synagogue, however, is irate. "There are six days to do work. Come and be healed on those days—not on the Sabbath day."

Jesus responds, "You hypocrites! Each Sabbath every one of you unties your cow or donkey from the stall and leads it to water. Then shouldn't this woman, whom Satan has tied up for eighteen years, be freed on this Sabbath day?" His adversaries are put to shame, and the people rejoice.

The Sabbath liberates every living being on earth. In *Exodus,* chapter twenty, examine who is set free: you, your children, your servants, your animals, and "the sojourner within your gates," strangers. To the freed slaves who were brought out from Egypt, God says, "As I set you free, on this day set each other free." Our human hierarchies disappear as we experience our equal status before God.

The exhortation to treat people with dignity, allowing them to delight in full rest, extends to us today. I can still picture the grateful look of surprise on the face of a gracious motel maid (also the manager) in Hope, British Columbia, when I requested that she not work for us that day.

"Take a break on our room," I explained. "It's our Sabbath."

Startled, she stared at me. "Why, thank you," she said at last, her eyes filling. "I truly appreciate it."

The Sabbath liberates the planet as well. In a time of global environmental concerns, it's good to know that God cares for the well-being of animals and His entire creation—not only for humans. At the opening of *Genesis,* when Sabbath

---

11. *Genesis,* chapter 5, New International Version.

first appears, God calls us to be caretakers of the earth. Later, in *Leviticus*, God institutes a sabbatical year: "Six years you shall sow your field, and six years you shall prune your vineyard, and gather in its fruits; but in the seventh year there shall be a sabbath of solemn rest for the land, a sabbath to the Lord; you shall not sow your field or prune your vineyard."

Niels-Erik Andreason says, "Every week on the Sabbath, as we contemplate God's created works, we do not turn *away* from the real material world, but *toward* it. We affirm this as our God-given environment, where life is nurtured, sustained, provided for, and made secure."

In addition, Sabbath liberates us from the effects of overstimulation. Blaming the complexity of our lives on the complexity of our environment, we may dream of flying to some remote island to relish the simple life, but the problem is not entirely our environment. The problem is in our anxious, disjointed selves. "We are tendencies, or rather symptoms," Emerson sighs. "We touch and go, and sip the foam of many lives." We are fragmented. We are torn and aching. Life doesn't work for us because we are without Jesus. The simplicity of Sabbath brings wholeness.

Sabbath is a day for all of us wrapped up in materialistic values. Establishing God's priorities sets us free. Judy Duncan tells a story of her little brother carrying to school two baby scorpions. "These scorpions," he said to the class, "are worth more than a big bar of gold." A hiss of skepticism rose from his classmates. "Yes, they are," he emphatically exclaimed. "It's because they have *life*."

Sabbath also liberates us from *boxes*. We may eat from a box, work in a box, type into a box, fill in the boxes, drive home in a box, live in a box, throw trash into boxes, be entertained by a box (yearning for box tickets), sleep in a box, and fittingly, be buried in a box. No wonder we feel unnaturally boxed in. At the end of the week the boxed lies, that we are ultimately in control of the universe and that the universe *owes* us, are hauled out and dumped; in grateful humility we acknowledge the freeing truth that every good thing comes from God. God Himself breaks out of the tiny, moldy boxes we've placed Him in and speaks to us because we are listening for the voice, the heartbeat. We experience God in the leaping dolphin, the cypress limbs, the moon rising over an open field.

Rachel Carson broke out of her boxed environment to experience an epiphany:

> My companion and I were alone with the stars: the misty river of the Milky
> Way flowing across the sky, the patterns of the constellations standing out

bright and clear, a blazing planet low on the horizon. It occurred to me that if this were a sight that could be seen only once in a century, this little headland would be thronged with spectators. But it can be seen many scores of nights in any year, and so the lights burned in the cottages and the inhabitants probably gave not a thought to the beauty overhead; and because they could see it almost any night, perhaps they never will.

Sabbath frees us for time to reflect. The difference between a parent who hits a child and a parent who doesn't is about ten seconds. We clear our minds, like rinsing brushes and rollers after painting, because we know the next job won't be as good if we don't clean our tools thoroughly. This clearing time for reflection makes us more effective.

Though we are hounded by time, the Sabbath liberates us to enjoy the eternal present. We no longer live in the past or the more debilitating future—wishing, wondering, and trembling. C. S. Lewis reveals in *The Screwtape Letters*, "The Present is the point at which time touches eternity . . . the Future is, of all things, the thing *least* like eternity. . . . Nearly all vices are rooted in the Future. Gratitude looks to the Past and love to the Present; fear, avarice, lust, and ambition look ahead. . . . [God's enemies] want a whole race perpetually in pursuit of the rainbow's end, never honest, nor kind, nor happy *now*."

Best of all, the Sabbath frees us to fall in love with God again and again. Now.

The Sabbath window enlightens; looking through it we receive new eyes. Seeing Jesus hanging on the Cross, we see ourselves as we are and as we can be, without excuse and with real hope. We give in to grace. Dispelling darkness and spiritual rigor mortis, we enter the fray again, renewed and emboldened by rest, assurance, and clarity. Rather than contributing to boxes of people plague, we stay distinctly and fully human. Instead of adding to the madness, we pull back and lift our sights to reflect on larger questions: where we came from, why we're here, and where we're going.

The Sabbath places our lives again on a higher plane. We experience transcendent love, knowing that we are accepted in the Beloved, feeling the rightness of being, and doing what will rejuvenate us for the week ahead.

Sabbath is the cool side of the pillow on a hot night.

God is restful.

. . .

O ambient Peace, walk with me in serenity through the chaos of my days. Calm my pulsing temples, that I may savor Your life. God, I need to slow down. I need to rest. I need deepening. Forgive me for playing in shallow mud puddles when an ocean of joy awaits me.

I need Your Sabbath, God. Please grant me discernment and give me courage to set apart this liberating day for eternal matters and lasting delight. You already hold my mind and heart, now I give to You my greatest gift—my time.

~

Of what use is immortality to a man who has not learned to live half an hour?

—Ralph Waldo Emerson

There are only two kinds of people in the end: those who say to God, "Thy will be done," and those to whom God says, in the end, "Thy will be done."

—C. S. Lewis

Estimated number of plant and animal species that have become extinct since 1980: 100,000.

—Harper's Index

"Would you tell me, please, which way I ought to go from here?"
"That depends a good deal on where you want to get to," said the Cat.
"I don't much care where—" said Alice.
"Then it doesn't matter which way you go," said the Cat.

—Alice's Adventures in Wonderland

To you it has been given to know the secrets of the kingdom of heaven.

—Jesus

When you speak of Heaven, let your face light up, let it be irradiated with a heavenly gleam, let your eyes shine with reflected glory. But when you speak of hell—well, then your ordinary face will do.

—Charles Spurgeon

We shall not cease from exploration
And the end of all our exploring
Will be to arrive where we started
And know the place for the first time.

—T. S. Eliot, "Little Gidding"

The light shines in the darkness, and the darkness has not overcome it.

—Jesus

~

10

HEAVEN IS NOT MY HOME

THE GREATNESS AND goodness of Christianity are not that it is right. We can be "right" and be small-minded, stingy, and smug as a mud turtle. The genius of Christianity is that it is liberating. "The truth," Jesus proclaims, "will set you free." This was a lesson I learned—and helped my students learn—the hard way during my last year of teaching grades seven and eight in Arroyo Grande, California.

It was the middle of the school year when I approached our principal, Leon Kopitzke, about a plan I had hatched, and I well recall his reply. "Sure, go ahead," he said. "It's your last year, anyway."

That day in the hour before lunch I made a brief announcement that fluttered like wet cement: "We need to add another school rule."

The students groaned. "We don't need rules!" they chorused.

"Okay." I smiled. "I'm tired of these rules too. Let's try something else. For just this class period, you make up all the rules."

The students grew silent, disbelieving. At last Bobby said, "You mean, seriously? Anything we want?"

"Yep," I replied. "But we all have to vote on them. And we'll have to follow two overriding guidelines: All activity takes place inside this classroom, and the experiment stops at noon. Agreed?" Heads nodded all around. I approached the chalkboard. "So, what's the first rule?"

Joey raised his hand. "We can put our feet on the desk." (The existing rule proposed that the instructor wished to see their souls, not their soles.)

"All right," I said, writing it down. "That's number one. What's another?"

"We can chew gum," called out Laura. (It had gotten thick under the desks.)

"Number three?"

"We can hold hands," said Jaime, casting alluring glances at Audra.

"Your own?" I suggested.

"No, somebody else's!" Jaime retorted. As we continued to pile up rules, the students' creativity blossomed. By the time we reached thirteen, the room was a sea of hands. I called on Eric.

"We can do anything we want!" he shouted.

Here my years of educational training paid off. "Hey," I said, "if we vote on just that one, all of the other rules would be covered and we wouldn't have to vote on them. That would save some time. Do you want to vote just on Number 13?"

Number 13 carried, with both hands from everyone and a few feet kicked in. It was 11:38 A.M.—a time burned into my brain until the day I die. "Remember to stay in the room," I reminded. "Okay, please get out your world cultures book and turn to page one hundred sixty-four."

The students' first impulse was to reach under their desks for their books. Then they hesitated. Leonard stood and began pacing across the back of the room. Kristyn reached for her novel. Angie grinned at me, raised her eyebrows, and meaningfully shook her head *no*.

Teachers are weird, of course; *I* wanted to teach world cultures, so I began. Many students got up from their seats. Jaime sat on Audra's desk, folded her hand demurely in his, and tilted his head at me in mock innocence. Two boys snatched Comet cleanser and a squirt bottle from under the sink and initiated a spirited water fight. A launched rubber band stung the back of a head. A pink eraser rebounded off a windowpane. I continued talking to nobody.

Soon things started heating up. Along with her novel, Kristyn received an unwelcome dousing. Two posters on a bulletin board were unintentionally ripped down. A shoving skirmish broke out. Loud, harsh voices intensified. The tail of a Comet attack covered unwilling participants.

I continued talking to nobody, writing precious notes on the chalkboard for no one, marking fascinating points to myself. Suddenly, Phillip appeared at my side. Phillip was normally as mild-mannered as a seventh grader could be, but this was not a normal day. Phillip adjusted his glasses, smiled grimly, stepped forward, and *erased what I had written.*

Flabbergasted, I looked down at Phillip and said calmly, "Phillip, please don't do that." He merely stood there, eraser in hand, and regarded me. I voiced to the rioting masses a few more invaluable nuggets, began chalking more notes on the board, and *as I was writing* Phillip began erasing my words. I looked down at Phillip, a head shorter and sixty pounds slighter, and like a bolt of fever the thought nudged me: *Hey, I can do anything I want too.* Gripping his wrist to halt the obliteration, I was gently pressing him into the carpet when a voice seemed to speak to me: "*What* are you doing?"

Pulling Phillip to his feet, I apologized and stood aside to collect my composure and assess the carnage. The uproar was deafening. Leonard and Sam pounded out a tribal rhythm on the countertop. Erin and Shana busily wrapped my desk and chair with transparent tape while Joey tiptoed across the tops of the desks. At that moment my colleague David B. Smith opened the door connecting our rooms. Assuming I was out of the room, he was about to bark orders to the rampaging horde when he noticed me standing to the side, watching, a benign look resting on my features. For some moments he strained to compute the scene before him. His head pivoted back and forth, from the unbelievable chaos to my silent witness. Finally he fixed me with a stare, said, "Blake, have you gone mad?" and stormed out, locking the door behind him.

I made my way to my desk and cut myself in, and as I sat there pondering, I noticed the most amazing thing. Danny was moving around the room *cleaning up* after people. He wasn't making a big show. He simply wiped the Cometose counter and windows, tacked up torn posters, picked up a fallen desk, blotted the drenched carpet, straightened an exploded shelf. He used his freedom to heal and redeem. I sat there awed.

At 11:54 a delegation of six approached my taped desk. "Mr. Blake," they begged, "we want this to stop now."

"I'm sorry," I replied, "a deal is a deal."

At 11:59, all the students sat in their seats, quaking with expectation. Randy shot one final rubber band at the ceiling. Each student was quiet, lost in thought.

At high noon I stepped to the front. "All right, we're going to do two things: We're going to talk about what just happened, and then we'll clean up for lunch. First, a question. How many of you got to do exactly what you wanted to do in the past twenty-two minutes? Raise your hands."

No one raised a hand.

"Why not? We voted on it, so you all had freedom."

A barrage of voices responded.

"I wanted to read and it was too loud!"

"They were throwing water on me!"

"He knocked my stuff over!"

"Oh yeah? How about you? You—"

"All right," I broke in, "so you didn't get to do what you wanted. Now, I have another question. How many of you think we need rules?"

Eyes wide, everyone raised two hands, and a few feet kicked in. If you asked any of those students the same question today, they would vote the same way.[1]

---

1. At the time of this writing, Danny and Shana are elementary school teachers. Erin is a pastor. Sam is in business management. Leonard is a firefighter. Bobby is in public relations. Audra is a dental hygienist. And Phillip wrestles professionally with the WWF as The Eraser. (Just kidding.) Phillip is a computer network administrator, deleting to his heart's content.

God and His "rules" are generally portrayed as limiting our freedom, smothering and constricting us. Serving God is viewed as picking up the ball and chain. The folly of this portrayal is evident when we consider which of the following is most free:

- A balloon filled with air and tied, drifting with each passing current
- A balloon filled with air and left untied, frenetically darting until spent
- A jet plane with seventy controls

Which is most free? The tied balloon is subject to the whims of its immediate environment. The untied balloon reacts merely to inner pressure. Only the jet can soar over the storms—*because* of its controls.

The Olympic gymnast is set free to do a back walkover on a high beam because of her disciplined habits. The professional flautist is set free to play "Flight of the Bumblebee" because of his fidelity to musical scales. Controls enable us to do much more.[2] People who decide to live under no controls—whether by shooting off guns or shooting off their mouths—inevitably find their freedoms curtailed.

The most basic and liberating controls for human beings are God's eleven commandments.[3] They show us the essentials in how to love. Yet controls are not enough. Without a pilot the jet sits useless, with all its frustrating potential apparent; an incompetent pilot will merely crash and burn. Only as we allow the right Pilot access to the controls do we experience personal sovereignty.

FLIGHT PLANS TO PARADISE

Paradise is a place where personal sovereignty rules, or so I'm told. I often wonder whether paradise makes any sense at all and how our view of paradise affects how we live in this life. What sort of preparations should we make? Do we need shots and a passport? What is the final destination like? The travel brochures are fuzzy on specifics. Unprepared travelers give rise to such stories as these, gathered from travel agents across the United States:

---

2. It is said, he who is a slave to the map owns the freedom of the seas.
3. The Ten Commandments, plus the eleventh commandment from Jesus: "A new commandment I give to you, that you love one another; even as I have loved you" (*John*, chapter 13).

A client called in inquiring about a package to Hawaii. After I went over all the cost info, she asked, "Would it be cheaper to fly to California and then take the train to Hawaii?"

A man called, furious about a Florida package we did. I asked what was wrong with the vacation in Orlando. He said he was expecting an ocean-view room. I tried to explain that this was not possible, since Orlando is in the middle of the state. He replied, "Don't lie to me. I looked on the map and Florida is a very thin state."

A woman called and said, "I need to fly to Pepsi-Cola on one of those computer planes." I asked if she meant to fly to Pensacola on a commuter plane. She said, "Yeah, whatever."

Making travel arrangements for eternity can be just as wild. I've asked people what they think the redeemed will do throughout eternity, and I've heard:

"They float on clouds and play harps, I suppose."

"They ski down million-mile slopes and never fall."

"They sit on Jesus' lap."

"I guess they walk the streets of gold and talk with Moses and David and other Bible heroes."

These may be interesting activities for a while, but would you want to do them forever? Images of heavenly harps, crowns, and gold paving used to trouble me as my tastes run more toward acoustic guitars, fishing hats, and foaming waves and sand beneath bare feet. Suppose I don't like the new neighborhood? C. S. Lewis notes that the Bible's harps, crowns, and gold are symbols, human attempts to express the inexpressible. Music suggests ecstasy and infinity. Crowns point to sharing God's powers and splendor. Gold embodies timelessness and precious value. If we take these symbols literally, Lewis contends, we "might as well think that when Christ told us to be like doves, He meant that we were to lay eggs."[4]

Sadly, in more ways than one, heaven has been unrealized. Too many envi-

---

4. Biblical images of heaven are described in terms familiar to the Bible's writers. Thus we read "the wolf and the lamb shall feed together, the lion shall eat straw like the ox" (*Isaiah*, chapter 65) instead of "every mouth-watering morsel of food shall be fat free" or "computer programs shall never know bugs."

sion life beyond the grave as unlike anything experienced in this life. In reality, eternity may be quite familiar.

Many years ago, my father watched from the sidelines while I shot baskets in an empty gym. I was feeling lazy, enjoying the echoing thud of my dribble and the squeals from my shoes, and I began carelessly, haphazardly flinging the ball at the hoop. My father, a superb basketball coach, observed a few moments before giving me advice that made a lasting impression. "Don't practice missing," he said. "You might get good at it."

What we practice matters. From "waxing on" karate moves to flicking turn signals to memorizing multiplication tables, our habits form us: We become our practices. Imagine, then, what we would think of a *swimming* coach who challenges her charges, "Okay, team, we have the big state meet coming up, so today we're going to practice the pole vault. When we're through with that, we'll work on picking up the four/six split in bowling. You never know when that will come in handy. Tomorrow, we'll attack some pesky dangling modifiers. Then, on to cross-stitching . . ."

As ludicrous as it sounds, many view God as this kind of coach. It's difficult to love someone who commands us to follow routines that appear pointless, incoherent, and superfluous. But would God have us practice things all our lives if He never expected us to use them again in the eternal game? What does God ask us to practice? The Bible describes the practices of those who inherit the kingdom of God: love, joy, peace, patience, kindness, goodness, faithfulness, gentleness, and self-control.[5] Could we need these in a perfect setting? Suppose we *can't* engage in all the activities we want at precisely the time we want. Is it possible that we'll need self-control?

In a perfect world, natural laws will still be in effect. This is what God has been trying to tell us all along: The universe is not tailored to fit us. We must adapt. Reality impacts us, sometimes painfully, because natural laws cannot be habitually canceled.[6] If we didn't slow down while skidding around a curve, we'd skid into oblivion. With gravity operative across God's universe, could someone drop something—accidentally? Might we then need to show gentleness and forgiveness? Could accidents take place in a perfect environment?

An intriguing old episode of *The Twilight Zone* depicts a compulsive gambler who dies and reappears in, of all things, a casino. Stunned and rejoicing, he

---

5. *Letter to the Galatians*, chapter 5.
6. D. N. Marshall submits, "We do not break the laws of the universe so much as we break ourselves upon them."

begins placing bets and, lo and behold, every bet he wagers—whether at black-jack, poker, roulette wheel, slot machine—he wins. He knows he's in heaven! After endless days of winning, however, he grows tired of the predictability. He misses the thrill of possibility, of scrambling after uncertain opportunities. At last he shrieks in desperation, "I want out of here! Let me go to hell!"

Everyone in the casino stops, turns, and glares at him. Finally one patron sneers, "Where do you think you are?"

We say we'd like everything in paradise to go our way, but much of life's pleasure comes from accomplishing tasks and pursuing goals that were anything *but* a sure thing. This is the message of *The Truman Show:* Human beings would rather endure risk and spontaneity than live by a predictable script, however safe and flawless. When Truman Burbank decides to leave his "perfect" pseudo-world, crowds cheer, the man in the bathtub splashes his glee like a baby, and audiences everywhere know the choice is right and true. Yet many continue to view God's paradise as a highly regulated environment, like *The Truman Show* biosphere, monitored by climate controls and populated by immaculate neighbors with smiley masks. That would be fools' paradise.

My home is not in heaven. My forever home is new earth, a material world that God proclaimed "very good" at Creation, which will be "very good" at its restoration. A holy city descends from heaven to this earth made new. The moving van is described magnificently in chapter 21 of *Revelation:*

> I saw a new heaven and a new earth; for the first heaven and the first earth had passed away, and the sea was no more. And I saw the holy city, new Jerusalem, coming down out of heaven from God, prepared as a bride adorned for her husband; and I heard a loud voice from the throne saying, "Behold, the dwelling of God is with men. He will dwell with them, and they shall be his people, and God himself will be with them; he will wipe away every tear from their eyes, and death shall be no more, neither shall there be mourning, nor crying nor pain any more, for the former things have passed away." And he who sat upon the throne said, "Behold, I make all things new."

Not much is written about life on new earth, but it's best that we understand our eternal home as a real place filled with surprises and subject to natural laws. Yes, we will have accidents and mistakes on the new earth, I believe. All will not go precisely according to our plans. We will need to overcome obstacles, but they won't be overwhelming, nor will we be tempted to despair. For example, though the perfect Jesus of Nazareth never sinned, He no doubt made mistakes. As a carpenter He worked with adz, hatchet, ax, bow drill, hammer, saw, chisel, plane, rule, file, and compass, and at some time He probably planed too deeply, dented a fingernail, drilled skewed holes, and measured wrongly. Especially as He learned the trade, He erred. A perfect worker is not one who never makes mistakes but one who learns from those mistakes. *Proverbs* confirms, "A righteous man falls seven times, and rises again; but the wicked are overthrown by calamity." This perfection carries more attraction than *The Twilight Zone* casino's sour certainty. In a perfect environment, surprise happens.

When accidents occur in paradise, how will we react? If someone drops a celestial rock on your toe, what will you do? How do we react now when a flight is delayed, our pathetic efforts to fix the leaky plumbing fail, or a close relative starts to aggravate again? Will today's practices fit us for new earth? Are we filling the hoop with godly habits, or are we practicing at missing? When I'm walking closest with God I know that, in every way, nothing is immaterial. *God's commands are neither pointless nor superfluous.* Every thought, word, and act moves my world.[7] C. S. Lewis comments, "Good and evil both increase at compound interest. That is why the little decisions you and I make every day are of such infinite importance. The smallest good act today is the capture of a strategic point from which, a few months later, you may be able to go on to victories you never dreamed of."

Actually, the idea of living forever isn't all that attractive to me. I have to trust God that I'll even enjoy living forever, because I cannot fathom relishing anything that long. Adults who are asked, "If life stayed basically the same, would you like to live another hundred and fifty years?" quickly decline the offer. Too many people find life too long as it is—they stop their breath abruptly with pills or commit slow suicide with cigarettes. It's not everlasting life we crave but enhanced quality of life—eternal life.

Webster's Ninth New Collegiate Dictionary defines *everlasting* as "continuing long or indefinitely," while eternal is "characterized by abiding fellowship with God." Eternal life—an intimate friendship with God—is ours now through Jesus. John explains in a Bible letter, "I write this to you who believe in the name of the Son of God, that you may know that you have eternal life." We can enjoy eternal life beginning today.

---

7. One of the most powerful examples of this is when Jesus neatly folds his head covering immediately after His resurrection. This might be one of the last things I would think of doing after my resurrection. But the headpiece becomes one more piece of evidence that thieves did not steal His body. It was also a sign carpenters of His day used to signify "the job is completed."

Hope Springs Eternal

In my first month of working at Review and Herald Publishing Association, I attended the funeral of a twenty-something young man, the son of a colleague who would later become a dear friend, who had committed suicide. Seated there, staring at the coffin, I wondered, *Why did this happen? What would cause someone to take his own life?* Only one reason came to mind. He had no hope.

Hope is the melody of our song, the spark that ignites our souls. Life without hope is a maze without an exit. Brennan Manning reports, "Hope is the good news of transforming grace now. We are freed not only from the fear of death but from the fear of life; we are freed for a new life, a life that is trusting, hopeful, and compassionate."

Especially when death claws at us, we long for hope. When Peter Marshall felt a sharp pain in his chest and was being carried into the night on a stretcher, he looked up into the face of his wife, Catherine, and said, "See you in the morning, Darling." The promise of being reunited with loved ones buoys us in the canyons of death's towering swells. Walter Lowen remembers:

> Let me tell you what the doctor who attended my wife did for me as I stood dazed and lost at the foot of her bed, knowing not only that the 37 years we had had together were over, but feeling also that all meaning had gone from life forever. He took my arm and held it for a moment. And then he said in a matter-of-fact voice: "You'll see her again." That was all.
>
> But it was all I needed to hear.

Our hope of rescue and vindication is born with our first breath—it's part of being human. *Realistic* hopes are most valuable, for though we may hope for world peace and hope to win the lottery, we know that the best way to make our dreams come true is to wake up. There is one hope so real that it wakes even the dead. It's the next appearance of Jesus—His Second Coming, our blessed hope.

His first coming brought hope to a dying world. In the future, "Christ, having been offered once to bear the sins of many, will appear a second time, not to deal with sin but to save those who are eagerly waiting for him."[8] God steps into history and thunders, "Enough heartaches. Let's go." The Second Coming is not principally a great event; it's a great Friend coming back for us. How certain is it to happen? "If it were not so," Jesus says, "I would have told you."[8] His Second Coming is as certain as His first.

---

8. *Letter to the Hebrews*, chapter 9.

When Jesus appears again, it won't be secretly, but "coming with the clouds, and every eye will see him."⁹ Paul of Tarsus explains what will happen next:

> We would not have you ignorant, brethren, concerning those who are asleep, that you may not grieve as others do who have no hope. For since we believe that Jesus died and rose again, even so, through Jesus, God will bring with him those who have fallen asleep. For this we declare to you by the word of the Lord, that we who are alive, who are left until the coming of the Lord, shall not precede those who have fallen asleep. For the Lord himself will descend from heaven with a cry of command, with the archangel's call, and with the sound of the trumpet of God. And the dead in Christ will rise first; then we who are alive, who are left, shall be caught up together with them in the clouds to meet the Lord in the air; and so we shall always be with the Lord.¹⁰

Astounding scene! Why does God go to such lengths to communicate specifics to us, to make the travel brochures less fuzzy? Because in the face of this stupendous future, each day we must battle against surrendering to perspectives that are too trivial to be true.

This morning I looked at a fly on our bathroom mirror and noticed that its reflection appeared to be about an inch from it, when in reality the fly poised directly on the silvered glass. Revelation describes the redeemed standing on what appears to be "a sea of glass mingled with fire," but it seems so far away. If we could know how close the other side is, what a difference it might make in our days.

Just surviving our days is difficult enough, so we concentrate on what "we can count on." We generally hold more faith in grocery bags than in God. Consumed by consuming, we wander aimlessly like sheep nibbling away, never looking up, focusing instead on what's under foot. Jesus urges us to keep checking the travel brochures, keep looking up, keep the hope so that we can rejoin Him. He assures us, "Let not your hearts be troubled; believe in God, believe also in me. In my Father's house are many rooms; if it were not so, would I have told you that I go to prepare a place for you? And when I go and prepare a place for you, I will come again and will take you to myself, that where I am you may be also." This is our mission: to boldly go where God has gone before.

"My Father's house" is the holy city New Jerusalem. Life in the holy city will

---

9. *Revelation,* chapter 1.
10. *First Letter to the Corinthians,* chapter 15.

be one of action, autonomy, and relationships. Isaiah says of the people in paradise, "They shall build houses and inhabit them; they shall plant vineyards and eat their fruit. They shall not build and another inhabit; they shall not plant and another eat."[11] Rather than thumbing harps on vaporous recliners, the city's residents are involved in active community.

The question may come to mind: We will live in a *city?* Though today's cities are a far cry from New Jerusalem (imagine, the city planner is God), spending afterlife in a city should not be totally surprising. Trend trackers find a community movement taking off. Instead of hunting for isolated, huge houses and virtual friends, many are seeking the connectedness of small towns. In the United States, intentional communities like Disney's Celebration are planned for close houses with front porches, wide sidewalks, and village greens. Cohousing developments, where residents design their community, are springing up like sunflowers in the countryside. The association between good health and a sense of belonging is medically documented and carries a label: the Roseto Effect, honoring the eastern Pennsylvania town where residents enjoyed astoundingly vigorous health as a direct result of living in a close-knit community.[12]

Heaven is really freshman orientation, where we learn the language of God and unlearn much of what we picked up on old earth. Our forever home base is new earth (with travel visas that are out of this world), this planet made over without a trace of separation from God. The thousand years the Bible says we spend in heaven before we return to earth is a time of healing and reconciliation. Perhaps we'll spend much of the time seeking answers. We'll ask questions such as, "Why didn't you step in when this happened?" "Why isn't my friend here?" And, "Whoa! What are *you* doing here?"

A WORLD OF DIFFERENCES

It matters that our final destination is not heaven but this earth made new, a place where we plant grapes, strawberries, pineapples, and mangos (and succulent fruits we've never before tasted); how we treat this planet is how we'll treat our home forever. When we understand this, we'll know why environmentalism is especially important to Christianity.[13] The new earth is second nature to

---

11. *Isaiah,* chapter 65. These features held special attraction in an occupied land under foreign rule.
12. When the social fabric of Roseto unraveled in the late 1960s, the health benefits of living there vanished.
13. In *Revelation,* chapter 11, verse 18, God is described as "destroying the destroyers of the earth."

us. As caretakers for the creation again, will we trash new earth, brazenly wasting and poisoning resources? If not, then we must not trash this earth either. Our eternal home is beneath our feet.

If our afterlife is in Nirvana, the absence of desire, or in a harmonic convergence of light atoms, then ultimately nothing matters. As far as I'm aware, a light atom doesn't need to be patient and kind. One of the most fundamental laws of the universe—cause and effect—is pointless if our end is to blend. God will not perform character transplants on us. Without those magnificent idiosyncrasies that define us—your crazy laugh, my loping walk—who cares? You wouldn't be you, and I wouldn't be me. If this is the end of all sentient matter, what a homogenized, slick, tasteless extract God desires. *Bleah.* You can have it.

Give me a universe where what I do matters and where differences are prized. As Bill Hybels delights in saying, "God is a variety junkie." The people who populate this planet made new will be more alive, clear-eyed, and distinctive than we can imagine. On the new earth we will be both like and unlike each other in far more ways than we are now: like each other in our trusting love for God, unlike each other in our personalities and pursuits because we have eternity to chase our dreams and change amplitude if we choose. The singer submerges in colors of sound while the cook plunges into a sizzling, steamy kitchen. The scholar probes the depths of thought, and the deep-sea diver spins through galactic oceans of space and teeming tidepools of planetary life.

There we will sincerely appreciate our differences, even differences of belief and species. Lively dialogues, untainted by rivalry, will lead to differing considerations and boundless growth. But if we want to be there, we must appreciate differences here. Palestinians and Israelis, Yankees and Red Sox fans, dog lovers and cat lovers will not only coexist but will also cherish distinctions. What a world it will be when "I like you—you're different" is the motto. Jesus lived that motto while He walked the earth, as Deborah Anfenson-Vance notes:

> Maybe the biggest change in heaven won't be in the place but in us and our ability to relate positively to the people and things around us. Maybe one of the most surprising things we can know about heaven is that it starts here, within us.
>
> I used to think Jesus was so narrow, precise, and strict that I'd have to limit myself severely enough to please Him. Now I realize Jesus has been limiting Himself for my sake—making Himself human, reachable, small enough not to frighten me off. And all the while He's slowly, carefully

pulling back the curtain, telling me, "It's all bigger than you think. I am bigger than you think. More broad-thinking. More open to variety and differences. More surprising."

Everybody will not be equal—at least in the realm of capabilities. In his chilling short story "Harrison Bergeron," Kurt Vonnegut shows what "all men are created equal" does not mean. His story opens:

> The year was 2081, and everybody was finally equal. They weren't only equal before God and the law. They were equal every which way. Nobody was smarter than anybody else. Nobody was better looking than anybody else. Nobody was stronger or quicker than anybody else. All this equality was due to the 211th, 212th, and 213th Amendments to the Constitution, and to the unceasing vigilance of agents of the United States Handicapper General.

The new earth will be characterized by acceptance of our relative strengths and weaknesses. We are God's misfits together, bonded by love.

. . .

A silly, superficial idea is afloat that "heaven" is tame. I recognized this idea again recently in the film *City of Angels*, the story of an angel (Seth) who falls in love with a pretty doctor (Maggie) and chooses to leave the employ of heaven. Angels in the movie are depicted as half-dead zombies. While open to reading thoughts, they remain closed to the more evocative senses—smell, taste, touch—and are thus infinitely less alive than humans. These angels wear drab uniforms and somber expressions. They hang out in public libraries. They show as much individuality as a school of tuna. Hearing chiming music in the sunrise comprises their greatest perk. That's it? Frankly, these sad-faced angels more nearly represent fallen human beings. Just look at those who are locked into addictive lifestyles or who endure a hopeless existence and you get the picture.

Seth falls for Maggie and decides to *fall*. He longs to feel hot showers, smell his beloved's perfume, taste ripe pears, catch the exhilaration of a thrashing ocean wave. He yearns for warm, aching sensations of sexual love. The poor angel wants his pores open. Later, after being asked if his fallen decision was worth it, Seth responds with quintessential ardor, "I would rather have one breath of her hair, one kiss of her mouth, one touch of her hand than eternity without it." Following Adam's archetype, he will give up eternity for his lover.

City of Angels makes the decision to give up heaven easy. This heaven assumes no individual rapture, no intense feelings, no breathless ecstasy. Moreover, every angel is out of the loop as far as the answers to *why.* God hasn't seen fit to communicate responses to hard questions, so Seth must ask his of a fallen angel. It would be difficult to come up with a heavenly prospect more hellish.

Can we possibly believe that God would deny feelings? God *invented* sensation, including throbbing sexual touch, ripe peach juice dribbling down chins, the aroma of cooking onions, the sparkling laughter of grandchildren. God wants us as He originally created us, when sex within marriage came before sin, taste entered before sin, healthy emotions appeared before sin. In afterlife every good sensation will be intensified. Without the deadening shroud of sin we will feel a thousand times stronger, see a thousand times deeper, communicate a thousand times clearer, hear a thousand times better, think a thousand times purer. If that's tame, I'll take it.

Like Adam, Seth was deluded. Falling for "that old black magic called love" is the classic "straw man" fallacy—build up a false concept and appear victorious when it is dismantled. God is discerning enough to take care of every need. We cannot entirely love a Super Bore. "I came," says Jesus, "that [you] may have life, and have it abundantly," forever and now. Adam would have gained his lover Eve and missed the heartache of a planet dying had he trusted God even in the realm of candlelight and blushing red roses.

Whether there will be actual sex in heaven and new earth no one really knows. In addressing the topic, C. S. Lewis gives an instructive analogy:

> I think our present outlook might be like that of a small boy who, on being told that the sexual act was the highest bodily pleasure should immediately ask whether you ate chocolates at the same time. On receiving the answer "No," he might regard absence of chocolate as the chief characteristic of sexuality. In vain would you tell him that the reason why lovers in their carnal raptures don't bother about chocolate is that they have something better to think of. The boy knows chocolate: he does not know the positive thing that excludes it.

Freedom is more than doing what we want to do. Freedom is doing what we ought to do. Danny was the only truly free person during my class's experiment because he wasn't enslaved by his chaotic environment. When I cannot stop lying, when I cannot stay loyal, when I cannot savor peace of mind, I am not free. Only when I grant God access to my life do I become free to enjoy fulfilling friendships. Free to develop a hobby to excellence. Free to educate a child in godly love. Free to live without worrying.

"For freedom Christ has set us free . . . only do not use your freedom for the opportunity for the flesh, but through love be servants of one another."[14] On the new earth, all will use their freedom to do what is loving. Ellen White observes, "In heaven none will think of self, nor seek their own pleasure; but all, from pure, genuine love, will seek the happiness of the heavenly beings around them. If we wish to enjoy heavenly society in the earth made new, we must be governed by heavenly principles here." But while rules can set us free and freedom rules new earth, it's unlikely that rules will be posted in the afterlife, spelling out prohibitions. Why not?

Picture a magnificent 15 million dollar mansion with gleaming pillars and three fountains. A driveway bends for a quarter mile, ending at six garages that harbor a fleet of extraordinary cars. Inside the house stand seven fireplaces (including three in bedrooms), rosewood floors, and *Architectural Digest* quality throughout. The kitchen is nearly the size of your entire house. You stagger about gaping in awe. There is one thing that disturbs you, however.

In every stunning room you note a different sign posted with the words "To Our Guests:" above explicit directives. "Don't spit on the floor" is mounted in an immaculate drawing room. "Don't toss scaly fish heads on the Persian rug" adorns a bedroom. The glittering dining room carries a notice: "Keep your dirty shoes off the table." "Change the car's oil *outside* the house" reads a kitchen message. You think, *Why would anyone post these commands? Given the exquisite beauty of this place, no one would consider doing these acts. The commands seem so . . . unnecessary.*

On a pristine new earth, no commandments will be posted to remind citizens, "Don't kill." "Don't lie." "Don't covet." "Celebrate Sabbath." "Worship only God." In this life they're needed; there they won't be. The laws don't need to be posted because, as God discloses, we are under an eternal New Covenant with Christ.

> I will put my laws into their minds,
> and write them on their hearts,
> and I will be their God,
> and they shall be my people.
> And they shall not teach every one his fellow

---

14. *Letter to the Galatians*, chapter 5.

> or every one his brother, saying "Know the Lord,"
> for all shall know me,
> from the least of them to the greatest.[15]

"The kingdom of God," Jesus says, "is within you." When God's laws of love are already in our feelings and thoughts, love happens as naturally as breathing. We don't have to "work it up." It's not a burdensome requirement. It simply is. Each morning when we get up we don't think, *Okay, I gotta remember to breathe today. Breathe in, breathe out.* . . . God's impulses become our impulses. Consequently we are treated as mature, responsible adults. Hans Steinmuss described to me a sign he saw posted above the door of an especially creative art department. The sign read, "You Are Allowed." With selfless love as our only motive, perhaps that sign will be the only one tacked up in the New Jerusalem.

A final reason the rules won't be posted is that they aren't the most important characteristic of eternity. Any relationship defined on the basis of what we do or don't do is legalistic. Friendship with God goes beyond a checklist approach. As Brennan Manning maintains, "Christianity is not primarily a moral code but a grace-laden mystery; it is not essentially a philosophy of love but a love affair; it is not keeping rules with clenched fists but receiving the gift with open hands." Our love affair with God isn't an arranged marriage to a demanding partner, a fate worse than death. It's more a rollicking adventure; like otters in the ocean, we swim in the assurance of deep, safe love.

FIT TO A T FOR ETERNITY

We call a perfect society a utopia, after the famous book *Utopia* by Sir Thomas More in 1516. The word derives from two Greek words, *ou* and *topos*, meaning "no place." More's book recounts three voyages to America of Portuguese sailor Raphael Hythlodaye with explorer Amerigo Vespucci. On the mythical island of Utopia they discover an ideal society where people are free, equal, educated, healthy, wealthy, and wise.

No place appears aptly named, for whenever utopian societies such as Brooke Farm and Oneida have formed, human pettiness and grotesqueries inevitably raise their heads, like hideous gargoyles come to life. Kathleen Norris reflects in *The Cloister Walk,* "Many communal ventures begun with high hopes have foundered over the question of who takes out the garbage."

---

15. *Letter to the Hebrews,* chapter 8.

Langdon Gilkey in *Shantung Compound* recalls life as a prisoner in a Japanese concentration camp in China during World War II. Two thousand captives—children and businessmen, priests and prostitutes—are herded together to form a society, and what emerges is a fascinating portrait of the human condition. The former trappings of status are worthless in the camp: of value are the character traits of generosity, integrity, creativity, industry, and toughness. Thus Mrs. W. T. Roxby-Jones, well-bred wife of a courtly gentleman, works alongside Mrs. Neal, the unschooled, earthy wife of a salty British seaman, and though they are as different as can be imagined, both operate with "the same undeviating honesty, sense of cooperation, and responsibility." Dick Rogers, an alcoholic, is a towering figure of honor who guards the food so that it will not be stolen at night. During the days it never occurs to him to take time off from work as everyone else does. After he finishes his job, he looks for other things that need to be done. Yet Gilkey recounts, "The irony was that many a pious diner, whose regular ration of good food depended on Dick's strength of character, still thought of him as immoral because he drank. One diner observed sadly, 'Pity, a man like that; looks so strong, but too weak to resist temptation!'"

During his months of internment, Gilkey journals the unguarded condition of people in the prison camp. He summarizes:

> The most important lesson I learned is that there are no cut-and-dried categories in human life, no easily recognizable brand names by which we can estimate our fellows. Over and over "respectable people," one of the commonest labels applied in social intercourse, turned out to be uncooperative, irritable, and worse, dishonest. Conversely, many who were neither respectable nor pious were in fact, valiant. At the same time, many obvious bums were just plain bums. It was the mystery, the richness, and the surprise of human beings that struck me the most. . . .
>
> It is truly fortunate that we are in the end judged by the Lord and not by one another!

In any utopian society we can realistically imagine, some personal qualities are called for, characteristics of love without which a utopia turns rancid. Unless these godly qualities unfold, cooperation mutates to competition, the wondrous magic of wedding vows evolves to snarling accusations in a cutthroat divorce. Our present cannibalism won't appear in afterlife. Yet because freedom is sacred to God, on new earth we will be forever free to be ourselves—even free to turn against God (as Lucifer did in a perfect environment). How can this be? Two character traits appear mandatory for new earth residency.

First, every new earth resident must be *teachable*. Everyone, even the most loving among us, has blind spots. We will all "retool" our thinking to adapt to God's universe, and to do this we must be willing to be taught. What gets most in the way of our teachability is pride—the first sin, the worst sin. Pride cuts us off from God. It distances us from ourselves and from others. This is not the pride that connotes dignity and self-respect; this is a glorying, preening pride, haughty, disdainful, immodest, a pride that vandalizes joy. Nothing on earth is so universally hated. Only one antidote exists for this poison, as we see in Philip Yancey's account in *What's So Amazing About Grace?*:

> During a British conference on comparative religions, experts from around the world debated what, if any, belief was unique to the Christian faith. They began eliminating possibilities. Incarnation? Other religions had different versions of gods appearing in human form. Resurrection? Again, other religions had accounts of return from death. The debate went on for some time until C. S. Lewis wandered into the room. "What's the rumpus about?" he asked, and heard in reply that his colleagues were discussing Christianity's unique contribution among world religions. Lewis responded, "Oh, that's easy. It's grace."
>
> After some discussion, the conferees had to agree. The notion of God's love coming to us free of charge, no strings attached, seems to go against every instinct of humanity. The Buddhist eight-fold path, the Hindu doctrine of karma, the Jewish covenant, and Muslim code of law—each of these offers a way to earn approval. Only Christianity dares to make God's love unconditional.

I have long wondered about the sacrifice of Jesus on the Cross. What *practical* difference does it make ultimately? Why does it have to be this way? How does it make sense? Here's part of the answer: Only through accepting the unimaginable sacrifice of God can we be residents of the new earth community. We don't deserve our passes. We are all guests in the universe, recipients of a priceless, interminable gift. *We own nothing about which to be proud.* No one on new earth will have earned one particle of presence. It's all free. All grace.

Paul of Tarsus points out in his letter to believers in Ephesus:

> God, who is rich in mercy, out of the great love with which he loved us, even when we were dead through our trespasses, made us alive together with

Christ (by grace you have been saved), and raised us up with him, and made us sit with him in the heavenly places in Christ Jesus, that in the coming ages he might show the immeasurable riches of his grace in kindness toward us in Christ Jesus. For by grace you have been saved through faith; and this is not your own doing, it is the gift of God—not because of works, lest any man should boast.

It is believing we don't have *enough* that makes us hostile and hard; where merit demands, gratitude appreciates. Christianity is the only religion that gives no reason at all for our boasting. No chakras to cleanse. No pilgrimage to Mecca. No reason for conceit. Just everlasting gratefulness to be here. This is not to say that only professed Christians will be on the new earth. Many who have not heard the marvelous story of God's love and freedom will, after encountering it, embrace it afresh. They will meet Jesus Himself, "and if one asks him, 'What are these wounds on your back?' he will say, 'The wounds I received in the house of my friends.'"[16] Only God knows who will be open to this new constant of having no claim on eternity.

Moreover, not all professed Christians will be there. Many have apparently not grasped one reason for Christ's sacrifice—to make us humble. The essence of humility is a genuine recognition of reality. As Mother Teresa maintains, "Humility is nothing but the truth." Jesus says, "Blessed are the meek [humble], for they shall inherit the earth." Only the teachable inherit the new earth. Those who are arrogant and exclusive in their intractable narrowness become unfit for heaven; in fact, they have not accepted the Messiah's sacrifice. The surest way to know that a gift has been accepted is to see it in use, whether it's a tie, a painting, or a perfume. God knows His gift of grace is accepted when He can see it in how we treat others—by graciously forgiving, accepting, and sharing. Otherwise, we don't believe.

Jesus cautions, "Not every one who says to me 'Lord, Lord' shall enter the kingdom of heaven, but he who does the will of my Father who is in heaven." Those who inhabit new earth will be eternally humble, eternally teachable. That's the practical difference the Cross makes. Forgiven, we are changed. Unencumbered by the sticky web of guilt, we live gladly.

(Here it gets tricky.) This change does not save us, however, for that also would give us cause to boast. God's grace alone saves us, and our responses flow from that sublime gift. The root of humility is *humus,* where roots grow and

---

16. *Zechariah,* chapter 13.

delicious fruits develop naturally. We don't love others in order to be saved, but because we are saved. Morris Venden points out, "An apple tree produces apples because it is an apple tree, never in order to become an apple tree." Lovers of God produce good fruits because they are grafted into the main plant.

It's not enough to be *right*, because neighbors who are right can be a pain in the community park. It's not enough to be *nice*, because nice people can be passive followers and ultimately disloyal, bringing down entire nations. When I look upon the soul-boggling sacrifice of Jesus, the God-man, small-town carpenter, healer of every disgusting disease, friend of all in need, I find my pride pummeled and spat upon. I find my inflexibility stretched, my self-worship spiked, my arrogance slammed to stone dust, my leathery heart punctured. But I am not left there. My wounds are then anointed with His sacrifice, and I am healed by His grace.

A QUESTION OF TRUST

The second mandatory trait that fits us for new earth is that each resident must be *trustworthy*. Every solid, growing relationship is based on trust. Parent-child, husband-wife, student-teacher, friend-friend, all healthy associations sprout as seedlings from the fresh, fertile soil of trust. Distrust breeds suspicion and repression. Imagine a "paradise" that includes untrustworthy people. It's impossible. We would be eternally doubting, eternally fearing, eternally loathing. In short, a world without trust is hell.

Dr. M. Scott Peck's research found that the primary ingredient in human evil is "hiddenness" that finds expression in pretense, denial, and intellectual deviousness. Trustworthy honesty does not come easily, though. A few years ago I visited the U.S. Postal Service to mail a package of books and a personal letter to my friend Gary in Australia. At that time, the books incurred only a "parcel post" fee, but a hefty surcharge was added if a personal letter was enclosed. I remember a postal clerk quizzing me.

"What's in here?"

"Some books," I replied. "And a letter."

She began weighing. "If you have just books here it's . . . $18.63. But if you have a letter it's . . . $26.31." She looked at me expectantly. I said nothing. Money can be a substantial concern in a teacher's life. *That much for a letter? Should I mail it separately?* She added, "We can just send it along as books," and waited. I said nothing. My brain and ethics seemed paralyzed. "Let's send it as books," she concluded, stamping the parcel. "That's $18.63."

I handed her a twenty. It all happened so fast.

Driving home, I didn't feel right. That night, I didn't feel right. Next morning, I didn't feel right. The following afternoon I drove to the post office and waited until the line suctioned me in front of the same clerk.

"Hi," I began, "I was in here yesterday and I said that a package didn't have a letter, but it did. Here's a check for $7.68 to cover it."

"Sir, I can't take that check," she replied tersely.

"Well, I'm going to leave the check here," I said. "You can put it toward another fund or a party fund or your child's education. I don't care. It's staying here. My integrity's worth more than any money."

"Okay, sir." She didn't appear to get it. I left the check anyway.

Lying is seamlessly easy and phenomenally costly. Our trustworthiness matters not in an ephemeral wispy wonderland of clouds and harps but in a real place with real people. How does God work it out? The grace of God's Son enables us to be teachable, the indwelling Spirit of God empowers us to be trustworthy, and the unconditional love of God the Father equips us to be loving.

The big question forming in the minds of the wondering universe is, "Can these new neighbors be trusted?" Though we are the renegade planet, we are not the only living, thinking beings in the universe. Jesus' life and death showed the universe what God is like—a Friend never to be feared, always to be trusted. More to the point, *can God trust us?* Who will be forever good neighbors to everyone? This is the practical question I believe God must closely evaluate. What a risk God takes with us! Many claim to be God's followers, whether Hindu, Jew, Baha'i, Christian, or Muslim, but how will they play for eternity? Could one unreasonable, malicious streak eventually bring down a galaxy? Once those who just want to be "saved" in paradise get there, what's to stop them from trashing the neighborhood? If we can't be trusted with little things here, can we be trusted with the universe?

God's ability to trust us—to have faith in us—is dependent on something that's highly unpopular in our culture. Loving God requires (gulp) *obedience.* "Trust and obey," the hymn attests, "for there's no other way." He gives us grace enough to trust and obey. While spiritual seekers throughout history have recognized the absolute necessity of obeying God, obedience has received a bad name with many in modern Western society, although anyone with children supports it as a matter of survival. Fortunately, this obedience is to Someone who desires that we possess our own minds and personalities.

Radical love—to the core of my being—is following God's whispered direction, living example, and written advice. Like an adoring son mimicking

Daddy's walk, we long to be in step with God, to hear His confiding laughter. "Come to me," Jesus implores, "all who labor and are heavy laden, and I will give you rest. Take my yoke upon you, and learn from me," Jesus beseeches, "for I am gentle and lowly in heart, and you will find rest for your souls." While we would profoundly appreciate "rest for our souls," most of us today can't relate to "take my yoke upon you." How might this yoke of obedience work in a modern example?

Recently I've taken up riding with my son, Nathan, who has taught me much about the world of cycling, including the disconcerting realization that I am getting old. In cycling, as do Canadian geese, the leader slices through the wind while anyone who follows "drafts"—that is, rides in a pocket of diminished air resistance. This enables the one drafting to conserve energy and to stay up to speed. Jesus promises us, "Let me lead, and draft with me, for my legs are iron and my lungs are vast reservoirs, and you will find rest."

Drafting Jesus is better than drafting any typical rider. In the film *Breaking Away*, a young cyclist drafts behind an eighteen-wheel truck until he reaches seventy miles an hour. Following Jesus on life's roads is like drafting an eighteen-wheeler; we're still pedaling hard, but our progress astounds. Yet it's only by following *closely*—within inches—that we receive the benefit. Following from a distance only increases our frustration, for keeping up on our own power is impossible. "Draft with me," Jesus urges, "all who pedal uphill and are fighting the wind. Honor me and my commandments, get in line with me, and I will give you peace and power."

Obedience is not for God's benefit; it's for our benefit. If we aren't finding Christianity restful, we are not drafting Jesus. Ellen White observes, "When you find your work hard, when you complain of difficulties and trials, when you say that you have no strength to withstand temptation, that you cannot overcome impatience, and that the Christian life is uphill work, be sure that you are not bearing the yoke of Christ; you are bearing the yoke of another master."

Some nominal Christians live by a "radar detector" mentality: It's wrong only if I get caught. This disobedience won't fly in heaven. If God counsels us in afterlife, "Please stay clear of the supernovas," or "Don't interrupt," or "Travel under 55 trillion light years per second," how will we react? Whether breaking speed limits or "borrowing" office supplies, many reveal their beliefs through their response: *This really applies to others, not to me.* God is not Master of their inner life. They let their dogs defecate on others' lawns, toss their gum on the sidewalk, spew blame and disharmony, and take unnumbered shortcuts at others' expense. No matter what, they want the best piece. When their car cuts you off and you notice a bumper sticker that heralds, "Christians aren't perfect, just forgiven," you know someone just isn't getting it. God never asks us to do anything unless He supplies the power to do it. Obedience to God is the joyful journey of a lifetime. Oswald Chambers declares, "What men call the process, God calls the end."

Observe religionists who do not love and obey but are instead toxic beyond belief and you will see the importance of obedience. Careful with their own salvation, such people care little about others who are less fortunate. They bring to mind the English girl's prayer, "God, make the bad people good and the good people nice." Mark Twain, who was often gloriously right and at times dead wrong, quips, "Heaven for climate, hell for society." On the contrary, the society of new earth will be unfailingly delightful. When we consider the perversity of incredibly selfish, deceptive, cowardly, mean, and arrogant people, one factor stands out—they won't be there.

Our family sometimes discusses what it means to be new earth people. We wonder, *Is this how a new earth person would act?* Are we choosing to invest in others? Are we enjoying the natural, the creative, the authentic? Are we drafting Jesus?

FOR GOD'S SAKE

Finally, what will it be like to enter the land of beginning again? Like a dappled bear sniffing the air we'll revel in exploring our new territory. No wheelchair-accessible buildings, no side-by-side cemetery plots, no barred windows or country clubs. What *will* it be like?

Marco Polo, the intrepid thirteenth-century traveler, was urged as he lay dying to recant the stories he had told about China and the Far East. He said instead, "I have not told half what I saw." Surely John the Revelator experienced similar feelings.

When Christ died on the Cross He broadcast His dramatic statement, "It is finished." Justice and mercy were fully demonstrated, Satan's charges were refuted, and humanity was set free. But without freedom from the presence of sin all was not finished. With the new earth, that too will be completed. Jesus frames it in the sweetest words ever spoken to human ears: "Well done, good and faithful servant; you have been faithful over a little, I will set you over much; enter into the joy of your master."

The travel brochures that some people believe, that beyond the grave we receive heavenly lobotomies, are false. Our practices matter; our characters will remain.

And while, thankfully, we won't carry a sinful nature—we aren't predisposed to a basic selfish bent—we will always be free to rebel. Because God will never take away our freedom—consider how much it has cost Him—we will be able to get into fights, shoot rubber bands, and hide, gossip, or tell God, "Forget you."

Actually, that's precisely what enables God to trust us—we can't forget Him. The constant reminder of the horrors of sinful choices are before us, even in the new earth. When we see the scars on Jesus' body, we recall with shame the fractured relationships, the racial tensions, the disparity between the rich and the poor, the screaming rapes, the wailing loneliness, and we freely choose *never to go back,* forever trusting God that His way is best. That is the substance in chapter 15 of *Revelation* of the fabled "Song of Moses and the Lamb":

> I saw what appeared to be a sea of glass mingled with fire, and those who had conquered the beast and its image and the number of its name, standing beside the sea of glass with harps of God in their hands. And they sing the song of Moses, and the song of the Lamb, saying,
> "Great and wonderful are thy deeds,
> O Lord God the Almighty!
> Just and true are thy ways,
> O King of the ages!"

In other words, "You were right, God. All along you were right."

God is practical.

The most anticipated event will be facing God with nothing between—no burgundy curtain, no clouded mirror, no sleight of mind. Marvel at His gentle, wise strength. Be amazed at His relentless tenderness. God's presence in the new earth will be so luminous that "the city has no need of sun or moon to shine upon it, for the glory of God is its light, and its lamp is the Lamb."

The question is, Do we love this being enough to serve Him for ever? Will we trust Him with everything we are, have, and can be? Is the pull of His extravagantly forgiving and accepting love enough? Not a God to fear, for fear would not last long. Not a celestial puppet to control, for it would not be God. Not a God to respect, for though we respect a charging mother rhinoceros, we find her difficult to love.

"How much do you love me?" God asks. How much do we love this reliable, personal, enlightening, liberating, compassionate, surprising, friendly, restful, practical, forever God who fell in love with us?

Paul of Tarsus writes, "It is the God that said, 'Let light shine out of darkness,' who has shone in our hearts to give the light of the knowledge of the glory of God in the face of Christ." Light and darkness cannot occupy the same place. A black hole is a region where even light, no matter how it bends, cannot escape, but there is a light that obliterates the darkness, no matter how dense. Jesus is the light. Jesus, the God-man, passed through the swirling black hole of death and separation from God to emerge incandescent and whole. We bask in the warmth of his radiant touch, and our lives are lightened. "For my burden," He says, "is light."

The sky is thick with light. Suns blast by me like light poles on a city street. The sense of terrific speed without wind resistance is strangely calming. A river of people, as far as I can see, flows around me, and soon the river is pooling ahead. I arrive beside a heaving ocean of glistening crystal, its foam mingling with fire. Waves lap at my feet, leaving warm, iridescent puddles. My toes wriggle in the creamy liquid, and with every movement I create popping flashes. Then God the Father is standing before us.

"My children," He announces with a voice like many waters, "it's so good to have you here."

At the word *here* I hear a rumble; it builds, growing in intensity, ever louder, stronger, rising in pitch, bubbling over, bursting out, erupting with emotion until every person is hugging another, crying with joy and thanking God for bringing us here. Here.

I glance at Jesus. A dazzling smile fills His features. And I notice that He is weeping, too.

Select Bibliography

Coles, Robert. *The Call of Stories.* Boston: Houghton Mifflin, 1989.

Colson, Charles. *Loving God.* Grand Rapids: Zondervan, 1983.

Conn, Charis, and Ilena Silverman, eds. *What Counts: The Complete Harper's Index.* New York: Holt, 1991.

Daniel, Orville E. *A Harmony of the Four Gospels.* Grand Rapids: Baker Book House, 1986.

Foster, Richard J. *Prayer: Finding the Heart's True Home.* San Francisco: HarperCollins, 1992.

Gilkey, Langdon. *Shantung Compound.* San Francisco: Harper & Row, 1966.

Golding, William. *Lord of the Flies.* New York: Perigree, 1959.

Hybels, Bill. *Too Busy Not to Pray.* Downers Grove, IL: InterVarsity Press, 1988.

Lamott, Anne. *Traveling Mercies: Some Thoughts on Faith.* New York: Pantheon Books, 1999.

Lewis, C. S. *Mere Christianity.* New York: Macmillian, 1952.

Lewis, C. S., *The Screwtape Letters.* New York: Macmillian, 1982.

Manning, Brennan. *Lion and Lamb.* Old Tappan, NJ: Revell, 1986.

Munsch, Robert. *Love You Forever.* Willowdale, Ontario: Firefly Books, 1986.

Peck, M. Scott. *People of the Lie: The Hope for Healing Human Evil.* New York: Simon and Schuster, 1983.

Pippert, Becky. *Hope Has Its Reasons.* San Francisco: Harper & Row, 1989.

Postman, Neil. *Amusing Ourselves to Death.* New York: Viking Press, 1985.

Stern, David H. *Jewish New Testament.* Clarksville, MD: Jewish New Testament Publications, 1989.

Ten Boom, Corrie. *The Hiding Place.* Old Tappan, NJ: Revell, 1971.

Terkel, Studs. *Working.* New York: Hearst Corp., 1974.

Thompson, Alden. *Who's Afraid of the Old Testament God?* Grand Rapids: Zondervan, 1989.

Wallis, Jim. *The Soul of Politics.* New York: Harvest Books, 1995.

Weisel, Elie. *Night.* New York: Hearst Corp., 1960.

Yancey, Philip. *The Jesus I Never Knew.* Grand Rapids: Zondervan, 1995.

Yancey, Philip, and Paul Brand, *Where Is God When It Hurts?* Grand Rapids: Zondervan, 1977.